Consumption and Social Change
in a Post-Soviet Middle Class

Consumption and Social Change in a Post-Soviet Middle Class

Jennifer Patico

Woodrow Wilson Center Press
Washington, D.C.

Stanford University Press
Stanford, California

EDITORIAL OFFICES

Woodrow Wilson Center Press
Woodrow Wilson International Center for Scholars
One Woodrow Wilson Plaza
1300 Pennsylvania Avenue, N.W.
Washington, DC 20004-3027
Telephone: 202-691-4029
www.wilsoncenter.org

ORDER FROM

Stanford University Press
Chicago Distribution Center
11030 South Langley Avenue
Chicago, IL 60628
Telephone: 1-800-621-2736

2 4 6 8 9 7 5 3 1

Library of Congress Cataloging-in-Publication Data

Patico, Jennifer.
  Consumption, values, and social change in a post-Soviet middle class / Jennifer Patico.
    p.   cm.
  Includes bibliographical references and index.
  ISBN 978-0-8047-0069-6 (hardcover : alk. paper) — ISBN 978-0-8047-6169-7 (pbk. : alk. paper)
  1. Middle class—Russia (Federation)—Saint Petersburg—Economic conditions.
  2. Professional employees—Russia (Federation)—Saint Petersburg—Economic conditions.
  3. Consumption (Economics)—Social aspects—Russia (Federation)—Saint Petersburg.
  4. Social change—Russia (Federation)—Saint Petersburg.   5. Standard of living—Russia (Federation)—Saint Petersburg.   6. Saint Petersburg (Russia)—Economic conditions.
  7. Saint Petersburg (Russia)—Social conditions.   I. Title.
    HT690.R9P38   2008
    305.5′5094721—dc22
                                                                        2008017709

Contents

Figures

Tables

A Note on Transliteration
and Russian Names

Throughout, Russian words have been transliterated into English according to the Library of Congress system. Exceptions include certain Russian words, particularly proper names, which are familiar in English. In these cases I adopt customary English spellings, for example, "Olga" instead of "Ol'ga," and "Anya" instead of "Ania."

All individual names used in the book are pseudonyms, drawn from the pool of the most common Russian names. For the most part, I have referred to individuals using first names only, although it is customary in many contexts—particularly in the workplace and when speaking with one who is older or in a position of higher authority than the speaker—to use first names together with patronymics (e.g., not just "Olga" but also "Olga Aleksandrovna"). Many of the teachers encouraged me to call them by their first names only, American style, and I have retained that habit here. In some cases I use full first names (e.g., Elizaveta), while in others I use diminutive forms (Liza). However, to avoid confusion for readers unfamiliar with Russian names, I have assigned one unique name (either a full first name or a diminutive form) to each person. Thus the reader can follow individuals across chapters knowing that "Liza" in chapter 3 is the same person as "Liza" in chapter 5, while "Elizaveta" and "Liza" are in fact different individuals.

Acknowledgments

To begin, this book would not have been written without the cooperation, support, and friendship of two cohorts of schoolteachers in Saint Petersburg. Though the women and men who contributed to this account shall remain anonymous, I am forever indebted to them for the openness and good humor with which they approached my research. They voluntarily invested many hours in this project during what was, for most of them, an extremely hectic and demoralizing year of financial hardship and general uncertainty. For this, and for many other kindnesses, I offer my deep gratitude.

Other friends and colleagues provided aid and advice in Saint Petersburg. The Department of Sociology and Political Science at European University was my institutional home in 1998–99; the faculty and students gave warm collegial support and practical assistance. In particular, I wish to thank Elena Zdravomyslova, who offered invaluable contacts and thoughtful guidance that furthered my work in the city. Olga Kalacheva was a lively and insightful interlocutor and a wonderful friend. I am indebted to her and other associates of the Center for Independent Social Research for their assistance in the transcription of tape-recorded interviews. With Anna-Maria Salmi of the Department of Sociology at the University of Helsinki, I shared many conversations about Saint Petersburg teachers and their exchange networks; thank you, Anna Maria, for your insights and friendship. Last but far from least, two Saint Petersburg families have provided homes away from home —literal and spiritual—during my research trips. I am inexpressibly thankful to the Pimkins and the Tarasovs for the friendship, wisdom, familial warmth, and hot meals they have given me over the years.

Though I am, of course, solely responsible for the shortcomings of this book, it most assuredly has been enriched through the guidance of a number of excellent scholars. I was blessed with a graduate committee at New York University composed of three wonderful anthropologists—Susan Carol Rogers, Lila Abu-Lughod, and Fred Myers—who offered me inspiration and pushed me further in countless and complementary ways. Special thanks go to Fred for getting me thinking about "value" as a frame for articulating what I had observed during my fieldwork. Susan was tireless as a reader and adviser, with her keen eye for detail and for the strengths and weaknesses in arguments. Her warm wishes of "bon courage" helped see me through the dissertation in good speed and good humor; thank you, Susan, for your wisdom and friendship. Mark von Hagen gave stimulating commentary on the dissertation as an outside reader, and Bruce Grant has offered incisive readings and warm support of this work at many stages along the way.

I am grateful for the feedback I have received on pieces of this book from many individuals at conferences and seminars over the years, but one person stands out as worthy of very special thanks. Melissa Caldwell has gone above and beyond the call of duty as a colleague, reading various incarnations of the project with close attention and offering wonderfully engaged and practical suggestions. Lissa, thank you for your unflagging energy and thoughtful feedback. I thank Michele Rivkin-Fish and, again, Melissa Caldwell for their extremely insightful and useful comments on the manuscript as readers for the Woodrow Wilson Center Press. The director of the Press, Joseph Brinley, saw this project through to the end, and I am grateful for his expert and responsive work as editor.

Selected material in chapters 1 through 4 and 7 appeared previously in *American Ethnologist,* volume 32, number 3, as "To Be Happy in a Mercedes: Culture, Civilization and Transformations of Value in a Postsocialist City," copyright by the American Anthropological Association and published under the auspices of the University of California Press. An earlier, abridged version of chapter 6 appeared in *Ethnos*, volume 67, number 3, as "Chocolate and Cognac: Gift Exchange and the Recognition of Social Worlds in Post-Soviet Russia," and is reproduced here by permission from Taylor and Francis (www.informaworld.com).

The ethnographic research upon which this book is based was made possible by two grants (1998–99, 2003) from the International Research and Exchanges Board, with funds provided by the National Endowment for the Humanities, the U.S. Department of State, and the U.S. Information Agency. Additional funding for research in Russia was provided by a PEO Scholar Award. A James McCracken Fellowship and Dean's Dissertation Write-up

Fellowship, both from New York University, funded the initial project through the writing stages. A summer research fellowship at the Kennan Institute, under the auspices of the Woodrow Wilson International Center for Scholars in Washington, granted resources for supplementary secondary research in 2001. Thanks are also due to the librarians in the European Reading Room of the Library of Congress, who provided assistance and valuable materials that have enriched the historical discussions included in this book. Space and time for working on initial revisions to the manuscript were offered by the Five College Women's Studies Research Center, South Hadley, Massachusetts, and by a Mellon Postdoctoral Fellowship at Haverford College. Later revisions were completed while I was on faculty at Haverford College and then at Georgia State University; I thank the members of both departments of anthropology for their camaraderie along the way.

This book is dedicated to my family—especially Denis, Eliza, Elaine, Alex, Kristi, Pam, Jim, Nick, Caroline, Hope, Matthew, Mary Kate, Clem, Chris, and Caitjan—for the love and nurturing they have given me, and by extension, this book. Denis struggled through a frigid Saint Petersburg winter to make this research possible, and he was a tireless supporter during the years of writing and revision that followed. The biggest *spasibo* of all goes to him.

*Consumption and Social Change
in a Post-Soviet Middle Class*

Chapter 1

The Price of Bananas and the Value of Postsocialist Subjects

[handwritten annotations: "bananas are kind of a crazy capitalist indexed fruit. (in the absence) intangible whatever?"]

"It is offensive that a PhD scientist cannot afford to buy bananas for her family." So said a Saint Petersburg research scientist in the spring of 1993. I was sympathetic: Bananas seemed like little enough for ask for, and at that time they were too expensive for her and her husband, both PhD chemists working in a local institute. Yet I was also intrigued: Why should this fact have been particularly bitter for her? How was it that bananas, of all things, had been mentioned as among the most "offensive," painful, and discouraging experiences of those first post-Soviet years of sweeping inflation and terrifying uncertainty? Imported bananas could hardly have been considered a daily necessity at that time, because they had begun to be sold widely in Saint Petersburg only in the preceding year or so, in the wake of the 1991 collapse of the Soviet Union. The chemist was aware, however, that in the West professionals with similar qualifications could afford to buy as many bananas as they wished; and it was this comparison that in part explained her resentment.

As I took in her words, and as I heard similar sentiments echoed by many others that spring when I was an exchange student in Saint Petersburg, I realized that such seemingly mundane dilemmas as the price of bananas revealed much about an emergent culture of capitalism in Russia. These matters came to people's attention in the course of their everyday movement through the city and in the pursuit of small domestic tasks, but they heralded far more overarching processes of local and global change. With the dissolution of the USSR and its centralized, socialist economy came several years of spectacular currency inflation; an explosion of imported goods available in local markets for the first time, but often prohibitively expensive to most residents; widespread job loss and unpaid salaries; and a general atmosphere of profound uncertainty and unpredictability, as people

1

wondered from day to day what dumbfounding developments might come next. How have Russians experienced and made sense of these economic and social transformations? As the material world around them takes on new contours, what kinds of meaning do people attribute to previously exotic objects—whether a bunch of bananas or a shiny new Mercedes? And what should those meanings suggest to those who, like myself, are attempting to track the broader dynamics of post-Soviet social change and cultural adaptation, or who are interested in the effects of post–Cold War globalization on the everyday lives of communities around the world?

The changing consumer landscape is only one aspect of the rather earth-shattering upheavals citizens of the former Soviet Union have faced since 1991, but it is a particularly useful entry point into the conversations they are having and the judgments they are making about what is happening to them and their compatriots. The contours and contradictions of social life, including the particular tumult of societies in transformation, tend to be crystallized in commodities and the practices that surround them. Indeed, as Jean Comaroff and John Comaroff paraphrase Karl Marx's nineteenth-century analysis of commodity fetishization, "the transformation of any society should be revealed by the changing relations of persons to objects within it" (Comaroff and Comaroff 1990, 196; Marx 1990). In this sense, even the most mundane consumer decisions and discourses can open important windows of insight into a historical moment. Hence this book examines how it is that through consumer products and the many conversations, desires, and worries these inspire, people reflect upon their own positionings—and their own socially and culturally defined *value*—vis-à-vis both local and global socioeconomic hierarchies that are themselves rapidly transforming.

By the late 1990s, when I began conducting the ethnographic research upon which this book is based, bananas had become much more affordable in Saint Petersburg. Along with other once-exotic imported commodities, they had quickly become taken-for-granted, unremarkable accessories to everyday life. Slick advertisements for commodities from Russian vodka to Scandinavian home furnishings now lined Saint Petersburg's streets, occupying corners that once were decorated only by Communist propaganda posters. Russian-language editions of *Cosmopolitan* and *Good Housekeeping,* published in Moscow, shared newsstand space with redesigned versions of *Rabotnitsa* (Working Woman) and *Krest'ianka* (Peasant Woman), women's magazines familiar from the Soviet era. Plastic bags advertising the brand names of cigarettes such as Marlboro or Peter I (a reference to Russia's early-eighteenth-century Westernizing tsar, Saint Petersburg's founder) were conveniently sold at the same store counters where shoppers had once brought out their own trusty *avos'ki,* the "just-in-case" bags they had toted in anticipation of serendipitous finds amid Soviet shortages. Outdoor markets (*rynki*) and indoor bazaars (*iarmarki*) sold relatively inexpensive clothing from South Korea and Turkey, while just a few steps away Benetton, Swatch, and Adidas stores showed their wares—all of these imports new to the local consumer scene but occupying different places in aesthetic and price hierarchies. Some aspects of the cityscape remained much the same; as before, Saint Petersburg residents took pride and pleasure in the grand architectural ensembles and picturesque canals of Peter's European capital. But by the late 1990s, my friend the chemist who had been so angry about the price of bananas a few years earlier, and many others along with her, had reoriented themselves to a new set of consumer options and prices—not to mention a new range of career and lifestyle choices in a more thoroughly marketized economy (figures 1.1 and 1.2).

But if in one narrow sense the banana problem had stopped worrying that chemist, the bigger questions it represented were far from resolved. The broader cultural ramifications of marketization were still very much in the process of being worked out, as people considered and reconsidered the nature and significance of social inequality—in the transformed society they were helping to create and in the new global scheme of things. What was the relationship between an individual's choice of productive activity (gainful employment) and his or her share of the material resources (goods, money) distributed among the members of the larger social body? According to what principles did people believe that such wealth should be doled out? Did one's level of material privilege roughly correspond to how well one was respected by one's peers—that is, did those two forms of value covary? Or were social and economic forms of value understood to be independent of one another, or even morally incompatible?

In this book, I examine how a particular group of people—two cohorts of Saint Petersburg schoolteachers—were taking up these questions. In the recent Soviet past, differentiation in consumption was naturalized and legitimated by virtue of its association with notions of socially useful work and professionalism. Schoolteachers, along with medical doctors and engineers, were part of what Vladimir Shlapentokh (1999) has called a "mass intelligentsia" (in distinction to the more exclusive intellectual elite). These strata enjoyed a certain kind of "middle-class" lifestyle—although they were never particularly well paid in relation to other categories of workers

Figure 1.1. A generic, Soviet-style storefront in Saint Petersburg, 1998: "Bakery-Confectionery." Photograph by the author.

and bureaucrats, and not coincidentally, both the teaching and medical professions were highly feminized (Jones 1991; Shlapentokh 1999). In the 1990s, however, these same groups were among those particularly affected by the disintegration of Soviet administrative and economic structures, as plummeting budgets for state-run enterprises including public schools and scientific institutes left many highly educated professionals with paltry or even unpaid salaries. With the rugs effectively pulled out from under their previous material security and vocational pride, they present a useful point of view from which to examine how marketization affects senses of self and social positioning. The world of these "old" professional classes, as I came to understand it through the lens of Saint Petersburg teachers' experience, was one in which the very logics according to which people once had set goals, evaluated prestige, and received their material rewards had been largely upended, resulting in no small measure of practical and symbolic disorientation.

For when there is, as we shall see, a perceived link between one's personal merit and its reflection in proper, civilized consumption, what does it imply to see oneself as suitably "cultured" yet be unable to afford the accoutrements of such culturedness? How is that situation explained, justified,

Figure 1.2. Across the street from the bakery, newer signs advertising American cigarettes and soda mark the entrance to a twenty-four-hour convenience store, 1998. Photograph by the author.

and/or critiqued, and who or what is held responsible? Has something gone awry at the macro level of market mechanisms and state institutions? Or perhaps one's own virtue might come into question? Most of today's Russian adults reached maturity with one set of assumptions about status, professionalism, respectability, and their rewards, but in the 1990s they found themselves thrust into a context where many of those assumptions no longer held, at least not in the familiar ways. For them, new consumer opportunities and unsatisfied desires have been bound up in a more fundamental deliberation about the relationships that they believe to exist—or which they feel should exist—between personal merit, social mobility, and their materialization in goods and wealth.

It is, indeed, largely through commodity consumption that Russians are addressing these issues, whether in relatively explicit conversations about just allocations of resources and wealth or in the more implicit realm of consumer discernment, taste, and decisionmaking. In the anthropological tradition of research on consumption and material culture, both commodities and other, less "alienable" possessions (e.g., family heirlooms and religious objects) have been recognized as playing central roles in how people articulate beliefs and affinities, signal membership in particular communities, and mark personal relationships or ritual transitions (Douglas 1984, 1992b, 1997; Levi-Strauss 1997; Sahlins 1976). Goods have been said to help people "make sense of the inchoate flux of events" as part of an "active process in which all the social categories are being continually redefined" (Douglas and Isherwood 1996, 43). Commodities do not merely provide a set of symbols that express social norms and categories that already exist as a priori, determining structures (Miller 1995a); rather, consumer practices are *themselves* constitutive of social experience and, potentially, of social change. Material culture is a key realm of action, perception, and discourse that provides part of the very "basis on which subjects come into being, rather than simply answering their preexisting needs" (Myers 2001b, 20–21; see also Miller 1987).

In other words, the significance of consumers' conversations about the price of bananas goes far beyond the objects themselves. Bananas and other commodities are being put to the service of much weightier judgments about the redistribution and meaning of resources, both material and moral, in contemporary Russia. As Judith Farquhar (1999, 358) observes, making a broad theoretical point that emerges out of her work in contemporary China: "Desires may be limitless, but resources are not. The economic is

It's hard to tease desire + ability [handwritten annotation]

therefore always political; it concerns loci of control over the stuff of which life is made, the power to allocate, consume, and produce the differentiated and unequal landscape of the social." In the same sense, my examination of consumer practices and discourses in postsocialist Saint Petersburg is at base a study of how emergent inequalities in wealth and status are being recognized, resituated, and perhaps increasingly naturalized as individuals' economic strategies, consumer possibilities, and political-moral sensibilities nudge against, and gradually begin accommodating themselves to, new logics of value: social cosmologies that help them to make sense of their own dilemmas and desires in unprecedented ways.

Logics of Value: An Approach to the Anthropology of Consumption and Transformation

What consumers are deliberating upon in contemporary Russia is what I shall call *logics of value:* the manner in which people in a particular historical context routinely consider measures of material wealth (money and possessions) and other kinds of value (e.g., moral rectitude, social respectability); and more to the point, how they understand the expected or legitimate *correspondence* of these value forms to one another in social life. Above, I asked: What is the relationship between an individual's productive activity and her share of material resources? Does one's level of material privilege correspond to the social standing and moral legitimacy one enjoys in others' eyes? How are displays of wealth, particularly through commodity consumption, assumed to bespeak individuals' moral standings and their relationships to others? Furthermore, how do people in a particular time and place interrelate such measures of moral and material value in the course of shopping, gift giving, and other daily practices of consumption and social exchange?

My concern with logics of value overlaps with theories of value developed by other anthropologists (Graeber 2001; Munn 1986; Myers 2001b; Verdery 2003; Weiner 1992). Many theorists have constructed "value" as a matter of the complex, dialectical relationships whereby persons and things define one another (Appadurai 1986; Munn 1986; Graeber 2001; Eiss and Anderson 2002a, 2002b; Myers 2001a). They have done so often as part of efforts to theorize (and trouble) the distinction between gift versus commodity exchange systems, building on the legacies of Marx and of Marcel

? why relevant? [handwritten annotation]

Mauss (Marx 1990; Mauss 1967; see also Weiner 1992, Thomas 1991, Gregory 1982, and Comaroff and Comaroff 1990).[1] But the meaning of value itself in anthropological thought is rather indeterminate and slippery; here, as in everyday English, "value" has been defined in at least three ways: as the value embodied in things (that which makes a given thing quantifiably "valuable" or desirable); "values" as a set of preferences and convictions about the "good" and the "proper" in social life; and in the linguistic/ semiotic sense, value as "meaningful difference" (Graeber 2001, 1–2). David Graeber argues that most previous works have erred by emphasizing only one or another of these aspects—treating value either in its strictly economic sense or in the Saussurian sense of meaningful difference—rather than seeing all these meanings as linked since they refer to investments of human energy and concern.

Whereas Graeber develops his own perspective on value as part of an ambitious and global theory of creative human action, fetishism, and social domination, this book examines concretely how people in a marketizing society interpret and construct the interrelationships between materiality and morality; between wealth and social standing; and between resources and respect in the course of their commodity consumption. In this subject-centered approach, I ask not how different forms of value or strategic "capital" (economic, social, cultural) are converted into another in social life (Bourdieu 1977, 1984, 1996) but rather how people explain to themselves, and thereby engage in, processes of structural and cultural reproduction and especially change.[2]

1. Following the lead of Arjun Appadurai (1986), a common objective (e.g., Keane 2001; Miller 2001) has been to problematize the relatively strict demarcation previously rehearsed between "gift" (affective, ongoing, embedded in rich social relationships) and "commodity"/money (impersonal, fleeting, individualistic, abstracted) forms of exchange. With a related agenda, Thomas (1991) discards "gift" and "commodity" as descriptors of "primitive" and "modern" kinds of *societies,* respectively, arguing that a multiplicity of economic forms is present in any society and that the really important question is how material artifacts get recontextualized over time and in situations of cross-cultural engagement such as colonization.

2. This stands in contrast to other, by now classic approaches to material culture studies. In the 1980s, Appadurai (1986; see also Kopytoff 1986) called for investigation of the "social life of things," advocating a kind of methodological fetishism in which the commodity status of a given object would not be taken for granted but would be tracked as the object moves through the multiple, power-ridden social contexts and agonistic "tournaments of value" in which its significance is hammered out. Hence the things' tumultuous "social lives" were hoped to illuminate the prevailing hegemonies and fault lines of the settings through which they traveled (see also Eiss and Pedersen 2002b).

In short, "value" refers here to how people perceive, produce, and correlate different measures of success, deservedness, and respectability, as they construct logical associations that form the loose explanatory frameworks—what Katherine Newman (1988, 19) has called "architecture[s] [for] interpretation"—that they employ to interpret post-Soviet dilemmas, including their own downward mobility. These frameworks are helpful ways into understanding how individual Russians' senses of their own personhood—what qualities they possess and how they are perceived by and related to other social actors—are directly engaged and challenged as they come to terms with a shifting market in labor and commodities. These engagements are not just "personal"; they are certainly political as well, as people's ways of understanding themselves and their social contexts are also ways of either legitimating or critiquing emergent structures of authority and resource distribution.

Reconfiguring Value in Russia: A Distinctive Perspective on a Global Phenomenon

Active deliberation over such questions is not unique to Russia or even to postsocialist countries. Rather, it is generally indicative of periods of socioeconomic crisis, upheaval, or transition (Newman 1988; Weber 1992). Indeed, many of the narratives conveyed in this book resonate with descriptions of commodification, resignification, and social restructuring that anthropologists have recorded for colonial and postcolonial contexts from Zimbabwe to Papua New Guinea (Burke 1996; Comaroff and Comaroff 1990; Foster 2002). During the past decade or so, postcolonial industrialization and the growing dominance of transnational capitalist markets have turned questions about commodity choice and the cultural significance of

---

This kind of sensibility is particularly appropriate to the question of how "desire and demand, reciprocal sacrifice and power, interact to create *economic* value in specific social situations" (Appadurai 1986, 4; emphasis added). The dominant imagery is that of movement and transfer, haggling, concrete acquisition or loss. Yet this "follow the thing" approach is rather less suited to providing a sense of particular individuals' subjective judgments of value or of how they formulate the logics that underlie social inequalities, which is the subject of this book. Thus while the politics of gift giving and other exchange relations are described in this book, I do not attempt to track these transactions per se but to consider material culture's overall relevance to consumers' moral contests and their direct experiences of social transformation.

mass-produced goods into key themes of anthropological research around the world (Berdahl 1999; Comaroff and Comaroff 2001; Howes 1996; Inda and Rosaldo 2002; Miller 1994, 1997; Watson 1997). At the same time, Russia's position as a long-standing colonial power in its own right places it differently on the periphery of the global economy than the other, typically postcolonial and modernizing societies most ethnographers have studied (Foster 2002; Gewertz and Errington 1991, 1996; Liechty 2003); and this positioning is reflected in the aspirations and dilemmas of its contemporary consumers. In this, Russia offers a new opportunity to revisit and resituate relatively familiar anthropological questions concerning how consumers conceptualize value and social difference, and to ask how they do this in relation to both global capitalist processes and the particularities of national experience and specific modernities.

How such questions of value are routinely framed gets to the heart of what it means to live in any economic regime—socialist, capitalist, or other. More than a century ago, Max Weber's *The Protestant Ethic and the Spirit of Capitalism* (1992; first published in 1904–5) made a similar kind of claim about the attitudes that accompanied capitalist styles of accumulation in seventeenth-century Europe. *The Protestant Ethic* proposed that a novel sort of moral logic had helped to create the conditions necessary for the development of modern capitalism. At that pivotal historical moment, Weber argued, people's willingness to direct their time and capital toward the growth of rationally organized capitalist enterprises did not depend upon a mere greed for riches. Rather, financial success and consistent, industrious activity combined with consumer asceticism became, for the emergent Protestant bourgeoisie, proof that one was in God's favor. As I would restate Weber's insight, the Protestant Ethic configured a particular relationship among bases of moral, economic, and symbolic value, such that hard work and financial success in this world were taken to be promising signs of one's fate in the next. More broadly, Weber's Protestant Ethic is echoed in contemporary American ideas about individual wealth as the product of one person's hard work, talent, or luck, explanations that tend to exclude more structural sources of inequality (see also Carrier 1997). Such moral valorization of commercial success was scarcely to be found in Saint Petersburg schoolteachers' conversations about the local nouveaux riches in the late 1990s. As we shall see, however, those commentaries were often highly ambivalent—and were already somewhat changed by the early 2000s.

On the face of it, twentieth-century Russia posed a stark contrast to the Europe of Weber's description: it saw the establishment and, finally, the collapse of a system that was purposefully opposed to capitalism and pointedly secular. Aiming to abolish social inequality in the name of the working class, the Bolshevik Revolution of 1917 was supposed to squelch selfish, bourgeois desires for the accumulation of material wealth (in which little virtue of the Protestant sort was felt to inhere). Marx famously viewed religious faith as "the opiate of the people," that is, as an illusion that distracted the exploited from fully recognizing and protesting against social injustice by convincing them that their true rewards would come in another life. In the Marxist-Leninist worldview, not only was the energy of the populace to be harnessed toward decidedly this-worldly endeavors, but it was also in the here and now—or at least, in the "bright future" when communism would be achieved—that people were to receive their just rewards. The Revolution's formal intentions were not fully realized in the USSR; nor, as time went on, were state agendas really oriented toward the possibility of their fulfillment. Indeed, the Soviet Union had its own hierarchies of distinction and privilege, and its own ideologies for their legitimation. These included not only the Marxist-Leninist valorization of productive (physical) labor but also the idealization of education, professionalism, and "culturedness" as bases of individual merit. This is what makes a Russian case study so distinctive as compared with other contexts of anthropological research on globalization, capitalism, and social change: post-Soviet consumerism and its rituals are not the product of recent modernization but to a great extent have been experienced and must be understood as part of a shift from one modernity to another, more market-driven one.

To paraphrase Michael Taussig (1980, 10), those of us who have been accustomed to living in relatively stable market economies tend not to reflect critically in our own workaday lives upon the logics of value that guide us. Social expectations and relations of power are more likely to be actively narrated, contested, theorized, and mythologized in situations of rapid, disorienting change. The rather abrupt nature of political and economic transformation in Russia since perestroika has provoked an especially intensive process of interrogating the correspondences between collective and private interests and between material and moral indices of value. Of course, if many Russians are engaging in a kind of cultural analysis of their own in everyday life, they do so—like Weber's bourgeoisie—from specific social positions and with particular (and high) stakes, as they investigate the standards of moral and material value according to which they and others might assess their *own* worth.

For it is not only the selection of available commodities that has expanded and been transformed in recent years. Because Russians are required to incorporate new market pressures and possibilities into their lives on an ongoing basis, many feel acutely the discomfort of having been *themselves* resituated vis-à-vis their fellow Russians and, indeed, an entire world of others. Russia's status as a former superpower and center of industrial modernity has given rise to particular brands of ambivalence for many Russians—perhaps especially those of the old professional classes, who as I found in the late 1990s were likely to share certain sentiments of social entitlement as well as keen resentment at having been "left behind" by market reforms. *— especially + the emergence no doubt the issue. "Market already existed*

Teachers and the Downward Mobility
of a Soviet Middle Class

The criteria upon which something like post-Soviet class identities might be based—and according to which observable inequalities can be explained and legitimated—have been common topics of public debate and private commentary in Russia. This was especially true during the financial crisis of 1998–99 (to which I return shortly), when I found myself in Saint Petersburg for fieldwork. I discuss "class" primarily as a folk analytical category that relates income level and the capacity to consume with professional background, education, and other measures of social achievement and orientation.[3] As such, class is treated in this account as part of the teachers' own "social imaginary" in transformation.

---

3. According to Max Weber (1946, 181), "class" refers more strictly to a person or group's positioning within an economy; "class" or "market situation" is "the typical chance for a supply of goods, external living conditions, and personal life experiences, in so far as this chance is determined by the amount and kind of power, or lack of such, to dispose of goods or skills for the sake of income in a given economic order." By contrast, "status" concerns communities of "honor" in which distinctive "styles of life" play a key role (ibid., 186–91). "With some oversimplification, one might thus say that 'classes' are stratified according to their relations to the production and acquisition of goods; whereas 'status groups' are stratified according to the principles of their *consumption* of goods as represented by special 'styles of life' " (ibid., 193). (For a concise summary of Marxian vs. Weberian treatments of class, see Liechty 2003, 11–19.) Bourdieu (1984) addresses a similar set of issues by identifying the different types of capital—economic, cultural, social, symbolic—that can determine a person's position in an overall social field. For both Weber and Bourdieu, economic

As Maureen O'Dougherty observes in her study of inflation, consumption, and middle-class identity in Brazil, such a class imaginary describes most aptly the way people talk not about who they "are" but about "what [kind of person] one would be or would not be" (O'Dougherty 2002, 9, 113). In other words, it refers not to a demographically locatable category of people but to a set of moral and material aspirations and orientations. Similarly, for Mark Liechty, the emergent Nepali middle class is less a distinct social entity than a "sociocultural project—material and discursive— in which members negotiate the apparent contradictions between what it means to be both modern and Nepali" (Liechty 2003, 61). Liechty analyzes class in Nepal as an essentially performative and narrative phenomenon; the middle class is "a veritable economy of circulating and contending narratives of honor, prestige, morality, suitability, and propriety" (p. 26). Similar concerns are at play in the post-Soviet Russian milieu, suggesting that the cross-cultural dynamics of middle-classness are ripe for further comparative analysis. This book contributes to that discussion by examining a situation in which what it meant to be "middle class" was extremely uncertain and by engaging the experiences of a group whose coming of age under conditions of Soviet modernity led them to expect a certain kind of "middle-class" identity, and yet who, in many cases, found it increasingly difficult to conceive of themselves that way given their positions in a new market in commodities and labor. This play of categories explains why the book's subtitle uses the somewhat awkward turn of phrase "*a* post-Soviet middle class" rather than "*the* post-Soviet middle class."

As the teachers' situation reminds us, to speak of class as a social imaginary is *not* to say that it can be adequately construed as a question of nothing than consumer lifestyle and creative self-presentation, as though workers' structural positionings in a system of production and employment as well as consumption were no longer relevant to our understandings of social inequality and the politics of identity. Comaroff and Comaroff (2001, 295) have argued that, "as consumption has become the moving spirit of the late twentieth century, so there has been a concomitant eclipse of produc-

---

and cultural/symbolic determinants of status tend to be interdependent and mutually reinforcing; though in specific cases (or in reference to specific social roles, e.g., the "starving artist") they may be relatively unbalanced or oppositional. For the purposes of this discussion, I have included both financial standing and sociomoral respectability within a loose definition of "class," as appropriate to the Russian discourses under examination.

tion. . . . The workplace and labor, especially work-and-place securely rooted in a stable local context, are no longer prime sites for the creation of value or identity." Yet this "eclipse," they acknowledge, may be at least in part a matter of production's *perceived* lack of salience as people around the world imagine themselves to be taking part in a global community of consumers. How this participation is informed and constrained by their positions in national and global labor markets is still a matter of direct import.

Saint Petersburg teachers' experiences on the job, including but not limited to their falling wages, have profoundly shaped their consumer aspirations and interpretations. In the conversations I shared with them in the late 1990s, these teachers made sense of their consumer preferences and possibilities by continually referring to their personal labor histories, qualifications, and beliefs about the usefulness of their own contributions to society as compared with others'. Thus it would be nonsensical to treat their consumption as an isolated repertoire of desires or symbols. Consumption must be understood in connection with professional identities and with labor markets as people have experienced and interpreted them in their Soviet and post-Soviet everyday lives. Such a study is necessarily situated from a specific social and temporal perspective—in this case, that of teachers, a downwardly mobile "middle class," at the end of the 1990s and early 2000s.

In the USSR, teachers bore a unique role as the molders of Soviet youth, mandated to convey proper social values to their students. The state regulated much of the content of their work, including the creation of curricula, choice of books for class use, and determination of "correct" attitudes and responses to be inculcated in pupils (Jones 1991, 156).[4] The more negative expression of this role was a stereotypical view, observable in popular films of the late Soviet era, of teachers as domineering, uptight, eccentric, and/or physically unattractive women.[5] As a group, teachers along with many

4. As Jones notes, some of the Russian words commonly used to describe teachers and education reflect this emphasis on socialization. The standard word for education, *obrazovanie,* comes from the verb "to form"; teachers (in my experience, especially nursery or elementary teachers) are sometimes referred to as *vospitateli,* "upbringers" (Jones 1991, 156) or "nurturers."

5. Images of eccentric, out-of-date, and/or lonely teachers (along with the occasional more youthful, attractive, and desirably soulful types) can be seen in Soviet and pere-stroika-era films such as *Dozhivem do Ponedel'nika* (We'll Survive until Monday, 1968), *Ironiia Sud'by* (The Irony of Fate, 1975), and *Dorogaia Elena Sergeevna* (Dear Elena Sergeevna, 1988). See also *Window to Paris* (1994) for a range of portrayals of post-Soviet schoolteachers. In the summer of 2003, a television serial called *Pyatyi Ugol* (The Fifth Corner) portrayed the conflict that ensued when a school principal, clearly por-

other publicly employed professionals experienced downward mobility in the 1990s. This was especially clear in terms of their personal finances, but neither did their education, professionalism, and authority within the schools any longer yield clear assurance of a stable status according to any other modes of social evaluation and consensus. Teachers were not the only ones to suffer such destabilization in the 1990s; but when I told local Russians other than my informants that my research would involve studying consumer practice among teachers, some reacted with surprise, believing that teachers form a "very specific" population, in part because of the negative image of the typical schoolmarm. A market researcher in Saint Petersburg informed me that people like teachers were not really on her firm's cultural radar, because they had little money and therefore simply were not consuming much. In all these ways, teachers were hardly on the cutting edge of post-Soviet consumer trends.

And yet, the fact of being constrained in their consumption makes teachers rather more typical of the post-Soviet Russian experience than not. Furthermore, the teaching profession per se does not determine uniformly the experiences of each woman and man who works in education. What it meant to "be a teacher" was highly variable. For though almost all the individuals who appear by name (or rather, by a specific pseudonym) in this book were employed at the time in public schools, only some of them were trained at pedagogical institutes and thought of teaching as a life's calling. Some of these career teachers had been working in Soviet and post-Soviet schools for as long as twenty or thirty years; and some had thought about changing tracks but deemed it "too late" to seek new, higher-paying careers. For others, working in education had been a relatively recent choice, based on the fact that Saint Petersburg's schools were in certain ways bastions of stability in the 1990s. "Teachers will always be needed," they said, unlike chemists and engineers, many of whom had lost their jobs when Saint Petersburg's scientific research and military industries shrank in the 1990s, and some of whom became schoolteachers thereafter.[6] Unlike in many other

---

trayed as an overly principled, out-of-touch member of an older generation, flagged down a taxi that turned out to be driven by a somewhat younger male teacher who worked under her supervision. She righteously criticized him for stooping to such a lowly job and hoped that he would not be so unfortunate as to pick up any of his students in the cab; he defended his right to earn extra money honestly and as he saw fit.

6. Amy Ninetto (2005, 444) portrays the research scientists of Akademgorodok, Siberia, as similarly concerned about "the loss of their elite status, prestige, and authority," which "added insult to the injury of their rapidly diminishing and often late salaries."

parts of Russia, Saint Petersburg public schoolteachers were receiving their admittedly paltry salaries on time.

Many teachers, especially English-language specialists, earned extra money as private tutors. In some cases, the lessons generated incomes significantly larger than their school salaries. Others had been less successful in attracting students or taught in fields where tutors were sought less frequently (strong English skills being in high demand in the labor market). As for their personal lives, some of the teachers were married, others not; most of them were women, and most, save a few younger women in their twenties, had either one or two children to support.

Despite this diversity in backgrounds and situations, the Saint Petersburg teachers' work within public schools did position all of them in a particular way. Casting themselves as relatively impoverished but at least cultured professionals, they tended to be both eager consumers and vociferous critics of the Russian market economy. Some among them felt painfully aware of an erosion of the social recognition and respect that their work was accorded in the late 1990s, not to mention of the material remuneration by which it was rewarded. Most of them identified themselves as "cultured," highly educated professionals, and they understood these associations as inherently meritorious, drawing in part on the assumptions embedded within Soviet institutional life. Yet in recent years they had also found themselves questioning the real relevance of those bases for self-evaluation, as they grappled with the apparent devaluation of their social contributions in a more market-driven environment where schools, pensions, and other social services received paltry and dwindling support and, as one teacher ruefully summarized, "nobody is thinking about us."

Their commentaries spoke of their own precarious positionings as professionals still dependent on the sinking ship of state-sponsored institutions in a privatizing former world power. Although teachers are not necessarily representative of urban Russians, then, they present a vantage point that is structurally revealing of particular processes of institutional decline (especially the diminishing of state funds for public education and employment) and marketization.

Marketization, Morality, and "Russian" Responses

What, then, is "Russian"—or perhaps, "Soviet"—about the ways in which teachers in Saint Petersburg experienced and participated in such processes of change? American anthropologists working in Eastern Europe and the (former) Soviet Union long have been concerned to debunk misinformed visions of what life was like in the "Evil Empire" and, now, its successor states—though they have also, inevitably, participated in the creation of new, still-partial truths (Clifford 1986) about who Russians are and have been.

American research on the region was dominated for most of the twentieth century by political science and the Cold War security concerns of Sovietology, with its emphasis on the inner workings of the Kremlin, the perils of totalitarianism, and the presumed failures of Soviet socialism (Verdery 1996; Sampson and Kideckel 1988). In response to these biases, American and British ethnographers working in the late socialist era endeavored to provide better on-the-ground descriptions of life behind the Iron Curtain, including both the acquiescence and resistance of citizens to official ideologies and policies (Kideckel 1976, 1993; Verdery 1983; Lampland 1995; Kligman 1988; Sampson 1976). Since the Cold War, ethnographers have worked in the shadows of experts on democratization, marketing, and civil society—ranks of Americans and Europeans who have set about nurturing the kind of infrastructures deemed necessary for overcoming East Europe's "dysfunctional" institutional legacies (Dunn 1999; Burawoy and Verdery 1999; Wedel 1998).

Under these conditions, anthropologists have usefully highlighted the continuing legacies of socialism, presenting these not as intractable, backward traditions nor as obstacles to future progress but rather as evolving sensibilities and strategies that may be *re*appropriated, adapted, and transformed as citizens confront the many new challenges that have arisen from reorganization in a capitalist mode (Creed 1999; Burawoy and Verdery 1999). They have observed and critiqued the practices of Western businesspeople and aid providers who tend to view their own methods of ensuring quality control in factory production or measuring the "success" of nongovernmental organizations as neutral, "efficient," necessary, and easily transferable across nations and cultures (Dunn 2004; Wedel 1998; Sampson 1996). Ethnographers have drawn attention to how such practices actually encode and depend upon specific ways of thinking about persons and social relationships—valuing individual over collective achievement and "transparency" over informal social networking—that differ from local norms. Often, these valuable studies have registered intense suspicion and moral opposition from Eastern Europeans to the same changes (including industrial privatization, a rapid influx of imported commodities, and the end of state price controls) that Western observers are likely to construe as commercial "freedoms" and signs of economic advancement (Berdahl 1999; Humphrey 1995; Caldwell 2002, 2004; Pesman 2000; Humphrey and Mandel 2002).[7]

This moral resistance is explained through reference to socialist experiences and ethics. Cathy Wanner (2005, 516), for example, writes in an article on money and morality in Ukraine that, "as new possibilities for making money open up, one of the most powerful legacies of Soviet culture is a moralizing lens through which wealth and consumption are evaluated." Along similar lines, Humphrey and Mandel (2002, 1) comment that, "having survived Western market-oriented 'shock therapy,'. . . the postsocialist societies still struggle to come to terms with the clash between deeply ingrained moralities and the daily pressures, opportunities and inequalities posed by market penetration." In the case of Russia in particular, scholars have observed that such struggles are tied to historically deep characteristics of national identity; in Russians' most impassioned discourses on the national self, they invoke the suffering, powerless, but morally aware "Russian people [*narod*]" and "Russian soul [*dusha*]" (Ries 1997; Pesman 2000; Humphrey 1995). In one of the earliest ethnographic works on perestroika and the collapse of the Soviet Union, Nancy Ries (1997) highlighted the long-term continuity of a Russian moral narrative about the dangers of money and the righteousness of poverty and suffering: popular ideology that incorporated both official Soviet platforms and pre-Soviet, including Orthodox Christian, ideas about collectivism and social justice (see also Caldwell 2004; cf. Ries 2002). Such rhetorics highlight Russian cultural difference from the West and seem to establish direct links between people's contemporary dissatisfactions and their enduring national traditions and touchstones, from Russian Orthodox religion and norms of village life to the classics of Russian literature such as Fyodor Dostoyevsky's *Crime and Punishment*.

7. Elizabeth Dunn (2004), in her ethnography of a Polish baby food plant taken over by Gerber, nicely problematizes how "freedom" has been (mis)understood in East European transitions: "Just as Poland is supposedly 'free to choose' whether it will join the European Union or participate in the global economy but in fact is compelled to do so because the only alternative is economic disaster, so too are individuals apparently more autonomous yet more stringently regulated than ever before. If marketers can successfully convince mothers that they can 'freely' choose between buying commercial baby food and poisoning their children, the choice is certainly constrained by the allocation of scientific authority to the baby food producer. . . . Becoming 'free' has thus made people less free than ever before or—freedom being hard to quantify—differently unfree" (p. 167).

All these very fine works acknowledge post-Soviet moral discourses to be multiple and sometimes contradictory. Still, discussions of Russian and post-Soviet "moralizing lenses" can tend to obscure how self-consciously "Russian" concerns for collective welfare, generosity, and "soulfulness," though clearly part of people's sense of national continuity and particularity, are not *always* invoked nor pitted so cleanly against the "outside" or "Western" world of commerce, profit making, and consumerism. The tendency to dwell upon such contrasts likely has something to do with enduring ideas about what "Russianness" entails (suffering, generosity, mystery, inscrutability)—ideas to some degree shared both by (many) Russians themselves and by ethnographers. Though it is important to recognize the cultural specificity of local responses to marketization and globalization, this project should not lead us too far in another direction, such that we tend to view the realms of "Russian culture" or of "traditional morality" as transcendent, somewhat timeless elements of identity that exist in simple opposition to an impinging capitalism.

Nor, indeed, should we underplay the fact that Soviet life involved its own structures of consumer access and its specific ideologies of justification, and that *these* ideas—which do not always condemn but rather frame and *legitimate* social inequalities in particular ways—continue to influence teachers' contemporary thinking about markets, value, and their own socioeconomic status (in addition to whatever market-hostile sentiments might deservedly be characterized as long-standing Russian mores). With this in mind, the better question to ask is not "How are market values affecting moral communities and traditional norms?" but rather "How are the connections people draw between various manifestations of value being reconfigured?" How do established logics of value shape people's experiences of large-scale changes over which they have little direct control, and how are those very logics gradually transforming as a result of such experience? What questions do people ask of the shifting tides in which they are swimming, and toward what shores do these questions lead them? How possible, desirable, and defensible do people find it to reconstruct their own senses of self and purpose to accommodate changing circumstances? I try to make anthropological sense of the very ambivalent ways in which social identifications and personal priorities are being aired in the multiple, sometimes contradictory, and certainly less mythologized situations of people's everyday lives, including many where—contrary to the more common portrayal—prosperity carries a *positive* kind of moral weight, the *shame* of poverty becomes quite tangible, and desires for material respectability are felt at least as keenly as the demands of the indomitable "Russian soul."

It is in this spirit that I examine, in the central part of this book (chapters 3, 4, and 5), how moral and material conceptions of value converged and diverged in teachers' aspirations to "culturedness," "middle-classness," and "civilization," ideals they shared with so many other consumers in the world but which also carried specifically Soviet/post-Soviet inflections (see also Stryker and Patico 2004; Fehervary 2002; Ninetto 2001; Pilkington et al. 2002). And I examine how sentiments of national pride (chapter 4) and of nostalgia for a recent past seen as more nurturing of social cohesion than today's marketizing Russia (chapters 3 and 6) continually play off more self-consciously global and consumerist conceptions of what constitutes a "normal life" in Saint Petersburg—in ways that have *converged* partially with certain Soviet middle-class ideals rather than being antithetical to them.[8] People took refuge in "Russian soul" arguments about how the have-nots were the ones who were truly meritorious, anyway; but they also found in their consumer environment less reassuring signals of their own social insignificance, impropriety, and humiliation.

The body of this book examines how teachers were embroiled in these questions during the particularly stressful "crisis" year of 1998–99. In the concluding chapter, however, I describe how just a few years later, during my return visit in 2003, the tenor of the teachers' judgments about Russian social life had shifted noticeably, throwing new light on the ambivalent tones of some of the teachers' earlier discussions, drawing attention to their temporal specificity, and highlighting the ongoing evolution of their views.

8. Such aspirations to global consumer "normalcy" have been examined in a few other postsocialist countries. Sigrid Rausing's (2000) work on consumption and "normality" in rural Estonia and Krisztina Fehervary's (2002) on the material culture of home renovations and the "normal" in urban Hungary nicely illustrate related themes of modernity and "Europeanness." In both contexts, the desire to consume Western (imported) or Western-styled goods and furnishings is understood as a matter of being "normal," and of claiming a "Western" identity that, people feel, really should have been theirs all along—but which must now be proven through respectable, "normal" consumption. In scholarship on postsocialist Russia, however, these convergences largely are occluded by more rhetorically powerful articulations of a classically "Russian" antipathy to crass materialism, making it all too easy to imagine that one traditional Russian (or, alternatively, hegemonic Soviet) morality stands in direct opposition to a new and overpowering capitalistic future. Exceptions include Shevchenko 2002a, 2002b.

Thus the teachers' commentaries of the late 1990s must be understood as responses to a very particular set of social and historical circumstances; they are not to be read as timelessly "Russian" or even as representatively "post-Soviet." To remind the reader of this, I use the past tense rather than the "ethnographic present" throughout the book, despite the fact that chapters 2 through 6 do focus upon the same "present" of 1998–99.

Saint Petersburg at the Millennium

In fact, I came to these teachers at a very particular moment. When I planned a 1998–99 ethnographic research project on consumption and social change in Russia, I had little idea that I would arrive in Saint Petersburg just as several years of relative stability and calm were giving way to a new period of drastic upheaval.[9] In the throes of the rapid depreciation of the ruble that began August 17, 1998, the atmosphere was one of dismay. In the first two weeks of September 1998, we witnessed 43 percent inflation.[10] The ruble fell against the dollar 70 percent in the first five days of that month alone, resulting in immediate and significant drops in real incomes (Simpura et al. 1999). Savings kept in rubles quickly depreciated, while people who had invested their savings in dollars found that these bank accounts were inaccessible indefinitely. For a time, certain staple goods, such as salt, rice, and flour, became difficult to find; reportedly, people were hoarding these items in expectation of the worst. Many grocery stores were half empty. Storekeepers spread a few soda bottles or boxes of candy widely apart on shelves in a feeble attempt to hide just how little there was to sell. Panic took hold not only among the poorer sectors of society but also among Saint Petersburg's more affluent residents, who scrambled to invest their cash in big-ticket items. A citywide scarcity of dollars for purchase during those weeks

9. Simpura et al. (1999) argue that the 1998 crisis was different from the jolt into extreme economic instability circa 1992, in that before 1992, "the old system restricted the freedom of people and provided them with some guaranteed benefits. In 1998, there was no old support system and the world was the same before and after the crisis" (p. 65). By that time, in other words, people had become used to weathering temporary drops in income and sudden job loss, which is not to say that situation has not brought its own challenges, instabilities, and humiliations for Russians—perhaps especially for state-employed educated professionals such as teachers whose salaries were barely adjusted to keep up with the rising cost of living after August 1998.

10. *RFE/RL Newsline,* September 17, 1998.

led consumers to "snap up items from cigarettes to cars as alternative stores of value" (Varoli 1998). The port of Saint Petersburg saw a dramatic reduction in incoming goods, as importers were affected by the uncertain value of the ruble and foreign partners sought to minimize their own risk. Some wondered whether food rationing measures were soon to follow, especially because approximately 60 percent of the city's (and Russia's) foodstuffs at the time were imported. It was a moment, then, when market values were destabilized abruptly, coming at the end of a decade rife with such economic, political, and social destablizations.

As it turned out, the shortages many feared never came. Within a few weeks, most goods had returned to shops and shelves were well stocked. However, the value of the ruble continued to drop and prices steadily rose, while adjustments in state salaries and pensions were slow in coming and relatively paltry when they finally did.[11] Though disappointed and exhausted by these events (which came to be known by everyone simply as *kriziz,* "the crisis"), most of the teachers who became my friends and informants in Saint Petersburg found that the economic reform programs, shortages, and rationing through which they had lived in the early 1990s had been more frightening and difficult than the current environment in which everything was available for a price. As one put it, "The scariest thing is not high prices, but deficit. Many people are afraid of high prices. . . . But when you need things and there isn't any [available at all], that is the worst. Especially medicines. Things have normalized now; everything can be bought, it is just expensive." At the same time, there was a general sense among them of not only economic but also cognitive strain, as they struggled to keep up with the pace of change, to earn more money by taking on extra work, and to make smart consumer choices with limited means.

To gain a sense of what all this has meant to people, it is worth highlighting again that urban Russia effectively displaces any simple notion of

11. The relationship between prices and exchange rates varied. Prices for some food products rose significantly over the course of the year but only slowly at first, especially those deemed "essential social goods" such as bread, for which Saint Petersburg governor Iakovlev issued a decree constraining price hikes (Shcherbakova 1999). Others, especially imported products, quickly rose during the late summer and early fall at rates equivalent to or even faster than the depreciation of the ruble. By the spring of 1999, the ruble's value had leveled out at about 24–25 rubles to the dollar, versus about 6 rubles in the summer of 1998. This refers to 6 "new" rubles, equivalent to 6,000 "old rubles." As of January 1, 1998, the three final orders of ten were wiped away for convenience. At this time kopecks (100 kopecks = 1 ruble), whose value had become so small that they had been impossible to use in preceding years, were reintroduced into circulation.

a hegemonic, globalizing Goliath and a culturally endangered David as the default model for understanding commoditization and cultural change. Russia stood for centuries as a colonial power in its own right, and in the twentieth century it was a center of industrial modernization where citizens were told that they enjoyed the highest standards of living in the world, shortages notwithstanding. Hence it constitutes a rather different kind of novice to the global economy than do the modernizing, postcolonial societies anthropologists more commonly study; it is one where a mass consumer society was long ago established, albeit under very different conditions than those that were taking form in the 1990s.

It is true that, to many of its citizens, Russia is situated not only geographically but also historically, culturally, and symbolically at the margins of Europe, forcibly detained by seventy years of Soviet rule from attaining the levels of technological and consumer sophistication enjoyed in the West and believed to be long deserved at home. In 1991, the city of Leningrad gave up its Soviet name in favor of its precommunist one, Saint Petersburg, signaling an explicit effort to place the social and political experiments of the twentieth century firmly into the past. As the hectic center of both politics and business, Moscow is at the forefront of post-Soviet economic transformation and consumer market expansion. Saint Petersburg is a quieter second; it is a center of arts and culture more than commerce. Whereas Muscovites tend to view Saint Petersburg as the sleepier of the two capitals, Petersburg residents refer to their hometown as the less brash, more polite, and culturally refined, and thus—in spirit as in architecture—as the more "European." In fact, the city has always been seen as Russia's most "European," by Peter the Great's design at the turn of the eighteenth century. The city thereby lays claim to a special place in Western civilization, though not primarily with a capitalist inflection (figures 1.3, 1.4, and 1.5).

Identifying perhaps even more closely than other locals with these cultural legacies of their city, Saint Petersburg's teachers commented on the bitter irony that they now seemed to be living in what had become just another "Third World country." Some spoke of having made their way fairly well in the "New Russia" through their own hard work, though they also contrasted their relative success in the mid-1990s with the subsequent blow that the 1998 ruble depreciation dealt to their finances. And by their own admission, many of them saw market economics as essentially necessary and positive. They appreciated that certain matters (How many hours would they work? How many jobs would they hold? What salaries would

Figure 1.3. Summer excursions on Saint Petersburg's canals. Photograph by the author.

Figure 1.4. Winter in the northern capital: the Peter and Paul Fortress on the frozen Neva River. Photograph by the author.

Figure 1.5. Apartment complexes built in the 1950s through the 1970s dominate the landscape as one moves away from downtown Saint Petersburg. Photograph by the author.

they accept?) had fallen more directly under their personal control. Indeed, having read sociological accounts that placed teachers among Russia's "new poor," I was struck by the degree to which my interlocutors accepted market competition as a normal, legitimate mode of human civilization—though to be sure, they would have liked the postcommunist Russian government to be taking far greater responsibility for its constituents' material well-being.

This is the story, then, of the contradictory positionings and deep ambivalence of the "cultured," relatively impoverished citizens of a superpower turned "Third World" nation. I see the teachers neither as victims of capitalist transition nor as pure agents of their own destinies within it; instead, I focus upon their experiences as interrogators and interpreters of shifting sets of expectations and values. Within their ambivalent interpretations of postsocialist life are some of the seeds of Russia's social and moral order as it is becoming: a perestroika, a rebuilding or restructuring, of much more than shop inventories and urban landscapes—yet intimately interconnected with those material artifacts all the same.

Notes on Researching Consumption and Everyday Life

If the diffuseness of the phenomena that can fall under the rubric of "consumption" is what makes this such a rewarding locus for investigating complex experiences of change, these same qualities present considerable challenges for ethnographic study. This is particularly true when research is to be conducted in an urban environment where social life is relatively atomized. To be sure, I planned to live in Saint Petersburg for twelve months (August 1998–June 1999, September–October 1999). But where to begin a meaningful investigation of consumption? There is no one place or context in which people "do" it; it is part of the ongoing flow of life, of relating to others, of creating oneself, of perceiving the world. How, then, to construct a viable ethnographic study?

I looked to a workplace as the starting point for my ethnography because such settings served as nodes of consumer networks during the Soviet period (Temkina 1996, 228), and I was interested to see how these work-based consumer mechanisms might be functioning or transforming more recently. Narrowing the field further, I chose to train my eye more closely on women than on men. As the infamous "double burden" carried by Soviet (and many post-Soviet) women indicates, women were expected not only to participate full time in the USSR's public labor force but also to maintain special responsibility for the care of home and family, including obtaining food and other necessities—no small business in the era of shortages and networking. This is not to say that husbands never participated in housework and shopping; on the contrary, it was not particularly unusual that they should help out with these tasks (especially if they should happen upon a lucky find when passing by a local shop, or when they could make use of their own workplace positions to gain access to desirable goods and resources). Nonetheless, when it comes to generalized social norms, expectations, and ideals, the work associated with care of the home (cleaning, decorating) and family (including cooking, shopping, and emotional support) has been understood to fall primarily to wives and mothers. It should be noted, however, that men also worked in the schools in which I ultimately decided to conduct my research, though in much smaller numbers; in addition, I met the husbands, children, and other family members of some female teachers. I gladly accepted their input and have integrated it into my analyses.

I have outlined above several reasons why teachers provide a useful perspective from which to understand the everyday experience of post-Soviet socioeconomic upheaval. From a methodological standpoint, a school was also a logical starting place in that the field of education is populated mainly by women. Many of those professions that were feminized during the Soviet period, including teaching, nursing, and medicine, have been among the hardest hit by recent drops in state funding (Eremicheva 1996, 162; Silverman and Yanowitch 2000). The fact that I could offer help with English classes provided an additional reason to focus on schools rather than hospital clinics or other workplaces; and this informal assistance, particularly welcome in a context where both time and resources for supplemental teaching materials were scarce, turned out to be important as a means of establishing friendly ties with teachers. It also allowed me at least partially to return their generosity in hosting and talking with me.

Within a few weeks of my arrival in Saint Petersburg in September 1998, academic and personal contacts gave me access to three schools. On the basis of the availability of teachers at each school, the receptiveness of administrators, and other logistical considerations, I settled on one school as the primary site for the project. Because few of the teachers I met had very much free time over the course of the workday, I decided to spend some additional hours each week at a second school, thereby expanding my base of acquaintances and providing opportunities for comparing the two collectives. Both schools were public, but they were better off than many others in the city, for their buildings were maintained relatively well and they enjoyed good academic reputations. Furthermore, it should be noted that they were both located in neighborhoods close to downtown that many considered desirable places to live as compared with the outlying bedroom districts; this, too, influenced the social makeup of their student bodies in favor of more prosperous families. Some of these families became benefactors that provided the schools with extra income, sometimes given in exchange for their children's admittance.

The site at which I worked most often (usually several days per week) was an English specialization school where students devoted extra class hours to English-language training (all other subjects were conducted in Russian). It had a rather large English faculty of about eighteen elementary, middle, and high school teachers (grades one through eleven). Many of my informants came from this group, a manageable subunit in which I could become acquainted with everyone and could easily schedule individual meetings and interviews (conducted in Russian). The head of the English Department served as my most important contact person at the school, occasionally arranging for me to meet a new teacher or to participate in English classes and school events, especially in the early months before I had established my own network of friends and acquaintances.

The other school I visited regularly (about one or two days per week) was an unspecialized fifth-through-eleventh-grade *gimnaziia*. Though it was a publicly funded school, its status as a *gimnaziia* meant that its students wore uniforms (not customary at most public schools) and were given the option of paying for optional classes such as "Design" and "Etiquette" that were not part of the standard public school curriculum.[12] It was significantly smaller than the English specialization school; it did not house any departments so large, and social interaction among teachers and administrators there was conducted through smaller, more closed cliques. Thus though I did gradually establish friendly connections with several teachers, I depended heavily upon one particularly close contact. This woman, who became a key informant and good friend to me, helped arrange appointments (especially with her own closer colleagues) and made sure I knew about school holiday events as well as inviting me to more intimate teachers' gatherings.

Over the course of my time in Saint Petersburg, I built a group of about twenty-four informants in all, about a dozen at each school. I conducted semidirected interviews with each of these informants (totaling approximately three to eight interviews in most cases, depending on each individual's accessibility). These addressed such topics as weekly shopping habits and preferences; the distribution of these responsibilities in the family; gift giving, holiday celebration, and hospitality; style and taste; family budgeting; self-evaluations of social status; and attitudes toward advertising. As a general strategy, I favored "small" questions that asked interviewees to report on concrete practices and weekly habits, for I was particularly interested to see how "big" questions (e.g., perceptions of class difference) were revealed implicitly, in bits and pieces, in the somewhat less examined and seemingly mundane choices and concerns associated with consumption. I came to each session prepared with a list of interview questions; but though all the preplanned questions were covered sooner or later in most cases, our discussions often ended up addressing many other questions that I had not

12. A post-Soviet *gimnaziia* "exist[s] within the traditional education system and experiment[s] with slight modifications of such internal elements as curriculum, teaching methods, parent and student involvement, and dress codes; . . . [but leaves] pre-existing funding and regulatory relationships with the ministry and regional departments of education intact" (Westbrook, Lurie, and Ivanov 1994, 108).

anticipated. As a rule, I followed the speakers' cues, taking the opportunity to ask impromptu follow-up questions whenever their comments spurred unexpected and relevant reflections. These in turn provided me with material for new, better-informed ways of posing questions in future discussions with other teachers.

I regularly lectured and led discussions in English classes at the English specialization school. As I had hoped, my status as a native English speaker was a boon to my work there. Not only did English language teachers appreciate my help with their classes but to some degree they came to view me as a colleague—a language specialist and teacher, like them—as much as a researcher with my own agendas. It is probably also true that their personal and professional interests in English made them more eager and somewhat less guarded about socializing with a foreigner than some locals might have been. Younger women who befriended me posed questions about makeup and fashion in the United States ("This brand is very expensive in Russia—is it considered one of the best in America, too?"), while older women seemed compelled by the idea of helping out a young American woman who had come to try to understand the hardships of Russian life for regular people like themselves.

I was included in school events such as faculty holiday celebrations and school assemblies, and informal contact with teachers led to many impromptu coffee breaks, discussions, and visits to informants' homes. With time we visited cafes, attended concerts, or went swimming together. Some invited me home for food and conversation (and in one case, to a bar with friends) almost right away, setting the foundation for friendships that developed over the course of the year. Several of the teachers became good friends, and their gracious willingness to participate in interviews as well as to involve me personally in their lives did much to deepen my understanding of the significance for them of consumption. Certainly it complicated my sense of the concerns that could arise in various kinds of decisions and social engagements. Visiting friends always presented the opportunity to ponder such questions, because it was common practice to bring a small contribution of cookies, cake, chocolate, or the like along to one's host. This was a matter of good manners; and in practical terms, it helped balance the expenditure of resources one's presence necessitated on the part of the host, for having tea— and snacks to go with it—was an obligatory part of home visiting.

Yet there were no hard-and-fast rules of reciprocity to follow. As Pierre Bourdieu observes, the logic of practice is not entirely logical in the scientist's sense, dependent as it is not only on shared cultural predispositions

but also on situational contingencies and judgments about the paths of action that will fulfill actors' various and variable goals most successfully in
concrete cases (Bourdieu 1990). To give an example, one family welcomed
me to their home often, and I knew that their resources were running low.
Should I bring extra sweets to them on my next visit to show my appreciation? Or would a slight extravagance make them feel worse the next time
they arrived at my apartment with homemade preserves (which I loved),
apologizing that they had had no time to buy a cake at the bakery? The
teachers themselves sometimes described similar uncertainties and shifting
expectations, which were particularly noticeable in the "crisis" context of
recent and ongoing instability. I have tried to do justice in the chapters to
come to the complexity and unsettledness of the teachers' consumer practices and discourses, and I have included as far as possible their own articulated rationales as well as the details of concrete situations that I observed
or in which I participated.

I accompanied some informants on one or more routine grocery shopping trips, where I observed individuals' choices of shops and markets as
well as some of their specific purchases. As useful as this methodology did
prove to be, it also presented certain dilemmas that were themselves revealing of the consumer climate of that moment. Scheduling the trip was
the first challenge, because teachers often said that while they were willing
to participate in theory, they were either very busy or had no money for
shopping just then. Some teachers seemed hesitant to take me at my word
that I would be interested in just tagging along with them as they stopped
off for bread or milk on the way home from work. More extensive shopping
trips were taken more seldom—especially given the fact that we were in the
midst of a financial crisis that had reduced the value of their salaries considerably—and it was such an excursion that they often seemed to think I
must mean when I said I wanted to "go shopping" (*za pokupkami*).[13] Just a
few seemed really uncomfortable with (or perhaps just inconvenienced by)
the idea, and they put the trip off into the future long enough that we never
got around to it. Yet these same people were quite forthright with me in conversation about the fact that their resources were depleted and acquisitions
paltry. One woman, having delayed our planned shopping trip a few times

---

13. Note that the term "shopping," directly transliterated from English into Russian,
had started to appear in glossy magazines, referring to the more leisurely process of shopping as a pleasurable activity. I did not use this phrase in our discussions, however, but
the more routine one: to go "*za pokupkami*," literally, "to go for [in pursuit of] purchases."

already, circumvented the problem by inviting me along when the school gave her a bit of money to buy supplies needed for an upcoming teachers' party, rather than including me on a personal shopping trip. Another friend, who was perfectly happy to stop into shops with me to pick up a few groceries or to browse for clothing in more spontaneous situations, hesitated when I proposed ahead of time to come along with her on a routine grocery shopping trip. "So how was it, were you disappointed with my purchases?" a third asked as we walked away from the market where she had let me observe her weekly shopping.

Such moments highlighted the fact that my position as a researcher, and perhaps much more important my understood privilege as an American, had an effect on how people presented themselves and their consumption to me. This kind of bias is inevitable, but I believe I have compensated for it substantially by generating a rich set of data collected in several different ways: by observing actions as well as hearing opinions, recording countless comments people made in passing as well as their more considered answers, and asking all kinds of "small," concrete questions in addition to the more open-ended ones that brought out people's relatively formulated opinions about the "Problems of Russian Life." The methodological tack of shopping was invaluable insofar as the trips prompted informant observations (about prices, salespeople, favored stalls and brands, etc.) that otherwise would have been difficult to draw out in conversation. These commentaries, even if they do not always represent realistic pictures of individuals' and families' concrete consumer habits, are quite useful as sources of information about the day-to-day concerns and explanatory frameworks through which people were able to make sense of their choices and decisions. Furthermore, the ways in which informants exhibited awareness of how their situations must have looked to an American researcher are notable in and of themselves, for they indicate how these urban Russians imagined a wider world of consumption and Russia's place in it.

More valuable than all these relatively systematic methodologies were the many leisurely evenings spent over tea or vodka with those teachers who became my good friends, and the hours spent walking with them or on my own through the streets and squares of Saint Petersburg. My work with the teachers was also supplemented with attention to relevant aspects of public culture, including television, street advertising, women's magazines, and urban shopping environments. However, I concentrated on learning as much as possible about the specificities of my informants' everyday lives, a choice whose wisdom I believe is borne out in the discussions ahead.

Plan of the Book

The rest of this book is organized as follows. Chapter 2 provides a socio-historical prologue to my examination of contemporary deliberations over logics of value by examining the Soviet and post-Soviet social positionings of schoolteachers. This discussion includes brief histories of Soviet social stratification and notions of "culturedness" and considers what being respectably "middle class" has meant and means in contemporary Russia, as people scramble to regain their social bearings. Chapter 3 examines in closer ethnographic detail some of the social categories and concerns most salient in teachers' workplace interactions as well as their consumer ideologies, showing that, for teachers, consumer opportunities, unsatisfied desires, and accounts of stereotyped lifestyles were bound up in a deliberation about values; specifically, about the relationships that exist—or should exist—between personal initiative, social mobility, and their materialization in goods and wealth.

Chapter 4 shifts to examine categories of value that are parallel in their logics but global in scale, as I describe the concrete dilemmas teachers faced in food and clothing shopping and the strategies through which they addressed these. Of particular interest are their concerns about the quality and safety of imported versus domestic foodstuffs and their techniques for avoiding undesirable or harmful goods. Here, consumers' commentaries pointed to a status hierarchy that ranked nations of producers as well as consumers, placing "civilized" Europe on one end and its antithesis, the humiliated developing world, on the other—and Russia somewhere ambiguously between. Standards of consumer civilization transposed the local/national deliberation over values seen in chapter 3 into a conversation about who deserved what in the global ecumene, reflecting subjects' timely and dynamic understandings of Russia's position at the end of the twentieth century.

Chapter 5 revisits themes of class inequality, culturedness, and propriety with a more explicit focus on the gender framing of consumption. By exploring how consumption is situated vis-à-vis domains of work, domesticity, and leisure that are both gendered and classed, this chapter provides deeper insight into how consumption plays into the demonstration, recognition, and contestation of privilege and of personal, gendered qualities such as culturedness and professionalism or laziness and superficiality. The deliberation over logics of value is here a matter of why, in the eyes of teachers, the "wrong" kind of women have had greatest access to the free time and material wealth it takes to be an attractive woman and good home-maker in contemporary Saint Petersburg.

Returning, finally, to some of the classic questions posed by the anthropology of value, chapter 6 explores gift giving, hospitality, and other modes of informal exchange. Though the social networks people once mobilized to obtain desirable commodities in the Soviet shortage economy were no longer much needed or advantageous, certain forms of networking and gift giving continued to be practiced in institutional and private arenas where privileged access and variable qualities of service were at stake. Teachers' gift relations illustrate vividly how social actors assessed one another and the terms of their relationships (or those they hoped to create) and objectified these stances through carefully chosen material objects. Centering on the question of why particular objects tended to be chosen for exchange in these semipublic contexts, the chapter culminates in an argument for why gift choices are so revealing of contestation about moral legitimacy and personal worth in Russia, and it asks what kind of "society" or societies people may thereby be reconstructing. Finally, chapter 7 describes how the tenor of the teachers' talk had shifted during my follow-up research in 2003 and considers how their logics of value are gradually transforming, with implications for how teachers and others conceptualize and legitimate relations of inequality in a changing Russia.

Mercedes Logic

At a teachers' New Year's celebration banquet in December 1998, late in the evening, the teachers and administrators began drifting home to make sure their children and husbands were fed. A smaller group of remaining revelers consolidated the scattered bottles of vodka and leftover appetizers of thinly sliced bread, prettily topped with orange salmon caviar or cold cuts and dill, onto one central, now more intimate, table. Amid toasts and anecdotes, someone raised a question for group discussion: Is it better to be happy (to be glad, *radovat'sia*) or to have a Mercedes? Several votes were offered for happiness. The head of the English Department pointedly asked me to contribute; I was the American, so what did I think? I concurred that certainly to be happy was better. Another teacher piped up triumphantly that it would be best to be happy in a Mercedes! Whereupon another corrected her that no, those who had Mercedeses were not happy, because they "aspired"—they were never satisfied but always aiming for more (*oni ne raduiutsia potomu chto stremliaiut*).[14]

The Mercedes question provided several minutes of distracting party conversation. It had an assumed answer, to be sure. But in the middle of an evening full of good wishes for 1999 and toasts praising the talents and hard work of the teachers' *kollektiv,* the debate also addressed nagging doubts and key dissatisfactions of the moment. The ritual of playing out possible responses allowed participants to come to an unusually unequivocal conclusion, more reassuring than those likely to be found in their workaday lives. Around the toasting table, the revelers had found that one could at least be glad not to have a Mercedes, for having one would mean sacrificing too much of oneself, endangering future happiness and the sustenance of any meaningful social relationships.

The debate's outcome that night did not mean, however, that the question was really closed. Mercedeses were not necessarily dismissed as not worth having, nor was the lack of them—along with a world of other luxuries (and some relative necessities) consumed by others both close to and far from home but inaccessible to the teachers—so easily accepted or understood. These questions remained open to ongoing consideration, and stances were articulated in explicit debate or, much more implicitly, in the ongoing decisions and judgments of everyday consumerism. As they came to terms with the institutional shifts under way in postsocialist Russia, people applied and incrementally reworked particular logics of cause and effect that helped to make sense of why some people were coming out ahead while others seemed to fall further behind.

The individuals whom readers will encounter here did not drive Mercedeses but only watched them drive by and reflected upon their significance. As such, they might not seem to be on the leading edge of a now-capitalist Russia—depending upon how one envisions its trajectories. Yet they have their own contribution to make to an anthropology of consumption, value, and social change. To put it most simply, it is my hope that the cognitive limbo my friends and informants in Saint Petersburg have faced will spur readers to reflect upon the "truths" and assumptions that inform their own positionings and life choices—shaped as they are by logics of value that all too often appear to us as the natural way of things.

---

14. It is worth noting that the term chosen here is not the common adjective *schastlivyi* (contented, fortunate) but the verb *radovat'sia* (to be glad, rejoice).

Chapter 2

Finding—and Losing—One's
Place in the Middle

"From thirty to thirty thousand dollars—cheaper at night!" Veronika quoted a commercial that had been running frequently on local television, advertising a downtown shop open long hours and claiming cheap (and not so cheap) prices for sheepskin coats. This seemed to her, an elderly elementary school teacher, truly ridiculous, and she continued: "Have you seen the new store on Kammennostrovskii Avenue?" I had, indeed, seen this recently opened establishment just a short walk away from the school, on a main commercial thoroughfare. Through an entirely glass storefront one could see racks full of particularly thick, luxurious fur coats; this was obviously an expensive boutique for a select few. Veronika called it *shikarnyi:* chic, impressive. I had been hesitant to enter it myself, not only because I had no need of (nor money for) an expensive fur coat but also because, as teachers too had complained, customers could expect to be glared at pointedly by salespeople in upscale shops if they were not dressed expensively and stylishly. Veronika noted incredulously that a sign in the store's window boasted "extra-high prices." How could they advertise that way, as though astronomically high prices were a *good* thing? Who was it supposed to be for? Veronika seemed to wonder.

Because I did not remember seeing that surprising sign at the shop, I walked by later to check and saw one in the window that read: "Super prices" (*super-tseny*). The prefix "super" has been adopted into Russian colloquial usage, often suggesting something prestigious or desirable as well as high, big, or extreme, as in "supermarket" or "superstylish." Thus the sign, which I had accepted as referring to "great prices," had been read by Veronika as touting "very high prices." This would have been an unusual advertising ploy; to her, it was shocking but also *plausible* in the context of all the other ways in which an older order of prices and allocations had been turned on its head. Veronika, an elementary school teacher who had passed retirement age but continued to work, often spoke indignantly about the measly salary raises that Saint Petersburg's teachers had received for the new 1999–2000 school year (postcrisis). "[Salaries were raised] by fifty rubles [approximately $2 per month]. . . . It's ludicrous."

Urban conditions including fluctuating prices provoked not only the most practical questions about how one might budget one's money from week to week but also doubts about where one fit into the general scheme of values. This chapter begins to examine more closely the subjective experience of socioeconomic transformation in Saint Petersburg in the 1990s: how people articulated and struggled to overcome a sense of general disorientation, and to discover the new logics according to which prosperity and respectability appeared to be distributed in postsocialist society.

The quantitative measures presented in this chapter—including teachers' average salaries, their relationship to official poverty thresholds, ruble/dollar exchange rates during the 1998–99 crisis year, and so on—inform readers unfamiliar with recent Russian events about the overall conditions of financial constraint and instability under which teachers and their fellow city residents were operating. But the more important question for this study is how teachers were *interpreting* and addressing conditions such as the diversification of local commodity markets, fluctuating prices, and declines in their own buying power. For people inferred from these developments knowledge about their *own* apparent worth and their places within shifting social hierarchies. What kind of resources or personal qualities seemed most to determine one's social place? Were teachers part of the "middle class"? Was this desirable, and what did it mean in a context where many old categories and hierarchies had become obsolete?

Before returning to these experiential aspects of post-Soviet marketization, however, it is necessary to examine the consumer logics and structures of inequality within which the adults described here grew up in the USSR.

Shortages and Social Networks:
The Soviet Consumer Context

The Soviet Union was plagued by ongoing shortages of basic foodstuffs and commodities that resulted in the hours-long queues that became, for the United States and other capitalist, democratic countries, such a striking symbol of the failure of socialism to fulfill citizens' needs and desires the very dynamics of shortage—and the practices people pursued to cumvent it—themselves partially arose from, and certainly reproduced, a kind of commitment to and investment in consumption that was particular to socialist Eastern Europe in the twentieth century.

The post–World War II Soviet economy concentrated state resources in heavy industry (energy, raw materials, and armaments) at the expense of production of consumer commodities. Overall economic growth was low during the period popularly known as *zastoi*, literally "stagnation," which was roughly coterminous with Leonid Brezhnev's leadership (1964–82) and ended only with Mikhail Gorbachev's call for radical economic reform in 1986 (McCauley 1997). Nonetheless, measured efforts were made to accommodate demand for commodities under Brezhnev (Millar 1990, 187). Consumption per capita by the early 1980s had almost doubled since Joseph Stalin's death in 1953, and significant increases had been seen in supplies of clothing, fruits, and vegetables as well as in ownership of consumer durables (Millar 1981, 97, 101). Gradually it became possible—if erratically so, and often only through considerable effort—to buy cars, refrigerators, and televisions. New housing was constructed, and tourism within the USSR was encouraged (Kelly 1998c). Still, production did not respond to consumer demand but rather followed centralized planning schema devised according to the regime's strategic priorities.

Nor did goods, once manufactured, flow freely to the distribution points where need was greatest. Instead, the economies of socialist Eastern Europe and the Soviet Union were organized centrally, such that shipments of scarce goods were directed to certain favored shops and important cities (particularly Moscow and, secondarily, Leningrad) and not to others. At the same time, retail prices were kept artificially low through state subsidization; raising them to levels more accurately reflecting actual demand was considered politically risky, in that it might have provoked greater popular dissatisfaction and unrest (Millar 1990, 188). Certain commodities, particularly the most underpriced ones for which demand far outstripped availability, were known as "deficit" (*defitsit*) products and were seldom to be found on shop shelves.

In this context, successful shopping required considerable stores of knowledge and expertise on the part of potential buyers, especially in the absence of indicators of quality of the kind used by consumers elsewhere in the world. For example, prices could not necessarily be read as meaningful signs of quality; one simply needed to know where food tended to be of higher quality and to ascertain and remember which stores had particular items in stock most often. In fact, deficit goods exclusively available in limited-access, elite shops and canteens could actually be priced *lower* than those more readily available to the general population (Voslensky 1984). Foods that were difficult to find were put away by citizens lucky enough to have obtained them for use on holidays and for special gatherings with friends. Alternatively, stores such as the specially stocked Eliseevskii in downtown Leningrad often had what could not be found elsewhere, as long as one was willing to stand in line for hours on end. People who had enough free time, such as retired senior citizens, could stand in shop lines all day to maximize their families' consumer possibilities. In cities less central than Moscow and Leningrad, certain products disappeared entirely for long periods of time; stores in provincial towns might offer only a few stale foodstuffs, while those in rural villages were likely to be entirely empty (Kelly 1998c, 255–56). As a teacher later remembered the visits of provincial Russians to Saint Petersburg and Moscow, "It was like a 'shopping tour' to the capital—just for sausage!" Whenever she traveled to smaller towns in those days, she brought along sausages as gifts ("just a normal sausage," she reminisced), and people always gave her a very warm reception as one of their own (*kak rodnoi*).

Soviet consumers were not entirely dependent on the formal economy and official allocations, however, a reality that was reflected in the jocular but revealing Soviet-era curse: "May you live only on your salary." People found channels other than state provisioning and official salaries through which to obtain scarce items, engaging in a wide range of informal economic practices that some scholars call the "second economy" (Grossman 1977; Millar 1981). Private commerce was not entirely prohibited in the USSR, but there were severe limitations on hiring others to work in enterprises for personal profit, on intermediary activities, and on private ownership of the means of production. Still, small-scale private enterprise was commonplace and took a variety of forms—from the legal use of private plots and sale of crops grown on them, to the legally ambiguous sale or barter of homemade and second-hand goods, to the straight theft of state resources. Indeed, these practices often defied clear categorization as either "legal" or "illegal" and "criminal" practices (Millar 1981, 91, 94–95). "Public property" could be manipulated in "private" ways, as in informal exchanges of state-allocated housing (Millar 1981, 88; see also Timofeev 1985).

Accordingly, wealth in the form of money was not the most advantageous kind of capital to have, because education, goods, and other signs of status could be obtained and contacts cultivated through alternative means; money would not get a person very far without also having the proper social contacts and access to state resources.[1] Access to resources at one's workplace could similarly be turned to private advantage, as in the case of the truck driver who diverted the load he was transporting away from its intended destination to sell for a profit, or the industrial director who bought and sold materials against the specifications of official allotments (Grossman 1977, 29). In some cases, people pilfered from their own workplaces or from warehouses scarce items such as sausages, coffee, soap, and caviar that were temporarily or permanently absent from local stores. They often spoke not of having purchased new things (even if they had exchanged them for cash) but of where and how they had managed to "obtain" (*dostat'*) them. Storekeepers and clerks held aside the most sought after and scarce goods for their own friends and acquaintances, often selling them for personal profit or as a favor to someone who might supply a return favor at some later time. Memories of hotly pursued sausages (*kolbasa*) and imported shoes came to mind most quickly when people in post-Soviet Saint Petersburg recalled the kinds of exchanges in which they engaged back then. A teacher in her midtwenties reminisced about a night in her childhood when there had been a knock at the door after she was already in bed. A neighbor had obtained some good sausage for them, and the young girl enjoyed some of it in a sandwich on the spot, right there in her bed. Another woman recalled getting a phone call in the dead of a freezing and snowy winter informing her that someone had succeeded in getting some good sausage for her. Despite the threatening weather, she bundled herself up and headed out to retrieve the prize.

The organization of all these activities drew upon and created ties of friendship, as well as proceeding along kin and family lines, common ethnic or territorial origins, and broker-client relationships. Exchanges were conducted through variously understood social channels: *na levo* (literally, "on the left" or "under the counter"), *na chernom rynke* ("on the black market"), *po znakomstvu* ("through a contact"), and *po blatu* ("through pull") (Millar 1981, 96; Sampson 1985–86). The key colloquial term *blat* referred

---

1. This point should not be overplayed, especially because some commodities, such as clothing and large household appliances, were quite expensive even through state outlets. Still, the limitations on money's usefulness, and the general avoidance of money in *blat* relationships (Ledeneva 1998) and careful ritualization when it was used in informal contexts, resulted in what Pesman (2000) has referred to as the "low moneyness of money" in the Soviet Union.

to a variety of practices but most often involved obtaining access to "deficit" commodities through personal connections. "Favors of access" were exchanged among friends and acquaintances in relationships of loose reciprocity. Such favors were framed by participants more as "helping one's friends" than as utilitarian profit seeking, representing ways in which "we" could help one another in spite of "their" unsatisfactory provisioning (Ledeneva 1998). Drawing on one's *blat* was not just a means of procuring goods and services that would otherwise be difficult to get, then, but was in fact also inextricable from the fabric of friendships, morality and behavioral norms, and social relations in general. Though all family members participated, women tended to spend the most time and to build the greatest expertise in these endeavors, for it was they who usually managed family finances and were considered primarily responsible for the maintenance of households. In short, consumption produced social identities in the USSR, as the acquisition of goods was itself a thickly social activity that required not only money but also the mobilization of other sorts of "capital," relationships, and know-how.[2] This is not, however, to suggest that Soviet consumption was a "collectivist" endeavor free from the stratifying effects more often associated with the consumer culture of the West.

— I feel like the US has . . . L of
Connection had Consumption too —

Hierarchies of Access

In Soviet Russia, work and professionalism were linked explicitly with privileges of consumer access. Having been won in the name of the working class, the Communist Revolution promised to bring full social equality to the citizens of the new Soviet Union through the socialization of property and rational redistribution of resources according to need. However, beginning in the 1930s, and yet more markedly in the postwar 1940s, Stalin and his administration committed themselves to partnership with a broader range of professional groups, constructing a system of graduated material rewards and marks of honor. These were distributed in recognition of individuals' work performance and in accordance with their membership in the professional groups deemed most vital to the USSR's economic growth and the continuing stability of the regime (Lane 1985; Zemtsov 1985; Dunham 1976; Fitzpatrick 1992).

2. Some of these networking activities continued into the 1990s and beyond, as I discuss in chapter 6; see also Caldwell 2004.

In the 1920s, opportunities for social mobility through access to higher education were provided to working-class people. However, these doors to advancement did not stay wide open for long, as emphasis shifted to placating the desires of the new middle class for security and material comforts. In the 1930s and 1940s, Stalin's administration was bent on rapid industrial progress and, after World War II, reconstruction; but these goals were endangered by conditions of poverty, devastation, and the threat of widespread discontent. A solution was found in cultivation of the loyalty of the newly created stratum of professionals and bureaucrats, whose skills and political apathy were considered important to Soviet stability and therefore progress. Likewise, this newly established middle class, apparently more interested in material prosperity than in political ideals, was susceptible to the material incentives offered for their productivity and docility. This "Big Deal," as Vera Dunham (1976, 17) dubbed it, came about because "neither the regime nor the middle class was interested in ideology or further revolutionary upheavals. Neither objected to a stratified society. . . . Both were interested in stabilization, normalization, and material progress."

Increasingly, differential incomes and consumer privileges provided incentives to bureaucrats, engineers, and other professionals as well as students, and this stratification appears to have been accepted by the population as legitimate, as a Western journalist traveling in Stalinist Russia confirmed:[3]

The Soviet student who receives a higher scholarship and can afford smarter clothes is not merely dressed better than his fellow students, but he is also, demonstrably, a man of greater ability; his smart suit is tangible proof of this. . . . On the whole, [Soviet citizens of the 1930s] accept achievement as the basis of social advancement, and they have a genuine and sincere admiration for the expert. (Mehnert 1962, 69, 100–1, 111)

Thus while Stalin did use his now infamous powers of coercion to fend off challenges to state authority, his regime also offered positive incentives to its allies—not only in the form of personal incomes and increased wage

---

3. Using Bourdieu's terminology, Fitzpatrick (1999, 105) argues that the Soviet intelligentsia and elites "misrecognized" their own privilege by thinking of it in "cultural terms." Stalin referred to the entire elite, including Communist officials, as the "intelligentsia"; "thus, the Soviet 'intelligentsia' (in Stalin's broad definition) was privileged not because it was a ruling class or an elite status group, but because it was the most cultured, advanced group in a backward society."

differentials but also via special commodities made available only to certain groups and the selective provision of superior, inexpensive social services such as dining halls and child care centers. Though Stalin's government continued to pay lip service to revolutionary agendas, it did not, in practice, extend the same offer of partnership to the postwar working class (Dunham 1976, 15).

In fact, there was a very noticeable dearth of available consumer commodities; heavy industrial production was the focus of the Soviet economy, at the expense of items for popular consumption. Throughout the Stalin era (from the late 1920s to 1953), particularly during World War II and its aftermath, most people in the USSR were hard pressed simply making ends meet and purchasing enough food for their families. Periods of growth and increased market activity were interspersed with times of extreme scarcity and rationing; and, particularly at these more strained moments, state-led hierarchies took root that distributed available goods differentially by profession and institutional rank. Those with the most privileged access shopped at special stores, where the standard products—along with more rarely found, higher-quality ones—could be had at prices lower than those typical elsewhere in the same cities (Hessler 1996; Osokina 1998).

Policies and economic conditions fluctuated in the postwar period; under Nikita Khrushchev (1953–64), income differentials were relatively small and new efforts were made to shape material culture in accordance with functionalist, socialist ideals. However, threats to stability in the Brezhnev era, including poor availability of consumer goods and dissatisfied bureaucrats, led the Communist Party to increase material incentives once again, to allow elites more "quasi-legal perks," and to turn a blind eye to illegal or semi-legal petty trade and other informal economic activities (Buchli 1999, 137–47; Millar 1990). While Brezhnev's tenure (1964–82) is popularly known as an extended period of *zastoi,* or stagnation, that is, of slowed economic growth and general social malaise, increased attention was finally paid to the production of consumer commodities. These were accompanied by a renewed enthusiasm for acquisitiveness, officially defined now as a legitimate aspect of a respectable, comfortable, "cultured" life.

Special buying privileges were allotted to people according to their workplaces; for example, particular collectives were allowed to purchase special packages of goods not available to the general public. Through the final decades of the Soviet Union's existence, Communist Party administrators and other privileged citizens had access to special shops and goods. *Berezka* stores sold the most exclusive items for foreign currency only, catering to tourists and to those selected citizens who were allowed to travel and to hold hard currency. At the highest levels, lush office furnishings, expensive cars, and connection to special telephone lines (separate from regular city lines) for the Moscow elite marked degrees of status and influence (Zemstov 1985; Voslensky 1984). These extravagances were less publicly and conspicuously flaunted than the riches of today's "New Russians," but people were aware that they existed; and party leaders' perks were not generally seen as legitimate rewards for work deserving of respect.

It is important, indeed, to remember that the distinction between "us" and "them"—where "they" are corrupt, power-hungry, uncultured, and undeserving (as teachers deride today's nouveaux riches), while "we" are simple, good people who help out our friends whenever we can—is not at all a new vision of Russian society, though the evaluative categories and valences shift. Dale Pesman (2000, 261), for example, draws a direct connection between how people in Omsk talked about Soviet-era party bureaucrats and about New Russians in the early to middle 1990s. Both were "said to be stupid and uncultured, to have no sensibility or scruples, and to be hard to distinguish from mafiosi." Likewise, there was a significant degree of skepticism about the system's efficiency (or lack thereof) and the real value of participation in the Soviet labor force, as expressed in the famous popular quip: "We pretend to work, and they pretend to pay us."

It is also crucial to note that the Soviet Union was, in fact, more equitable in its distribution of resources than its twentieth-century counterparts in North America and Europe (Shlapentokh 1999, 1170; Lane 1990). Gaps in incomes and standards of living, though appreciable, were smaller in scale than those prevalent in the United States in the twentieth century; nor were they so visible as those that took hold in Russia in the 1990s. Of particular importance, virtually all Soviet citizens could depend on the state for salaries and services adequate for their basic survival. Still, despite the regime's continuing, stated commitment to the values of equality and social justice and the interests of the proletariat, differentiation in consumption was naturalized and legitimated by virtue of its association with notions of socially useful work and professionalism. A new kind of hierarchical structure had been institutionalized and naturalized, organized according to individuals' educational backgrounds, professional identities, and statuses in the Communist Party, and it was maintained through the differentiated distribution of not only monetary compensation but also of more direct consumer privileges and allotments. In this way, ongoing conditions of social inequality were ensured and even strategically encouraged by the state.

Moreover, people were encouraged to interpret the relative worth of their contributions to society in terms of the material privileges to which they were granted access.

Thus, though some scholarly accounts of Russian culture emphasize its valorization of collective suffering as morally superior to individual achievement and acquisitiveness—and though it is clear that such an ideology has long played, and continues to play, an important role in Russian discourse and consciousness—it is also clear that another, somewhat contradictory, logic of value coexisted with it in Soviet life and continues to influence how many people experience contemporary Russian capitalism.

The Relationship of "Culturedness"
to Consumption and Stratification

Though in the Russian language "culture" (*kul'tura*) can signify "an achievement of the intelligentsia in the sense of high culture, a synthesis of ideas, knowledge, and memories," "culturedness" (*kul'turnost'*) came to refer to a code of public conduct, a template for conduct and for the proper relationship of individuals to material possessions (Dunham 1976, 22). "Admonitory and educative," it began under Stalin's leadership to refer to a combination of polite manners, hygiene, and basic knowledge of high culture, as well as sanctioning a particular kind of consumerism that took root in the 1930s and remained a central aspect of social and moral life from that time forward (ibid.; see also Fitzpatrick 1999). The masses to whom the USSR was to bring "culture" included not only Russia's rural peasants, many of whom were moving to urban areas, but also the peoples of other republics and regions (including Central Asians and the nomadic groups of the Siberian north) who were considered "backward" or uncivilized (Slezkine 1994a; Fitzpatrick 1999).[4] Thus "culture" was linked not only to social distinction but also to notions of progress and civilization that set European Russian urban lifestyles as the standard to which other Soviet peoples were to aspire—even as cities like Moscow and Saint Petersburg themselves were being rapidly industrialized, urbanized, and "civilized."

---

4. According to Fitzpatrick (1999, 105), "Beds, gramophones, sewing machines, watches, and radios were all goods that helped raise their possessors out of 'Asiatic' backwardness and into 'European-style' modernity and culture" (1999, 103). A worker from the Soviet republic of Tadjikistan boasted that "I don't live in a my old mud hut anymore—I was awarded a European-style house. *I live like a civilized person.*"

From the 1920s, state-sponsored discourse, including books of advice on etiquette and home decorating, promoted the ideal of culturedness, with emphasis placed on the importance of simplicity, cleanliness, and hygiene in home life. The attainability of domestic "coziness" (*uiut*) for Soviet workers was touted as an achievement of the Revolution (Buchli 1999, 43–45). At the same time, acceptable objects of and attitudes toward consumption had to be distinguished from unworthy ones, because the eradication of "petit-bourgeois" lifestyles and mentalities had also been a key Communist revolutionary goal (ibid., 55–56; Kelly 1999a). Related efforts were made to improve workers' standards of living while doing away with the remnants of bourgeois life in Soviet cities, as evidenced, for example, in architectural projects of the first twenty-five years of the USSR's existence. New housing complexes were constructed, and many of these were organized as dormitories with communal dining halls, libraries, and leisure facilities (Kelly 1998b, 227–28). These functionalist structures, which were built to provide maximum sunlight in each apartment and to avoid the ornate details of pre-revolutionary, upper-class urban dwellings, were not only cost-effective but also were "symbolically representative of [the regime's] . . . determination to sweep away the unhygienic, disorderly, and socially divisive nature of the old city and replace it with a new collectivity based on the egalitarian and rational use of social resources" (ibid.).[5]

Ultimately, however, plans to fully communalize urban residences, which would have included socialization of all domestic labor previously performed within private family units (child care, cooking, laundry, etc.), were deemed financially unfeasible and inconducive to social stability. Emphasis shifted, instead, to the separate provision of various public services, including day care programs and the establishment of inexpensive cafeterias for the benefit of some citizens. By the 1930s, these services came to be understood not as an absolute right of all citizens but rather as rewards granted to particularly enterprising, productive workers (Buchli 1999, 35–36; Dunham 1976, 14). "Enlightenment" (*prosveshchenie*), a key word of the 1920s and early 1930s, was replaced by *vospitanie,* that is, "upbring-

---

5. Plans for communal living, including full socialization of child care and housework, were also related to the goal of women's emancipation. In accordance with Engels' theorization of female oppression under capitalism, the bourgeois "domestic hearth" was to be dismantled, freeing women to come "out" to take on roles in the public sphere (Buchli 1999, 25). However, the "domestic hearth" was ultimately to be left intact, though transformed; see chapter 5.

ing in conventional morals and mores—culturedness" as a broad goal of the education of Soviet citizens (Hessler 1996, 337).

Kul'turnost' played a special role as the moral foundation of a renewed emphasis on acquisitiveness,

> embodying a slick decorum and a new kind of self-righteousness—stable, prudent, heavy. *Its special function is to encode the proper relationship between people through their possessions and labels; between mores and artifacts. . . .* Most of all, kulturnost helped to bestow on material possessions attributes of dignity and virtue. (Dunham 1976, 22–23; emphasis added)

As time went on, new material comforts ("crepe-de-chine dresses, old-fashioned dinnerware") were cited as indicators of improving standards of living and even an increase of "happiness" in Soviet life—just deserts for "the marching enthusiasts of the new Stalinist order" (Boym 1994, 105). Thus while material prosperity and "civilized life" were most accessible to the new administrative elite, the ideology of *kul'turnost'* stressed that these things were available to everyone in exchange for hard work—or would be in the near future (Kelly and Volkov 1998, 295; see also Fitzpatrick 1992, 218, and Boym 1994, 105).[6]

Consumer commodities and sought-after domestic conveniences gradually did become more widely available under Brezhnev in the 1960s, as greater priority was given than ever before to the production of these goods:

6. "*Meshchantsvo*" had been a primary target of the Communist Revolution; the term approximated "petty-bourgeoisie," but also referred to a "social type" that devoted excessive attention to material perks and social climbing at the expense of intellectual interests and spiritual qualities. Though historians' views vary somewhat as to how those negative traits came to be reframed and rehabilitated and to what ends (or to whose greatest benefit), as Dunham's notable account has it, it was a very *meshchantsvo*-like middle class, "public in employment but private and inner-directed in its strivings," with whom the Stalin regime began formed a long-term partnership (Dunham 1976, 20; cf. Fitzpatrick 1992). On a related note, Fitzpatrick writes that in the 1920s, Communist intellectuals argued over whether emphasis should be placed on the building of a new "proletarian" (as opposed to bourgeois) culture or rather on the development of "culture" viewed as transcendent of class, i.e., as an absolute value that was found to be regrettably lacking in Russia. The latter view ultimately won out, and culture was seen as "something immensely valuable and beyond class, in the ascendant. But it also left a tacit agreement that the meaning of culture was something that should not be probed too deeply. . . . It was the complex of behaviors, attitudes, and knowledge that 'cultured' people had, and 'backward' people lacked. Its positive value, like its nature, was self-evident" (Fitzpatrick 1999, 79–80; see also Fitzpatrick 1992).

Their Excellencies the Refrigerator, the Washing machine, the Television set, the Record player, and most coveted, the "Volga" [automobile model] made their appearance. More and more people began to worship the goods in showrooms and strained to think them now, perhaps, within their reach. Cookbooks with tempting color plates, featuring jellied sturgeons festooned in radish rosettes and live daisies, were followed by chapters on *kulturnost.* (Dunham 1976, 244)

Eschewing such desirable things in favor of more ascetic behavior could now be interpreted as a lack of *kul'turnost'* (Dunham 1976, 52). Meanwhile, as shortages of particular commodities continued, people turned their professional positions, official allotments, and social contacts into resources for the procurement and exchange of hard-to-get goods. By the 1970s, commodities from the West became more available and greatly desired—even fetishized—items on the black market (Boym 1994, 64–65). Goods from foreign countries (especially, but not only, from the socialist countries of Eastern Europe) were on sale in official shops as well, though like other items for which demand was high, they could be difficult to procure except through social contacts.[7] This is not to say that citizens were fully content with the goods available to them on the official and unofficial markets. Shortages of certain items, such as shoes, persisted and worsened.[8] Nor was there only one standard of acceptable aspirations and taste. For example, youth cultures emerged, especially in the 1980s, that subverted notions of staid consumer propriety and gender roles in favor of more inventive styles of dress and comportment (Pilkington 1992, 1996a, 1996c).

Meanwhile, official discourses still strove to frame materialist preoccupations with reference to particular values. Simplicity and modesty accompanied honesty, moral purity, mutual respect in the family, and intolerance for injustice in the *Moral Codex of the Builder of Communism* (Sharov 1965). Writings on ethics and etiquette, though not particularly consumerist in outlook, reconciled substantial attention to one's own appearance with communal interests through an emphasis on good grooming as a signal of one's respect for others.[9] Limits were set: One Soviet commentator on ethics described *dukhovnoe potreblenie* ("spiritual needs") in terms of the interest in and respect for knowledge, art, nature, one's own and others' labor, and other people in general; these proper orientations were absent, he

7. See, e.g., "Importnaia Veshch'," *Rabotnitsa* 1990, no. 1: 23–24.
8. *Rabotnitsa* 1985, no. 1: 16–17.
9. Sagatovskii 1982; Dubrovina 1989. See also "Domashnii Kaleidoskop," *Krest'i-anka,* February 1986, 8.

said, in the superficial and selfish "slave of things" (*rab veshchei*) who pursued material possessions with slavish devotion and judged other people on the same basis (Sagatovskii 1982).

By the end of the 1990s, similar reminders about respect for others and the importance of tact and moderation (whether in one's dress and comportment or in one's telephone manners) continued to be voiced in publications such as *Rabotnitsa* and *Krest'ianka* as well as in new American- and European-affiliated women's magazines, and these even became important topics of discussion in some cases. Yet room was also created in magazines and etiquette guides for greater attention to one's "*imidzh*" ("image") as a worthy concern in its own right and as a means of advancing one's personal or business interests. Though susceptible to these urgings, teachers in Saint Petersburg still drew upon notions of *kul'tura* and *kul'turnost'* as they described and questioned how they were positioned by the social and economic structures emerging in the postsocialist era.

For them, *kul'turnost'* implied being educated, having an interest in high culture (museums, literature), and being "*intelligentnyi*" (loosely: knowledgeable, cultured, of the intelligentsia)—although these qualities could also be, at least rhetorically, divorced from *kul'turnost'*. For example, one teacher, Nastia, explained that the word *intelligentsia* indicated a "store of knowledge" (*zapas znaniia*) as well as referring to people who are "sufficiently cultured" (*dostatochno kul'turnyi*). When I asked her to go on to explain what it meant to be "cultured," she described someone who "knows how to behave in a given situation" and who has interests "other than the everyday, mundane ones" (*krome povsednevnykh, bytovykh*)—"cultural values" such as literature or the theater—"everyone has their own thing (*u kogo chto*)." Another acknowledged that everyone understood "intelligentsia" in her own way but ventured that for her it referred to (formal) education, behavior that showed respect to a person of any group, lifestyle (including interest in literature and art), and type of work (mental rather than manual). But mainly, she concluded, it described relations between people; an *intelligentnyi* person felt his own dignity and worth (*dostoinstvo*) but also respected others'.

Intelligentnost', in Liza's estimation, went beyond this to encompass a base of knowledge from which a person actively draws in her life. "I give knowledge and *vospitanie* [good upbringing] to children. If I work as a governess [*guvernantka*] and give it to just one child—this is a different matter. That is called a servant [*prisluga*]!" Liza proclaimed with a laugh. "I have the need to be useful to society [*potrebnost' byt' nuzhnoi obshch-*

estvu]," she continued. "That's why I didn't become a salesperson at a shop [*lavka*]—it's not a way to realize my possibilities." Professionalism and being "needed" by society were positive bases of identification and sources of pride, at least rhetorically counterbalancing the demoralizing effect of teachers' low salaries.

But Lena said that because of financial and time restraints, she could not go to the library or theater often; this state of affairs made her "not 100 percent intelligentsia," because she did not live under the necessary "conditions for self-development." Another woman, Lidia, referred to doctors and teachers as part of "our class, which is pretty [*dostatochno*] *intelligentnyï*"; but she too cited the problems one encountered in pursuing one's intellectual interests today. Now there were films, books, theater, the press, open speech, and choices, and in that sense things had gotten easier, she reflected. "But now," she qualified, "we have to think more about money. Everything is free [*svobodno*] now, but there is less time precisely for intellectual or spiritual things—there simply isn't time! It's hard to compare [the periods]; these are just absolutely different times." The irony, then, was that more had become available for consumption—including things of "spiritual" value— but one did not have the time or money needed to take full advantage of them.

At least as troubling was what they perceived as a lack of *kul'turnost'* in contemporary Russian society at large, a complaint that amounted to a more overarching critique by teachers of postsocialist institutional decay and capitalist marketization. A woman whose family was applying to emigrate to Canada invoked "culture" in identifying reasons for contemporary Russian disorder and her own desire to leave. She wished that life in Russia could be more "like in the West," a world in which one would be able

to live quietly [*zhit' spokoino*]. To know that there won't be any reforms . . . to have certainty in the future. To know that you can put money in the bank, and the banks won't [close], and you can get this money after ten years. To be able to rent an apartment, and not sit in a communal one. Uncertainty is the most terrible [scariest] thing [*samoe strashnoe*]. That's why we're leaving. . . . Why is it that problems that can be solved in the West can't be here? Are Russians simply fools?

Or perhaps, she asked herself, it was that "they [government leaders] don't have enough culture [*kul'tura*] or upbringing [*vospitanie*] when they sit at the Duma [federal legislature]?"

I return to the question of *kul'turnost'* as social critique in chapter 3. For the moment, the critical point about "culturedness" is that through it, good intentions, respect for others, interest in high culture, education, and status were thought of as organically and properly related to one another, in a specific logic of value. For teachers, a particular kind of social trajectory (education, specialized training) and choices about how to spend one's time (including "leisure" activities such as going to museums) were understood to be linked with the explicitly moral importance of being respectful, kind, and *kul'turnyi*. At the same time, in the context of financial crisis, this sense of the proper way of things was being defined in the breach more often than not, as so many circumstances of everyday life seemed to be jarringly changeable and out of whack.

Crises of Disorientation

During the last few months of 1989, all the Eastern European socialist regimes were overthrown, to the surprise of the world. In the Soviet Union, Gorbachev's policies of perestroika (restructuring) and glasnost (openness) had, by the late 1980s, opened the floodgates to previously forbidden forms of economic activity and public discussion. Privatization of some of the USSR's state-owned industries and resources was proceeding apace; at the same time, chronic shortages of consumer goods were worsening. Wages were inflated and the production of consumer goods was declining, leading to cycles of panic buying and hoarding at all levels of Soviet society. Official and market ruble/dollar exchange rates began to diverge swiftly, encouraging underground currency speculation and adding to the general sense that the Soviet economy was spinning out of anyone's control. Though the official rate was maintained at 0.66 ruble to $1, the "tourist rate" in 1991 was about 27 to 35 rubles to the dollar; and by December of that year, the free exchange rate had reached 100:1 (Nove 1992, 417). Meanwhile, prices of foods and other goods that long had been kept artificially low through state subsidization were finally readjusted, though still controlled. On average they were doubled, though some of the most highly subsidized rose more dramatically; the price of beef more than tripled, and that of the cheapest rye bread quadrupled (ibid., 413–14).

Nancy Ries was the key ethnographic observer of this process in Moscow just as the USSR was dissolving; as she reported, people were speaking then of the "complete collapse" that seemed to be overtaking the country. In daily conversation, women described their biggest shopping successes as amazing feats; these were narratives in which the shoppers became the heroines of an upside-down kind of "fairy-tale" Russia (Ries 1997, 49). Rationing cards (*talony*), as Saint Petersburg teachers later recalled, dictated how much grain, meat, tea, vodka, tobacco, soap, and other products each family in Saint Petersburg could buy each month during the year leading up to the USSR's collapse. Even if a person did not really want vodka, she would buy it because she had the right to it (and would receive nothing else in its place), then pile it away for a special occasion. Extra bottles of vodka could be used as payment to an electrician or plumber whose services might be required around the house. Sometimes it was possible to find someone who had a surplus of the kind of *talony* one desired, which could be exchanged for one's own unwanted tickets. The lines to purchase rationed goods were "wild" (*dikie*), "even eight hours long"; and people had to wait in other lines to receive the *talony* themselves. A teacher in his midthirties recalled for me a joke that had circulated at the time: A person walks into a store and asks, "You're out of meat?" The salesperson replies, "No, we're the one out of fish. It's across the street that they're out of meat" (*net miasa—na protiv*). The joke, in other words, was that shops could be distinguished most aptly in terms of the goods they carried only in *theory* though not in fact, because in *fact* no one had anything.[10]

By the close of 1991, the Soviet Union was no more. Russian prime minister Egor Gaidar's new program of price liberalization and rapid privatization, or "shock therapy," became the experiment of 1992. In its wake, galloping inflation completely devalued many citizens' life savings in just a few months. Real wages fell, social services disintegrated, and domestic production declined (Silverman and Yanowitch 2000). Previously ubiquitous queues in front of shops disappeared for the most part; the shops were now full of goods for sale, including exotic fruits that had never been seen in Soviet shops and increasing amounts of imported, packaged foodstuffs. (Snickers bars, among the first of these, were extremely well known and on sale everywhere in Saint Petersburg in 1993.) Social contacts became both less necessary and less expedient in obtaining these commodities, which were no longer scarce but rather, for many people, had become prohibitively expensive. Cash resources began to play a far more determining role in

10. That this joke also has been traced to the Brezhnev era highlights how the shortages of the early 1990s were in some ways an instance of plus ça change (Boym 1994, quoted in Caldwell 2004).

people's lives, and the consumer advantages and resources to be gained otherwise were relatively few. In short, it became more difficult to get the things one wanted—while at the same time there was suddenly much more to want than ever before. And as the chemist's complaints about the bananas hinted, professional and educational status no longer ensured a respectable standard of "middle-class" living. Being an expert in one's professional field did not necessarily imply earning enough to feed one's family. Thus a previous logic of value—one that associated professional achievement with material privileges—was being challenged.

The mid-1990s saw a period of relative normalization in which inflation slowed and budgeting for the future became possible. Teachers remembered that during those years, circa 1995–97, they had been able to work extra hours as tutors and successfully save up for new color televisions. Such large purchases requiring advance planning and significant amounts of cash on hand (credit was rarely available) had become impossible for most of them in 1998–99. Furthermore, from the perspectives of these educated professionals it was still, by the end of the 1990s, disconcerting to find that business and even criminal activity had become viable, apparently permissible paths to prosperity, inasmuch as they yielded the newest and most visible kinds of success and security available in post-Soviet society. It often seemed to teachers that Russia's most respectable, deserving subjects were unable to consume in a befitting manner and that the converse was also true: Unworthy individuals were consuming beyond far what they appeared to deserve. Teachers, along with many others, reviled the post-Soviet nouveaux riches or "New Russians" as "uncultured" (*nekul'turnye*) and "not well brought-up" (*nevospitannye*).

In other words, wealth began to be redistributed among members of society in ways that did not seem to be based on any notion at all of who *should* be deemed most deserving of those privileges. This is not to suggest that the average Soviet citizen had viewed Communist Party elites, who indeed led relatively privileged lives, as particularly worthy or morally deserving of their perks; but post-Soviet disparities of wealth and poverty have been greater and far more visible to the public eye, and have challenged familiar logics of value. Soviet patterns depended on both informal, popular tactics and official, fully sanctioned rewards for achievement—all of them accustomed, intelligible aspects of how society had worked. Now myriad new chances to consume glisten invitingly from market stalls and behind store counters— "freely" available and yet still largely inaccessible, becoming tangible signs of one's somehow having been left behind in the global scheme of things.

The year 1998–99 was an especially charged moment. I had known, in seeking out teachers, that I would be encountering a population severely affected by postcommunist market transition; but the 1998 financial crisis struck them a new and unexpected blow. Actually, I was surprised to learn how positively many of them retrospectively assessed the year before August 1998's ruble depreciation. Many of the teachers spoke of their lives' gradual improvement since the shocks and shortages of the period just before and after the collapse of the Soviet Union (i.e., the early to middle 1990s, especially 1991–93). During those years, they said, they had gradually adapted to new market conditions and to the need to search out work for themselves, and they had managed to make long-awaited purchases such as new televisions or videocassette recorders. Some of them had been teaching many private lessons and squirreling away the extra income for larger future acquisitions, such as a small apartment to replace an unsatisfactory rented room or a Soviet-style communal apartment still shared with other families.[11] One music teacher said that while there had been some faith that life was improving up until the crisis of 1998, she now had little hope that anything good would happen in the country for a long time to come. For her family and many others, she expected, life would continue to be about getting by rather than getting ahead. At the same time, some teachers spoke quite positively about the changes wrought by the transition to a market economy, the recent financial chaos notwithstanding. They were glad to have the choice to take on as many private students as they wished and to

11. The fact that people evaluate the period preceding the crisis as a prosperous one (i.e., from informants' postcrisis perspective) does not necessarily mean that informants actually held such rosy views of their situations before the crisis hit. However, my informants' comments to this effect are supported by similar findings from interviews conducted in the spring and summer of 1998 by a Finnish-Russian research team in Saint Petersburg. Their interviews showed attitudes among "middle-class" people (including teachers, other highly educated state wage earners, and small business owners) were "slightly optimistic. Many of the respondents said that for the first time in many years they had some confidence in the future and that they could make plans at least for a few months ahead. Some families could have afforded a trip abroad or durable consumer goods, such as furniture" (Simpura et al. 1999, 57–58). The researchers add: "It is worth noting that the economic development in the 1990s never reached the pre-1991 levels, neither as measured by GNP indicators or estimated by the everyday living standards of a vast majority of the population. There was, however, a brief period of growing optimism in 1997, with an 0.4 per cent increase in the GDP, and a corresponding increase of industrial production of 1.9 per cent. The annual inflation rate slowed down from almost 50 to 15 per cent, the gross debt of the state remained stable, and the budget deficit was at seven per cent, showing a slow decline" (p. 51).

improve their situations through their own efforts and choices. They seemed proud of the progress they had made before the crisis.

At the beginning of the 1998 school year (i.e., just a few weeks after the abrupt ruble depreciation that jolted the nation on August 17), official teaching salaries were about 800 to 1,100 rubles a month, depending on a teacher's seniority, how many hours she worked, and what additional responsibilities (e.g., being a class teacher) she had taken on. Very small raises were given in the spring 1999 semester, by which time the salaries represented far less buying power than they had the year before. The value of a 1,000-ruble salary dropped from approximately $167 in August 1998 to about $42 in the winter of 1999, with most ruble commodity prices rising accordingly. As one teacher recounted in February 1999:

> Even in September [1998], I could buy more [than I can now]. I could buy fruit for the kids, for example. Now bananas are twenty rubles a kilogram. I can spend no more than fifty rubles per day. So I can choose: I will get a kilogram of fruit and a piece of cheese, and that would be it! So I buy [less expensive items such as] grain, cabbage, bread, milk. I try to find cheap apples, with spots—you have to go around and look for them [*nado khodit', iskat'*].

Some tutors lost private clients due to the fact that almost everyone was cutting corners in the wake of the crisis. Others retained a good number of pupils but felt they would lose them if they raised their fees significantly. Instead, they might take on extra students if they could find them, in an effort to make up the lost difference in real income. Those without any additional income at all found that it became harder and harder to get by.

Estimates of the minimum monthly income per person necessary for subsistence, as calculated by Saint Petersburg's Committee on Labor and Social Protection, help concretize the nature and magnitude of some of the changes that took place during the year of my fieldwork. These living wages are calculated in rubles according to prices recorded locally for a standard "consumer's basket" of foodstuffs plus allowances for housing costs and other basic necessities (e.g., clothing) and services.[12] The figures below are

12. This measure of subsistence, formulated in 1992, "was developed by estimating the value of a basket of food that guaranteed a sufficient number of calories and whose composition conformed to Russian tastes and the recommendations of the international health (World Health Organization—WHO) and food (Food and Agriculture Organization —FAO) organizations" (Silverman and Yanowitch 2000, 43).

the estimated minimums deemed necessary for the "average person" (separate calculations are made to determine the differing levels of need of the average man, woman, young child, and senior citizen or pensioner):

1998:		*1999:*	
July	512.2	February	1,142.3
September	800.8	July	1,306.6
October	745.5	August	1,242.8
		September	1,213.3

[handwritten annotation: Always seems to be presented as a Russian problem... but is it really?]

Temporary drops in the cost of the baskets (in October 1998 and in August and September 1999) are likely the result of seasonal shifts in food prices (particularly produce); according to *Nevskoe Vremia,* though inflation was steady in the fall of 1998, certain food prices had gone down in the warm summer and early autumn months, lowering the October subsistence level as compared with September's.[13] In any case, these figures make clear how difficult it became to support oneself—let alone dependents—on a teacher's public school salary alone (roughly 700–1,000 rubles). In fact, the figures above may be underestimations. *Nevskoe Vremia* reported in July 1999 that it had determined that 4,764 rubles (per person, per month) was the level of income currently needed to sustain a "normal life," while the actual average income per person in Saint Petersburg was 1,075 rubles.[14] (A more complete rendering of these findings, including data from 1991–99, is presented in tables 2.1, 2.2, 2.3, and 2.4.)

The change in quality of life after August 1998 was noticeable for most of the teachers. Olga rued the fact that the year before she had been able to spend more on small luxuries, such as going to cafes. She claimed not to suffer too much from their lack now; yet, she admitted, she had begun to feel depressed and was no longer inclined to set goals because she was sure that they would not be successful. Most notably, she had been saving for a few years already to buy an apartment—or even just a room in a communal flat—for herself and her daughter; they had been living in a rented room that Olga

13. "754.5 rublia i nikakikh khlopot," November 12, 1998.

14. Tatiana Protasenko, "Uroven' normal'noi zhizni 4764 rublia," July 1, 1999, 4. On February 12, 1999, a local paper (*Vechernii Peterburg*) reported that according to the Saint Petersburg city administration, income levels for 22.6 percent of the urban population had fallen below the poverty line. At that time, the majority of citizens were said to earn between 600 and 900 rubles a month; about 40 percent made from 300 to 600 a month (this figure appears to be per wage earner, not distributed per person in a household).

Table 2.1. *Views on Standards of Living in Saint Petersburg, 1991–99*

Answers to the survey question "Given the current level of prices, what average monthly income per family member do you consider sufficient in order to 'live normally?'"

Currency	December 1991	January 1992	January 1993	January 1994	February 1995	November 1995	March 1996	April 1997	January 1998	April 1998	October 1998	January 1999	April 1999
Rubles	1,379	2,440	34,958	255,693	684,490	1,101,000	1,410,000	1,910,000	1,821.3	1,990	3,128.0	4,254	4,764
Dollars		24.9	61.6	164	151.7	239.5	288.0	332.2	303.6	329.4	208.5	189.1	191.3

Note: Figures are presented in rubles and in dollars, according to the exchange rates in effect at each stage of the survey. From January 1998, ruble figures refer to "new" rubles (1,000 pre-1998 rubles = 1 ruble after January 1, 1998).
Source: Tatiana Protasenko, "Uroven' normal'noi zhizni 4764 rublia," *Nevskoe Vremia*, July 1, 1999.

Table 2.2. *Average Real Incomes per Capita in Saint Petersburg, 1991–99*

Currency	December 1991	January 1992	January 1993	January 1994	February 1995	November 1995	March 1996	April 1997	January 1998	April 1998	September 1998	October 1998	November 1998	January 1999	April 1999
Rubles	365	551	6,781	73,731	257,700	474,900	487,400	580,200	728.8	776	813	787.5	811	946.5	1,075
Dollars		5.6	11.8	47	57.1	103.2	99.5	100.9	121.5	128.3	54.2	50.8	46.3	42.1	43.2

Note: Figures are presented in rubles and in dollars, according to the exchange rates in effect at each stage of the survey. From January 1998, ruble figures refer to "new" rubles (1,000 pre-1998 rubles = 1 ruble after January 1, 1998).
Source: Tatiana Protasenko, "Uroven' normal'noi zhizni 4764 rublia," *Nevskoe Vremia*, July 1, 1999.

Table 2.3. Subsistence Level as Calculated by the Saint Petersburg City Administration's Committee on Employment, 1994–99

Currency	January 1994	September 1994	February 1995	November 1995	April 1996	April 1997	January 1998	April 1998	September 1998	October 1998	November 1998	January 1999	April 1999
Rubles	46,342	89,182	203,500	291,400	350,000	450,000	470	513	800	750	776	1,016	1,209
Dollars	30	30.2	45.1	63.3	70.0	78.3	78.3	84.8	53.3	48.3	43.4	45	48.5

Note: Figures are presented in rubles and in dollars, according to the exchange rates in effect at each stage of the survey. From January 1998, ruble figures refer to "new" rubles (1,000 pre-1998 rubles = 1 ruble after January 1, 1998).
Source: Tatiana Protasenko, "Uroven' normal'noi zhizni 4764 rublia," *Nevskoe Vremia,* July 1, 1999.

Table 2.4. Subsistence Minimum as Percentage of Average Real Income of the Population of Saint Petersburg, 1994–99

January 1994	September 1994	February 1995	April 1996	April 1997	January 1998	April 1998	September 1998	October 1998	November 1998	January 1999	April 1999
62.9	41.6	79.0	66.2	77.6	64.5	66.1	98.4	95.2	95.7	107.3	112.5

Source: Tatiana Protasenko, "Uroven' normal'noi zhizni 4764 rublia," *Nevskoe Vremia,* July 1, 1999.

strongly disliked. Almost all the teachers described needing to be more frugal in their food purchases than they had been during the previous year (table 2.5). Prices for certain items such as cheese had risen even more swiftly than others, such that their families' consumption of these needed to be curtailed significantly. Some families had access to fruits and vegetables grown in garden plots at their small dacha cottages in the countryside near Saint Petersburg. Like many other urban Russians, the teachers enjoyed spending summer weeks at the dacha for relaxation; but getting to these villages by train had become costly, like everything else, and garden produce did not significantly relieve financial pressures (cf. Zavisca 2003). None of the teachers went without enough to eat that year (at least to my knowledge, though one family had to borrow money to avoid such a circumstance), but they regretted that their children were missing the extra snacks and sweets to which they had become accustomed, including the tasty, nicely packaged, imported yogurts many of them had learned to prefer. Most families had also reduced their consumption of meat, sausage, and fruit. Though some had taken economy bus trips to Finland or Western Europe before the crisis in the summer of 1998, few could afford such indulgences in 1999.

This situation strained both familial and collegial relationships. Nadezhda, a long-time teacher in her forties, told me in December 1998 that she was receiving an official school salary of 820 rubles a month, whereas in a good month (i.e., when none of the children cancelled their lessons) she could make as much as 2,000 rubles in additional private income. Her ex-husband paid about 500 rubles in support of their two children, and her mother received a 650-ruble pension. All in all, then, despite the exhausting hours Nadezhda worked in addition to her regular school day, she and her family brought in less than 1,000 rubles a month, per person. She had warned her children that she would not be able to give them presents for New Year's, the most important holiday of the year (along with birthdays) for gift exchange in Russia. Meanwhile Nastia, a very busy and well-respected English teacher and tutor, observed that during the previous year, 1997–98, there had been enough private students to keep all the teachers as busy as they wanted to be. Now everyone, including pupils' families, had less money, and some parents had decided to end their children's extra lessons or could not pay fees that kept up with inflation. Increased competition for students had led to resentments and suspiciousness among colleagues at her school, Nastia complained. They had become hesitant to reveal to other teachers who their students were and how much they were charging them, for fear of their rates being undercut and pupils usurped.

Table 2.5. Price Fluctuations for Common Foodstuffs in Saint Petersburg, 1998–99

Foodstuff	December 1998	May 1999	September 1999
"Petmol" milk, per liter			
0.5 percent milk fat	8.0–8.9	9.7–11.4	
3.5 percent milk fat	10.2–10.7	10.8–12.7	
Buckwheat groats, per kilogram	8.6–18.6	31.0–35.0	
Popular breads, per loaf			
Khleb darnitskii	2.6–3.8	3.4–3.8	4.6–5.4
Baton podmoskovskii	2.3–3.4	3.2–3.4	
Baton gorodskoi	2.1–4.0	3.1–4.0	3.6–4.4

Note: This table shows the typical range of prices of a few basic and popular foodstuffs in 1998 and 1999 at local markets in Saint Petersburg (especially in the Petrograd Side area, where the author and many informants resided). All prices are given in rubles. The given items were chosen based on the fact that they were widely available brands or varieties and came in standard packaging (as opposed to goods such as produce that differ significantly in size, quality, etc., from market to market and day to day); this allowed for comparison across locations and time. The breads listed as well as Petmol milk are produced in Saint Petersburg.

As the year wore on, it seemed that for many of the teachers, life had returned to a more or less stable tenor—but a demoralizing one, characterized by financial strain and emotional fatigue. The fact that prices had changed so dramatically over the course of the 1990s, and more recently since the ruble depreciation of August 1998, encouraged a high degree of attentiveness to prices and could bring confusion and frustration. "Everything changes!" one teacher said in exasperation at the *rynok* (outdoor market), trying to find her accustomed brand of mayonnaise without luck and to recall at which stall she had seen the lowest price for rice. Another woman examined cuts of meat behind the counter at a local shop and realized that she could so seldom afford to buy it that she did not know whether the prices listed were high or low. A third teacher observed that the correspondence of prices for various types of goods in general had changed radically; whereas, in the Soviet Union, stylish clothes had been very expensive and difficult to find but food had been entirely affordable, today a greater range of clothing was available at relatively affordable prices but those for food had risen dramatically. In this sense, the different categories of goods had become "more the same; . . . [with the same money, one can buy] a skirt or a sausage [*kolbasa*], it's all the same!"

In light of the rapid proliferation of new products and advertisements that had flowed into Russian cities since about 1993, it had become somewhat less clear to people than it once had been which consumer items were *sup-*

posed to be most desirable, stylish, and worthwhile. For some, the sheer range of commodities now available and the expanded diversity of popular consumer tastes was a source of befuddlement. In the summer of 1999, Nastia told me that she needed to buy a new dress for herself as well as something for her daughter to wear to an upcoming function: "But I don't know what people are wearing at all. It used to be basically clear what people were wearing, and now everyone wears everything. You see it, right?" Such a sense of disorientation and shiftiness was more common among middle-aged and older teachers (in their forties through sixties) than among their younger counterparts (twenties to thirties), who had lived a greater portion of their adult lives in postsocialist conditions.

One of their colleagues, Lidia, an English teacher in her forties, addressed these confusions in vivid detail when I asked her about her taste and habits in clothes shopping:

> JP: In general, who might give you advice about what suits you and what is better not to wear, or what is fashionable, for example? Friends? Or family members?
>
> Lidia: You know, I really . . . it's hard for me to answer that question, because I dress very little from the point of view of fashion. To really dress fashionably you need a lot of money. . . . And in general, what is fashion now?! Can you imagine what fashion is now? Now there are so many different styles, and such absolutely different clothing. If before—I remember in the 1970s, 1960s—miniskirts were fashionable. Everyone was in miniskirts. A person in a long skirt?! This was . . . well, people would look at her just wildly [*diko*]! Do you understand this? "Now this isn't allowed [*ne mozhno*], now people don't wear this." Then pants came into fashion for women. *Everyone* started wearing pants. . . . They wore skirts too, of course, but pants were considered fashionable clothing. You see? There was a notion that "this is fashionable now." I couldn't say—if you would answer this question, I would be grateful—I couldn't say what is fashionable now. Now, probably, what is fashionable is what looks good on a person. People wear so many different things: one wears short, another long, someone wears pants, someone. . . . Well, take a look, even sometimes you look at fashion magazines—what is fashionable? What color, for example, is "in?" "In colors:" and they list: "This season light blue, pink and brown are in fashion." That

is, they list half the colors. That is, it's practically wear what you want, as long as it looks good on you. You see, because for me now the idea of "fashionable" is eroded [*razmyto*] and unclear [*neponiatno*], right now, in the nineties. Understand? Because again here you are talking about "advice," but I very seldom ask for advice at all. I don't need it, I already know now, at my age, what suits me. Because . . . here [*u nas*] in general it isn't really done, to go the store 'with someone' and specially pick something, go to a fashionable store and choose. We almost don't have that at all.[15] This can be afforded by. . . . You shouldn't be addressing this question to *us,* this should be addressed to people who dress from fashionable stores. You see, at stores—I don't even know their addresses! (laugh) You see, I don't have any opportunity to do that . . . in this magazine here. Well, they're again offering us [products for] hair, but all their shampoos. . . . I don't know, I can't say, they are all very expensive, but somehow I can't say that they really work well. That is I wash my hair with the most ordinary, and if I use these shampoos—well, I don't feel any difference. That is. . . . It seems to me that [they] just need to sell all this. . . . Yes? That's why they advertise, but there's basically no difference, right?

Lidia's monologue exemplified certain features of the market environment in Saint Petersburg and the general processes of disorientation and reorientation it had set in motion. Though many of the teachers spoke of their desires for more time and money with which to clothe themselves better, buy good makeup and tasty food, and generally care for themselves and their families, they did not see themselves as naive victims of marketization. Rather, they questioned the quality of newly available goods, both imported and domestic. They were often suspicious of advertisers who "just needed to sell" things. They wished to master all this new knowledge and tended to find it important to be well-informed consumers and to maintain as far as possible dignified, "cultured" lifestyles.

At least in retrospect, clear answers about which goods should be chosen had been readily available to consumers in the relatively stagnant, less

---

15. Lidia was contradicted on this particular point by other teachers, however, who said that when they went shopping for relatively important and expensive items such as winter coats they consulted the opinions of close friends or family members.

mercurial, and less pluralistic Soviet economy. Such answers could be sought now but were likely to be much more ambiguous and individual. In asking what was fashionable and whether advertising had anything to do with the true qualities of goods, Lidia was also demonstrating her understanding that the relatively predictable structures that used to constrain and channel consumer desire and access were no longer in effect. The question was, what kinds of logics were replacing them?

Finding a Place in the "Middle"

In the early 1980s—that is, just before perestroika—teachers were considered part of the "mass intelligentsia," along with doctors, engineers, cultural workers, and certain white-collar and blue-collar workers (Shlapentokh 1999, 1171). According to a narrower definition, the Soviet "intelligentsia" could refer to a more elite set of top intellectuals, academics, scientists, and bureaucrats; primary and secondary education was less prestigious. Teachers received among the lowest salaries given to professionals. In fact, in the USSR and in post-Soviet Russia, both the teaching and the medical professions have been highly feminized; 73 percent of teachers in 1985–86 were women (and the proportion of men at the Saint Petersburg schools where I worked in the late 1990s was yet lower).[16] On average, women in the Soviet Union earned 70 percent of men's salaries and were unlikely to hold high posts of authority in any field (Jones 1991, 155; Shlapentokh 1999, 1174). Professionals' salaries were often similar to or surpassed by those of manual laborers (Vinokur and Ofer 1987). In 1985, teachers earned an average of 150 rubles a month, versus 210 for construction workers and 236 for industrial workers.[17] Though pay raises were awarded to teachers later in the 1980s (the 1991 average teaching salary was 214 rubles a month), their relative statuses in the occupational structure as measured by wages did not change much (Jones 1991, 154).

16. Other fields in which women predominate have included service professions, light industry such as textiles, and clerical work. Heavy industry, mining, and construction are dominated by men and have been significantly better paid than "female" jobs, especially in the post-Soviet period (Silverman and Yanowitch 2000, 60, 68).

17. Note that these ruble figures should not be confused with the more recent salary levels cited in this chapter and elsewhere in the book; 150 rubles in the Soviet Union represented significantly more buying power than did the typical 800 to 1,000 rubles paid monthly to teachers in 1998–99. See table 2.1.

Still, as Anthony Jones observed of the 1980s, "teachers benefit from being defined as part of the intelligentsia. . . . Although teachers have fairly low status within the intelligentsia, their membership still conveys high status in the general occupational structure" (Jones 1991, 164). Despite the broad range in the educational backgrounds of the mass intelligentsia and their low standing in salaries and perks compared with the elite, they shared a similar, relatively "dignified," "middle-class" lifestyle:

> The middle class [shared] the same type of housing (usually a small individual flat), furnishings and durable goods such as television sets and refrigerators. Some owned cars, though this remained a much envied possession through the 1970s and 1980s. Most middle-class families had small private plots, . . . or at least a garden to grow fruit, vegetables and flowers. They took the same types of holidays, mostly in state resort homes. . . . Their leisure time was also spent in much the same way, visiting friends, watching films and reading. . . . Most children went on to study at the college or university level. (Shlapentokh 1999, 1171)

In the 1990s, much more paltry salaries and the need to work long hours and extra jobs made such relative leisure and comfort less attainable for teachers. Somewhat more freedom in classroom instruction came along with a drastic drop in institutional resources, as well as the opening of private schools whose academic rigor public school teachers seriously questioned. Meanwhile, the primacy of private business as the path to financial success diminished the previously central role of education in determining people's career options and social status. Sometimes these were exacerbated by dynamics of gender and age; women over about thirty-five to forty years of age were presented with fewer options for employment in the private sector than their more youthful counterparts. For example, job announcements for positions such as administrative assistantships openly advertised that only young, attractive women "without hang-ups" need apply (Azhgikhina and Goscilo 1996). Some English teachers gave this as a reason why they could not parlay their (otherwise highly marketable) English language skills into lucrative jobs in the business world.[18]

---

18. The proportion of women among the unemployed is somewhat contested, ranging from about 50 to 80 percent, as explained in chapter 4 (see Shlapentokh 1999, 1174; Ashwin 2000; and Ashwin and Bowers 1997. For similar data on East Europe, also see Einhorn 1993; Gal and Kligman 2000). By the late 1990s, women's wages were on

Even for those still employed in the public sector, the dependability of wage payments and the quality of services such as health care had seriously declined. Teachers and other members of what was once thought of as the middle-class or mass intelligentsia were now more often categorized as part of the "new poor," because as a group their income levels had suffered considerably since the initial jolts of economic reform in 1992 (e.g., Golenkova 1998, 4–5; Silverman and Yanowitch 2000, 90; Balzer 1998). Pensions were still paid but were often late and insufficient to meet the real needs of elderly people. Destitution, poor living conditions, and a lack of sufficient medical resources had resulted in new epidemics of diseases such as tuberculosis. The Soviet social contract, which hinged on citizens' obligation to participate in the public labor force and, in turn, the state's "system of social distribution of goods and services through the workplace . . . and a sense of identity and belonging to a labour collective," had to a great extent been dissolved (Piirainen 1997, 141). Though in the Soviet Union graduates of pedagogical institutes were assigned their job placements upon graduation, today there are no assurances of job security and each person is on her own in finding a position (though social contacts often come in handy in finding desirable ones; see Lonkila 1997; Alapuro 1998).

Yet there is a continuing demand for teachers; several of the women at these schools had been teachers in provincial cities and had migrated to Saint Petersburg within the past several months or years. For them, a consistent need for teachers in the city meant that they had been able to find steady jobs and to support their children, many of them as single mothers. For those who considered leaving teaching for other, more lucrative jobs, retooling was not a simple matter. A few English teachers in their forties rued their low pay but noted that despite their expertise in English—a highly marketable skill—they would not be offered jobs in the private sector due to their relatively advanced age.

Meanwhile, other Russians had become infamously and ostentatiously wealthy. It was estimated in the late 1990s that about 1,000 Russian citi-

---

average reported at only 45 to 50 percent of men's (compared to 70 percent in the 1980s); it appeared that men were still more likely than women to occupy higher-paid positions and to work in industries that were more lucrative across the board. According to Goskomstat, the official state organ for statistical data collection, the ratio of disparity in income between the top and bottom 10 percents of the Russian population rose from 4:1 in 1990 to 15:1 in 1994 (Shlapentokh 1999). Shlapentokh notes that these rates of income disparity are similar to those of developing countries such as Brazil, Venezuela, and Mexico.

zens earned yearly salaries in the millions of dollars, and "for all those who have crossed a certain boundary, the purchase of a 'Mercedes 500' or 'Mercedes 600' becomes obligatory; in the Moscow region alone, more of these cars were purchased between 1992 and 1996 than in ten years in all of Western Europe" (Medvedev 1997, 64, 66). The so-called New Russian post-Soviet wealthy elite was said (as of the mid-1990s) to be composed of three layers: politicians, entrepreneurs (who helped finance political campaigns and mass media), and security services (who maintained order by enforcing contracts) (Krishtanovskaia and White 1999, 43). The new entrepreneurial class included former apparatchiks and professional or scientific intelligentsia as well as some "underground" businesspeople whose trade networks had roots in the Soviet era (Silverman and Yanowitch 2000).

In the late 1980s, when economic reform efforts gained momentum as part of Gorbachev's policy of perestroika, new legislation legalized small-scale cooperative enterprises. In April 1991, several months before the Soviet Union was declared dissolved, a more sweeping law allowed individuals to trade and to employ others freely (such activity had previously been punishable as "speculation" and "exploitation") (Nove 1992). Members of the Communist Party administrative and managerial elites were able to parlay their positions of authority into select credit advances, partnership in joint enterprises with foreign investors, and ownership of valuable resources as state enterprises began to be privatized (Krishtanovskaia and White 1999; Medvedev 1997, 58–63).

In addition, the emergence of cooperatives in the late 1980s gave rise to an illegal protection racket in which both criminal groups and, unofficially, government agents were involved. In 1992, subsequent to the collapse of the USSR, private protection firms were legalized, diversifying the kinds of organizations and individuals involved in these legal and illegal business dealings. According to all reports, even small businesses can scarcely be run today without involvement with a protection organization, and ties to criminal groups appear to be common. In this arena of "violent entrepreneurial activity," as Vadim Volkov calls it, business contracts are guaranteed by protection groups' management of violence (Volkov 1999, 2001). These "security agents" or *okhrana* were in many cases, especially in Leningrad/Saint Petersburg, recruited from the ranks of former athletes such as wrestlers and weight lifters (ibid., 746). Teachers often referred to these *okhrana* as the least intelligent, most stereotypical examples of the tasteless but wealthy "New Russian."

Meanwhile, in both everyday conversation and the mass media, one heard in the late 1990s that due to the current disparity between rich and poor there was "no middle class" in Russia, a state of affairs said to have been exacerbated by the 1998 financial crisis, when many people lost jobs or effectively lost their savings. This lack of a middle class spoke to the increasing social injustice of postsocialist Russia; yet the "lack" was in fact difficult to determine, particularly because demographic data are notoriously undependable and class models are variously defined. In fact, assumptions about what "middle-class" identity entails have varied widely, the applicability of the term to Russian society remaining uncertain throughout the 1990s (Simpura et al. 1999, 56; Balzer 1998, 167, 171).[19]

The assumption in many of these discussions has been that given the advent of capitalism, a middle class such as that understood to exist in the West is bound to be the next step—sooner or later—in Russia's development. In April 1998, an entire issue of the news magazine *Itogi* was devoted to looking for the new middle class in Russia. Did it exist? What did it look like? A cover photo and story portrayed one vision of what a middle-class family in contemporary Russia might look like, picturing a home replete with comforts and conveniences: from comfortable, stylish, but simple clothing to a home computer, personal compact disk player, and open textbooks for courses in hotel management. But according to the magazine, that graphic portrayal was not based on any "typical" family it had managed to discover. Rather, the image derived from those created by Russian advertising agencies, and readers were warned: "We have represented this 'Euroclass' as it would be if it lived by Western standards."[20] In the absence of a recognizable local middle class, a semifictional "Euroclass," as yet alive only in commercial advertising, had been articulated (and forecast?) for Russia.

---

19. Harley Balzer (1998, 177) suggests that the content of families' consumption may be a more reliable indication of "middle-class" status than income figures, whose accuracy are difficult to judge due to routine underdeclaring of salaries for the purposes of tax and mafia evasion. He notes that "Russian marketing professionals consider the 'real' middle class to be those who will purchase a videocassette recorder (VCR) during the coming year." The VCR criterion clearly reflects the orientations of those professionals, for whom actual or predicted purchases would constitute the most salient aspect of class identities; it also makes sense insofar as Russian families must be relatively affluent or save long-term in order to make such purchases, because they generally do not have the option of buying on credit. Along similar lines, a sociologist quoted in the Moscow-based newsmagazine *Itogi* suggested the ability to purchase everything but real estate as a provisional definition for the middle class such as it did exist in Russia (quoted in Startsev 1998, 10).

20. "V Poiskakh Srednego Klassa," April 21, 1998, 6.

A journalist explained why the question of the middle class in today's Russia was so complex, in effect articulating the problem of upended logics of value:

> It is unclear how our middle class is forming, since the chain "education-work-income-status" does not operate in our country. Education does not guarantee employment with opportunities for growth. Work does not guarantee income: the salaries of representatives of one profession in the private and state sectors differ dramatically. Income does not guarantee status: few will consider a "shuttler" [*chelnok*] who trades at the market to be a respected member of society. (Startsev 1998, 10)[21]

Startsev's commentary further suggests that contemporary Russia is set apart from (and less orderly than) both prosperous "Western" societies where middle classes flourish and its own past of assured employment and valued education. In such contexts of normalcy and stability, it is presumed, a "chain" of social cause and effect prevails that is not dependably at work in Russia, where the interrelationships of work, money, consumption, and social recognition or respect are more open to question.

The matter of definitions is further complicated by the fact that the Russian word for "middle," *srednii,* can also denote "average." Thus among sociological commentators and in general discourse, it can be unclear whether this "middle class" is supposed to represent the situation of those who are literally in the "middle" of Russia's socioeconomic scale or rather to serve as an absolute, even international standard of "middle-classness" that indicates certain kinds of employment (i.e., professional, including law, advertising, and so on), income, political orientations (emphasis on stability and protection of financial investments), and consumption levels (property ownership, car ownership). In the latter case, it was usually decided in the late 1990s that the Russian middle class did not exist "yet" (Startsev 1998, 8–10).

If sociologists, marketers, and pundits had trouble determining what the middle class might be and whether it even existed, the changing social and economic conditions that underlay their confusion also presented considerable challenges to those who, as they navigated the same shifting terrains in everyday life, were figuring out how to situate themselves and others on

---

21. A *chelnok* is a petty entrepreneur who makes his or her living by personally traveling abroad to buy cheap commodities and bringing them back to Russia to sell at a profit.

a post-Soviet social map. Some teachers did, in fact, describe themselves as middle class. Their usage of the term was as murky as sociological commentators', however, depending in some cases upon measures of disposable income and/or consumption and in other instances emphasizing professional identity. Often, those who did declare themselves to be middle class seemed to be applying a relatively generous notion of what might qualify someone for that category.

Anya, who was in her twenties, divorced, and living with her mother, talked about herself and her friends as *srednie* and said that she thought that these *srednie* were people who had what they needed but could not often afford traveling abroad or completing significant renovations in their apartments. Another teacher, Katia, in her late twenties and living with her boyfriend, remarked: "Middle class? Probably that's me. People who can adjust, who have work, . . . who have some kind of earnings, which aren't a lot but they're there." And finally, Olga, a divorced single mother in her thirties, stated: "That's probably me, *srednii klass*. People who can't afford to travel where they could before [i.e., before the 1998 crisis], . . . before I could travel to the south [of Russia]. Now that's over." Still others considered themselves to be lower than middle class; one family told me in the fall of 1999 that over the course of the year I had known them, they had gone from "poor" (*bednye*) to "destitute" (*nishchie*).

Conversely, being middle class could also be cast as a matter of one's professional affiliation—though that aspect of one's social self could easily be blurred together with particular consumer styles held to be typical of the middle as opposed to the extremely wealthy and the extremely poor. Lidia suggested that doctors and teachers typically could be expected to consume at a middle level, explaining that the European bus tour she had recently taken had been filled with people of these *srednie sloi* (middle "layers" or strata), such as doctors and teachers. These were people, Lidia explained, who could afford to save up over the course of a year the $200 per person the trip cost. Wealthy people did not go on such tours; rather, "they travel on planes and go to different countries, more expensive ones of course—Spain, Italy."

Having guests visit one's home had become very difficult now for the middle class in which teachers were included, Lidia went on, because such people had so much work both day and evening that they had little time or energy left over. When I asked her how typical she thought her hosting practices might be compared with those of people in Saint Petersburg generally, she replied that it was difficult for her to make a judgment about everyone because there were other groups and therefore, she imagined, customs: from the New Russian nouveaux riches to the red-faced men she frequently saw standing around beer stalls at the marketplace. "I can just say for my own class," she said, "which is considered middle class, of a pretty *intelligent-nyi* level, with particular interests and concerns, . . . not necessarily just teachers, but people who are connected with culture, enlightenment." In this, Lidia's comments recalled the Soviet system's emphasis on professional status as a determinant of both social respectability and the distribution of resources.

They also pointed to the continued centrality of this logic of value for many people: It was a framework that continued to "make sense" at one level, while not necessarily proving to be very useful for explaining contemporary realities. Education and good personal qualities no longer translated dependably into material compensation and society's respect; the pursuit of market "freedoms" and self-determination had been disconnected disturbingly from meaningful social relationships and the values they represented. That perceived disjuncture was a key characteristic of this mass intelligentsia's social imaginary, describing a world in which the logic according to which people once set goals, evaluated prestige, and received their appropriate material rewards had been largely unraveled, necessitating the adjustment of personal expectations and strategies. As we shall see in the concluding chapter, that social imaginary was already transforming further by the time I returned to visit the teachers in 2003.

"Now It's More Fashionable to Be Bad"

Teachers' efforts to secure for themselves a modicum of comfort, capital, respectability, and dignity constituted a much more multitextured and dynamic engagement with socioeconomic upheaval than their diminished status in economic terms might seem to suggest. They had acquired new consumer knowledge and skills, had observed and interpreted systemic social and market shifts, and were consistently aware of how mechanisms of differentiation had shifted and continued to evolve. Their aspirations and measured successes—the very fact that they had so much to lose after August 1998—indicated that their lives as consumers, professionals, and individuals were richer and more hopeful than any images the label "new poor" is likely to evoke. By the same token, consumption is not only "about" class difference (Miller 1987, 1998) but also helps produce more diffuse and personal experiences of morality, propriety, and human dignity. Varying measures of relative worth—including income, consumer choices, professional qualifications, and social contributions—were being applied and reapplied in people's evaluations of one another, and in their decision making for their own lives.

In the process, contradictory answers were produced about who might be "middle class," what kind of middle-classness would be desirable, and, most fundamentally, about where the most authoritative and morally defensible sources of value in postsocialist society lay. Some teachers felt that many, if not all, Russian citizens "still" respected education as a general value and realized that it could lead one to many prestigious careers, such as law. Others noted that students and their parents seemed to look down on teachers and to see them as "losers" (*bezudachniki*) because of their pitifully low salaries. Elizaveta reflected that the category "*intelligentsia*" once referred to people who were involved in intellectual occupations, but now,

> borders have blurred, in that a former engineer will work as something else. . . . Before . . . his work, manners, and knowledge all went together. Now someone can have a [good] position but behave obnoxiously [*kakoe-to byvaet khamstvo*]. Before there were traditions through generations, but now a lot of traditions are being lost. . . . Before the intelligentsia were respected and people aspired to be like them. Now it is more fashionable to be bad [*modno byt' plokhim*]. To not respect anything, finding everything humorous and becoming higher than certain accepted [*priniaty*] values. To show that, "I am like this. You be however you want" [*Ia takoi. A vy kak khotite*].

Thus while teachers may have defended their own worth as agents of socialization and *kul'tura,* they did so amid discomfiting uncertainties about how their contributions to society would be valued by others, many of whom appeared to be dismissing education and other "accepted values" in favor of individualism and "being however they wanted."

As we will see in the next chapter, the specific social roles these women and men played in Saint Petersburg's schools informed their interpretations of socioeconomic upheaval in significant ways. As teachers, they were brought into close interaction with an array of students and their parents. In this context, they became acutely aware of social processes and changing lifestyles beyond those in which they directly participated, and they had cause to dwell upon what set them apart from some of their wealthier compatriots. Simultaneously, through their consumer experience, they came to know themselves and their immediate social environments as part of a larger society and world regulated by standards of moral legitimacy as well as material sophistication.

Chapter 3

Teachers and Bandits: Logics of Value at School and Beyond

Olga was a divorced, thirty-five-year-old English teacher with a teenage daughter to support. When I met her, she had been living in Saint Petersburg only a few years, having moved there to pursue graduate study (which she had had to drop because it did not fit with the schedule she was required to keep as a teacher). Her daughter had stayed behind at first in the small provincial city north of Saint Petersburg where they had lived, but now she had moved in with her mother and attended the school where Olga worked.

Olga's financial situation was difficult. She had an apartment back in her hometown, which was her only significant base of capital, and which she hoped to exchange for an apartment or even just a good-sized room in a communal apartment in Saint Petersburg (preferably, she explained, one with nice neighbors, or at least no drunks or drug addicts, though as long as they kept to themselves even drunks could be OK). Unfortunately, there were few buyers interested in leaving the northern capital for a smaller town in the provinces, and because Olga had been wary of jumping on the first deal with which she had been presented, she had yet, after more than a year of looking, to find an exchange with which she felt satisfied. After a long stint renting a room in another woman's apartment, she was able to switch midyear to renting an entire spacious, if somewhat shabby, apartment that she jokingly dubbed the "underground," comparing it to an unrenovated sort of bohemian night club. She taught private English lessons, which was an important source of extra income for her, though she had lost some clients in the wake of the recent financial crisis.

Still, she expressly tried to put a good face on things, and she allotted some money and time whenever possible to do things such as hear music at a jazz club, have a beer at a cafe with friends, or visit the theater or a museum, and sometimes she asked me to join in these activities. Indeed, the very first day I was presented to the teachers at her school, she had introduced herself and invited me to come out to a club. As we became friends, I often stopped in her small classroom between class periods or when I knew she had some free time. She would quickly plug in an immersion heater, go down the hall to rinse out the plastic cups she kept under her desk, and set out a small tin of coffee. While we drank, Olga, always sociable and talkative, would tell me about the latest developments in her life, such as her continuing search for an apartment or the new brands of imported coffee she was curious to try. She seemed continually interested in some measure of self-improvement, whether finding affordable aerobics classes or visiting the local chapter of the British Council for new lesson plan ideas. Though in the "crisis" context she economized on certain grocery items she previously had enjoyed on a regular basis, she found occasional visits to fitness clubs and tanning salons worth saving for.

One day, I came to her apartment as we had agreed for a relatively formal interview. To my surprise, she came to the door in a breathy rush, with her hair pulled back from her face with a headband. "Just a minute," she apologized; she was having a facial and the cosmetologist had showed up very late, ruining her carefully planned schedule. The woman was still in the other room waiting to finish the job; could I wait in the kitchen for a few minutes? After hurriedly putting out something for me to nibble on, Olga ran back into the other room. Once the cosmetologist had left, we headed to a cafe across the street to have our interview over a drink. While we ordered and sat down, Olga told me how the visit of this cosmetologist, a woman whom she had never met before but who had been recommended to her, had turned out to be awfully unpleasant. Not only had Olga not much liked the facial she had gotten but she also had been upset about something the woman had said: that she should change her whole image because she was a "provincial" and it showed. Her makeup and hair were all wrong, the cosmetologist had advised. Olga thought the woman had been rude, but she nonetheless found it difficult to shrug off the words. "People tell me I have good taste," she said, and I tried to reassure her that I thought they were right. "I don't know, maybe I know nothing in this life, . . ." she worried. "Maybe it's my loud teacher's voice," she mused, that gave the impression of "provincialness."

Olga found another cosmetologist. "I try to put myself in order," she told me another day, "as far as possible." When she had a bit of money, she would go for a session at the tanning salon (a practice relatively common among women in this northern climate—women talked about tanning lamps as lending health effects as well as an attractive glow), visit one of her favorite hairdressers, or plan new garments with a seamstress friend who would make things for her cheaply. "For me, clothing is connected with my mood," she told me in the spring of 1999 (i.e., after several months of "crisis"), going on that recently she sometimes felt wretched and poverty-stricken (*ubogii*) because of not being able to buy things. "It makes me so sad to talk about this," she admitted, but reassured herself by affirming that "in her soul" she was still a woman.

In the course of our conversations about shopping and consumerism, Olga complained about acquaintances who had money and were not saving up for major purchases such as apartments yet lived "primitively" all the same. She gave the example of a friend who had a large income, even after the crisis, but did not like to spend money on going places such as the theater or out with friends. She only spent the money on "rags" (*triapki*) like new stockings. She bought things and always called attention to them—"it's like kindergarten!" she complained. This is a particular "type," she said, and "it drives me crazy."

A final scene. In the fall of 1999, we were discussing the different kinds of stores found in Saint Petersburg—some modeled on Western-style supermarkets, with checkout lines and free access for consumers to shelves of goods; others retaining the more traditional, complicated *kassa* (cashier) system where goods were locked away behind counters and customers stood in multiple lines to order, pay for, and finally receive their purchases; and the open-air markets (*rynki*) whose merchants carried a broad range of everyday necessities including fresh produce, usually at relatively low prices. Olga did most of her shopping at the *rynki;* she lived close to one and did not have much extra time, so she just walked over there whenever she found she had run out of something. There was also a "minisupermarket" nearby, into which she stopped from time to time for ice cream cones, but it was much more expensive than the *rynok;* it was clearly, she pointed out, appropriate for those of a different financial stratum (*sloi*). I pushed further: What would she prefer if the prices were the same? "Of course it is better at the [inside] stores [*magaziny*]," where there were no lines or crowds. "I'd put my purchases in a basket *kul'turno*"—in a cultured way—"and go."

Olga's standards of respectability in both consumption and behavior resonate with middle-class imaginaries around the world, but their specific contours come to light only through reference to both Soviet institutions and the post-Soviet dilemmas of social welfare and restructuring. As described in chapter 2, the objective of the "culturalization" project in Stalinist Russia had been for Soviet citizens to achieve a sort of "self-civilization" (Dunham 1976). At the end of the twentieth century, Olga was involved in a similar endeavor, "putting herself in order" as much as she could, given restricted financial means even as compared with some of the other teachers. Maintaining her appearance was connected, for her, to being cultured, tasteful, and sufficiently worldly. In addition, her comments illustrate how appropriate consumption and self-presentation were understood as important aspects of being a mature, well-bred individual. Certain kinds of displays, such as messy hair, loud voices, and bragging about new purchases, were attributed to a lack of culture and criticized on those grounds. Olga further acknowledged that a proper physical appearance was not enough without maintenance, too, of one's knowledge, social contacts, and activities such as going to the theater—some of the less material evidences of social usefulness and inner integrity that helped to define a particular kind of self. For her own part, Olga had received a Soviet higher education in English pedagogy and had worked hard to maintain a tolerably enlightened and enjoyable life for herself and her daughter in the big city. The fact that the tide seemed so often against her these days left her feeling "wretched" and doubting the strength of her claims to sophistication and even femininity (a topic to which I return in chapter 5).

In concrete situations, individual actors or communities certainly can judge the proper balance among these elements of cultured selfhood differently; what is to one woman a measured concern to maintain a nice physical appearance, a fashionable wardrobe, and an active social circle might appear to another as evidence of excessive and even uncultured self-involvement. Yet the fundamental objective of living a respectable, cultured life on limited means was one close to many teachers' hearts and frequently on their minds, as manifested in our most focused conversations in 1998–99 about consumption as well as in their unprompted comments and interactions at school.

At times, the teachers' complaints about the suffering patiently being endured by the kind, impoverished Russian people, combined with their frequently pointed critiques of the local nouveaux riches, might seem to suggest that they viewed material prosperity and its pursuit as utterly separate from—and indeed *competitive* with and *detrimental* to—meaningful social relationships and collective well-being. Nancy Ries (1997) has described similar discourses, common during the perestroika era, as constituting an everyday oral genre of litany whereby Russians responded to the political chaos of the USSR's collapse and the shocks of economic "shock therapy."[1] Ries and others have highlighted Russian narratives that resonate with both Soviet and pre-Soviet ideologies in demonizing money and business and valorizing poverty and suffering (Humphrey 1995; Ries 1997; Pesman 2000; Caldwell 2004). Indeed, as discussed in chapter 1, these traits are often seen as central to the modern imagination of Russianness and the mythologized "Russian soul." Echoes of such litany resonated in the Saint Petersburg teachers' reflections about Russian life at the end of the 1990s.

But what of the more ambivalent and conflicted ways in which material and moral objectifications of value actually overlapped with and depended upon one another? A closer look at how teachers were negotiating and reflecting upon their own social identities in the late 1990s highlights certain basic ways in which they *did* assume or expect material standards of living and social or moral attributes such as culturedness and professionalism to be fundamentally interconnected, and even reflections of one another.

Two interrelated frames of reference took center stage in teachers' talk about these issues: culturedness as a measure of persons' worth and a positive locus of identification; and critiques of the (eminently "uncultured") New Russian nouveaux riches. Both discourses articulated the specific relationships perceived to exist between material things or styles of consumption, on one hand, and the consuming subjects' moral or personal worth and social contributions, on the other. Through these frames, individuals assessed the relationships of different kinds of people, how they could be compared with one another, and the logics according to which these relationships were governed. In many cases, such talk took the form of more or less essentializing descriptions of social "others" and their evils. Though such descriptions themselves tell us little if anything about the *actual* lives of the financially successful Russians whom teachers were critiquing, they are informative insofar as they express teachers' views of post-Soviet marketization in a condensed and powerful form. At the same time, as we shall see, indignant, moralizing discourses did not hold exclusive sway, for the teachers also entertained less black-and-white visions of post-Soviet reality and, like Olga, took some of the shame of what often felt like a "wretched" degree of consumer exclusion upon themselves.

1. Also see Ries 2002 for a later account of Russian discourses on business, corruption, morality, and cynicism in the 1990s.

Kul'turnost' as Social Critique

In the course of daily life, I probably heard about *kul'turnost'* most at school; for example, when teachers were decrying, and apologizing to me for, the inattentive behavior of students in our English classes. "This is *beskul'tur'e* [lack of culture]," one teacher muttered as a particularly unruly group of children was dismissed. Such complaints sometimes also were lodged against pupils' parents. Liza provided the example of a parent who had come in for a meeting with her. Judging initially by her appearance, Liza thought the woman to be *intelligentnaia,* an impression that was shattered as the woman became irate at what she heard from Liza. Recounting the episode, Liza pointed out that she had only been conveying information to this woman, simply transmitting something that had already been decided by the school's higher administration. Yet the woman started to shout that these decisions did not suit her. Liza scolded: "If you are used to yelling that way, do it at home." The woman continued, Liza telling her with derision, "even more quietly, please!" Finishing the account, Liza summarized: "This is a lack of culture—simply boorishness [*khamstvo*]!"[2]

Kul'turnost' was thus construed as a personal quality more inherent to a person than social status, educational background, or physical self-presentation—despite the fact that education, style of dress, and other acquired characteristics informed expectations of whether a person was indeed cultured. *Kul'turnost'* was difficult to imagine, for some, outside the context of an educated individual; but it could be cultivated aside from social status, job, or formal education, driven as it was by an individual's inclinations and instincts. Though social and hereditary factors were understood to play a significant role, then, individuals implicitly were held responsible for their own level of *kul'turnost'*. "A lack of culture" was an admonishment for bad behavior.

Veronika lived with her daughter and son-in-law, both scholars at a local university, and their daughter in a relatively large and pleasant apartment close to the center of the city. When I visited them in their home, they complained about the arrival of some unwelcome neighbors. Over tea, Veronika told me about a health club that would soon open in their apartment build-

2. In speaking about New Russians, people sometimes cited a proverb that implied that such boorishness (*khamstvo*) was a worse fate than poverty, and that riches did not ensure cultured behavior: "Better a lord become a *kham* [boor, lout; here, in the sense of a rough, uncultured, or lowly person] than a *kham* become a lord [i.e., wealthy] [*Luchshe pan v kham, chem kham v pan*]."

ing. Amenities such as a sauna were being installed, and these projects were drawing on the building's water supply with the result that residents periodically were left without water. Unfortunately, Veronika's daughter pointed out, the owners of that business had money behind them; thus the rest of the residents were powerless to counteract their demands or get them kicked out. The younger woman cited this as an example of "the absence of culture in relations between people in this country." If there had been "more culture," such humiliations and the absence of legitimate authority would not have had to be suffered. Here it was the business owners who presumably lacked "culture," but the family's complaint also was directed more diffusely: Whatever normative code of ethics existed for people like themselves, it did not appear to be operating powerfully enough to curb such rascals' pursuit of stark self-interest.

Nowadays, *dobro* (goodness, kindness) was pitted against a kind of cruel practicality. The latter, as a few teachers told me, was referred to euphemistically by those who benefited most from it as "knowing how to live" or "the ability to survive" (*umenie / umet' zhit'/ vyzhit'*). To the teachers who lodged these complaints, Russians who touted their own survival "abilities" were indulging in a mystification of reality that conveniently allowed them to justify and to mask the nature of their morally questionable pursuits from themselves. One woman described a prosperous relative involved in (some vaguely imagined) "business," who was laboring under the delusion that people like *her,* who remained poor, were just lazy and unwilling to take any initiative in the new Russia. Because she was currently struggling to work three jobs simultaneously (one as a school psychologist, another as a social worker, and yet a third as a survey interviewer for a marketing firm) to make ends meet for her small family, she found this assumption entirely inaccurate and more than a little insulting. The talent for "survival" was related to people's lack of time for the "cultural" and the "spiritual" (*dukhovnyi*) and it brought up questions about just what one was willing to do to succeed financially. In this usage, "spiritual" need not refer specifically to religiosity; rather, it can evoke notions of intellectual life, warm interpersonal relations, and morality, suggesting a quality that stands in opposition to pragmatic materiality.

Ivan and Larisa, a couple we meet more intimately below, took up this issue one evening. Ivan argued that in Soviet times there had been less interest in material things and that people had gone to the theater, read books, gotten together, and argued a lot. Though they had not believed in communism, they had believed they would do something to make the world better. His wife Larisa interjected that there were some for whom life had become much better in the 1990s than it had been then; and though Ivan could not but admit that in material terms this was true, he continued on by saying that there had been a general change for the worse in spiritual life and that people now did not understand what the point might be of doing anything at all (*za chem, voobshche, za chem sdelat' chto-to*). Larisa held that, all the same, certain things were "eternal in any regime": children, family, education. But she affirmed that, in general, those who had made money were not spiritual people; for to succeed in that sphere, one had to transgress certain spiritual rules (*perestupat' dukhovnye pravila*), that is, to violate widely accepted moral norms surrounding interpersonal relations in favor of one's own advancement.

Meanwhile, the teachers felt the indifference of their compatriots who held power and wealth; the teachers' cultured worthiness and contributions to the wider society sometimes seemed increasingly irrelevant. "No one is thinking about us," one teacher said, asking rhetorically: "Who lives better here [*u nas*]? One who produces or sells, or works in a bank. We don't produce anything concrete. It works out to: Go ahead and live, however you want." Elizaveta expressed a similar fear that cultural standard-bearers such as teachers were becoming obsolete and ignored: "Before, the intelligentsia were respected and people aspired to be like them. Now it is more fashionable to be bad [*modno byt' plokhim*]. To not respect anything. . . . To show that, 'I am like this. You be however you want [*Ia takoi. A vy kak khotite*].'"

This vision of the reversal of a previous logic of social rewards became especially clear in the words of Veronika, who declared that things had been more "cheerful" (*veselo*) before the August 17 crisis had wiped out a middle class that just had begun to form and to "get on its feet." I asked whether she included her own family in this number (her daughter and son-in-law were academics at a prestigious university, one holding the qualification of *doktor nauk* and the other *kandidat nauk*).[3]

"Well, a *doktor nauk* and *kandidat nauk*—before such people got pretty high salaries, prices were low. . . . What is this that a *kandidat nauk* makes 600 rubles [per month], when lamb costs 100 rubles a kilogram and rabbit 140?"[4] Educators and researchers certainly were not among the wealthiest

3. A *kandidat nauk* is roughly equivalent to an American PhD; *kandidaty* who go on to become *doktora nauk* normally do so only further on in their careers, once they have established themselves as already accomplished academicians.

4. It is pertinent that lamb and rabbit are far from being considered staple goods. Meat of any kind was widely acknowledged as overly expensive, particularly after the crisis, and chicken, beef, and liver seemed to be more common and somewhat less ex-

members of Soviet society (though professors of higher education were better rewarded than schoolteachers), but the notion that such a highly educated person as a PhD scientist should be paid only the equivalent of 6 kilograms of lamb per month represented, for Veronika, a perversion of reasonable logics of value; for the fact that such expensive goods should be on sale and accessible to certain locals—those who had enough money, however useful or harmful to society their professional activity—and yet be so inaccessible to highly placed scholars suggested an utter discounting of the culturedness associated with education and intellectual life.

Yet as Veronika's commentary also indicated, such talk about the dislodging of accustomed structures of respect and rewards did not imply a general championing of ascetic spirituality over materialism, as accounts of Russian cultural life sometimes seem to suggest. *Kul'turnost'* pertained in part to displays of material culture, though it was also compatible with *dukhovnost'*, spirituality. Culturedness and proper self-presentation were conceived as linked to and through appropriate *styles* and *subjects* of consumption. Self-presentation through consumption was a key if often implicit part of the expression of culturedness—even if teachers insisted that nothing material was *essential* to *kul'turnost'* and that *kul'turnost'* could not be reduced to the sum of its material signs.

Recall, for example, Liza's story of the obnoxious, deceivingly *intelligentnyi*-looking parent who had visited her at school. In the same conversation, Liza stated that taste in things like clothing was not necessarily related to being *intelligentnyi* ("a person can be obnoxious, know nothing about theater, but be prettily and attractively dressed" or can be knowledgeable and *kul'turnyi* but *bezobrazno*, messily dressed). What, then, had she meant when she had said that the lady at school looked *intelligentnaia?* Liza offered a list of concrete characteristics: The woman had a neat hairdo and wore a business suit, cut simply. She looked at Liza intelligently, not blankly. She was made up in moderation, not vulgarly, and she wore clothing that was appropriate to her age. More succinctly, teacher Maria explained that a person of cultured appearance "dresses, maybe, not richly [*bogato*], but with sufficient . . . taste, cleanliness, neatness [*opriatno*]. And, basically, worthily [*dostoino*, i.e., with dignity]." Another woman noted that though there existed people who were not educated but put on airs—usually businessmen—there were others, on the opposite side of the spec-

---

pensive choices. A kilogram of any kind of meat, however, would have put a sizable dent in a salary of 600 rubles per month in 1998–99.

trum and equally mysterious to her, who were not interested in material things at all but rather were buried in books and valued their occupation above all else in life. "Professors and I don't know what. . . . I think they're crazy."

Consumer aspirations were not, then, uniformly suspected but were seen to have a proper place. It was not acquisitive consumer culture so much as inappropriate distributions of wealth that were so unsettling. Both the inevitability and the desirability associated with the expanding consumer market were clear when teachers talked about the elusive material gains currently being enjoyed by only a few as part of *everyone's* future and as representative of progress. When I asked Elizaveta whether she read any special catalogs to find out about goods on the market, she said no, but she added that there were some that came free of charge to residential mailboxes. With this, she pulled out such a publication, a glossy catalog called *Rio,* from a pile on her office desk. As we continued to talk, she leafed through it, and as she did I caught glimpses of Gucci watches, expensive furniture, and lobster dinners. With the catalog open to a picture of furniture in a showcase home, Elizaveta remarked that all this was "not for us. We will wait." Though she had noticed that some people did not even bother to bring the catalogs in from the mailbox, she liked to take a look from time to time: "You have to, in order to see how people live and find out how far behind you are." She tried not to think about everything at home that needed renovation, however, because it would drive her crazy. Later, I brought Elizaveta my own copy of a current women's magazine for her to peruse. She leafed through it, apparently with some interest, pausing at one point to sigh, "Yes. I have to change my job [*nado meniat' rabotu*]." Of the expensive furniture, appliances, and other goods depicted there in the magazine, she predicted: "This is real life, our future before our eyes."

Given that teachers spoke about Russian standards of living as lower than European and American ones, Elizaveta's comment did not (or did not only) contribute to a conversation about class and social mobility per se (as in Americans' "keeping up with the Joneses"), but rather reflected broader understandings of material prosperity and "civilized" lifestyles as indicators of absolute progress and development. Certain privileged lifestyles were seen, then, not only as desirable but even as inevitable, as part of a brighter future of sophisticated goods already being enjoyed elsewhere in the world. For the moment, however, the future seemed to be leaving the teachers behind, while some Russians were already living there. Through their references to *kul'turnost',* teachers marked themselves as worthy subjects of such respectable consumption; and the fact that this consumption remained out of reach spurred pointed social critiques of the contemporary status quo as well as introspective self-questioning.

The School as Social Field:
Teaching Post-Soviet Raskol'nikovs

At school, teachers interacted with a great number of urban dwellers: colleagues, students, and students' parents, who in many cases enjoyed socioeconomic situations quite different from their own. The fact that teachers were among those responsible for socializing children and imparting knowledge to them made them particularly attentive to the dynamics and deficiencies of families in question. At both schools, teachers agreed that a majority of their students were relatively well-off (*obespechennye*); as one teacher pointed out, the poorest children attending her school were those of the teachers themselves.[5] Yet the teachers also believed that the relative prosperity of the student body was accompanied by a range of problems.

Some teachers expressed this indirectly, contrasting certain problematic families with the "many" or "most" who were "*intelligentnye*" people. Nadezhda, for example, explained that she did not like working as a tutor (which she did anyway, for the money) because she thought it spoiled children and allowed them to be lazy. "They get used to doing nothing in school and then go for their private lessons and everything is explained to them," Nadezhda complained; "the tutor explains and their parents pay." Yes, of course these were relatively well-off families, but some them of them were also, happily, *intelligentsia,* she said, whereas others were (uneducated) New Russians who had suddenly gotten rich. Liza complained after a teachers' meeting about the announcement by one of the head administrators that students' grades were too low throughout the school. Just a few weeks ago, Liza fumed with frustration, the teachers had been informed that grades were too high! The low grades were the administration's fault anyway, Liza insisted, because they chose to accept the children of New Russians whose parents gave money to the school, children who were unprepared scholas-

---

5. From time to time, I visited a third school, which was located in a less central part of the city. The building itself was in far poorer condition than were the relatively prestigious schools in which I worked more regularly. The teachers at the former school affirmed that their pupils were mainly from (what they called) "proletarian" or "simple" families, and the teachers I met there seemed to be living under more strained conditions, as well.

tically and then had a difficult time adjusting. Still, the parents at this s
were "mainly *intelligentnye*" people who wanted good educations for their
children and knew which classes were worthwhile, Liza qualified—not like
the New Russians who paid for additional, prestigious-sounding, but (in the
teachers' estimation) pointless or superfluous courses such as "Dizain" (Design, presumably a course on clothing and/or interior design).

In addition to academic difficulties, children of wealthy parents were said
to have attitude problems, for which teachers held the parents to blame. A
school psychologist described wealthy children's socialization problems
with conviction and in particular detail. "Children of wealthy parents suffer problems such as that of [*Crime and Punishment*'s] Raskol'nikov," Anna
said, referring to the antihero who kills an old woman as he grapples with
the question of, as Anna put it, "what I have a right to (do)" (*na chto ia imeiu
pravo*) as opposed to being a helpless executor of fate. "This is also the main
question for such families: what they have the right to do, having money."
Their children are given the idea, often subconsciously, that they can do
whatever they want, Anna continued, observing that those families typically
understood freedom as equivalent to omnipotence (*vsemogushchestvo*).
Furthermore, these children were overly concerned at a young age about
"who is higher, who is lower." A first-grader might ask other children at
school: "Do you have a computer? What kind of car? Who is your papa?
Who is your mama?"

The teachers told of a small boy who had seen a workman doing repairs
at the school, to whom the child had referred as "my worker." Liza inferred
that having gotten used to his family employing people, the child found it
natural to think in terms of "my" worker, and even "my" teacher. Here the
possessive pronoun was offensive to her in that it was interpreted to express
just that: *possession,* or perhaps simply—and no less offensively—*personal
employment* of a teacher by a family rather than by the state or even a specific educational institution. Indeed, Liza complained that while she thought
most people generally had a good deal of respect for teachers, especially for
English teachers in rigorous and prestigious schools like hers, wealthy parents expected things of her that were not part of her responsibilities. They
think, Liza went on, that once they have paid the school, she, the teacher,
has to do exactly what they want. In Soviet times, by contrast, as another
woman put it,

> A teacher was something like a tsar or lord, . . . whereas now it is like
> *working for a family.* Even if the parents know nothing about the educa-

tional process, they will allow themselves to criticize it. . . . At private schools teachers work under even closer parental control, because people who are paying money want successes, results. (emphasis added)

Unpleasant encounters with parents thus threw into relief the coercive power of money and the devaluation of teachers' cultural capital as professional educators in post-Soviet market society. Wealthy parents' demands appeared as examples of—and also symbols for—how teachers themselves had been repositioned in Russia.

It was not at all the case that teachers unequivocally condemned, or took no advantage of, the fact that parents had money and wished to pay for schools' and teachers' services. Teachers understood the need for sponsors, or "*sponsory,*" wealthy parents willing to give money to the school. Such funds could supply new furniture, renovations, or supplies that government money did not. Although both schools were technically public, a variety of fees were paid by parents, including payment for classes outside the required program and taught in the late afternoons (e.g., English courses based on British textbooks more expensive than those used in the regular curriculum). Teachers earned additional monthly income by teaching such classes. Parents also often paid unofficial fees to administrators to have their children admitted to the schools.[6]

Many teachers accepted students for private tutoring, and English-language teachers were in particular demand. Some were able to draw relatively large numbers of students thanks to their good reputations and/or referrals from other students or teachers, and as of 1999 they were charging hourly rates as high as $10. The significance of these lessons as a source of income becomes clear when one considers that teachers' official monthly salaries were often in the area of 1,000 rubles, or about $167 before the 1998 financial crisis and about $42 by the spring of 1999. (Teachers who took on a maximum of optional duties at their schools could earn up to 1,500 to 2,000 rubles in salary.) Successful tutors could earn much more in that capacity than they did in their official jobs as teachers; for example, one woman, a single mother of two, reported receiving about 800 rubles a month from the school and 2,000 rubles in a good month from private tutoring. Still, school positions remained central because they provided stability and a pool of potential private pupils. In some cases, teachers prepared students for par-

6. This "payment" can take the form of cash or gifts; see chapter 6.

ticular oral exams—which they might themselves be helping to evaluate—
holding themselves to varying degrees responsible for assuring that a student would get the desired course grade. In short, their positions within
schools gave teachers a certain degree of marketable power; high grades
helped students get into good universities and departments, and these were
teachers' resources to distribute.

Yet it was distasteful to those teachers to think that a wealthy family
might try to "*employ*" them—that, in the teachers' perception, it would assume it could control them because it had money to pay, in effect hiring a
teacher as a private employee no different from a chauffeur or nanny. This
was a blow to the teachers' sense of the broader social value of their knowledge, qualifications, and so on, as (ideally) conferred by their institutional
status as well as by popular understandings of the importance of education
and culturedness. They sensed that their own sociomoral claims to status,
respect, and satisfactory material rewards had, like the ruble against the dollar, fallen to an unfavorable rate of exchange vis-à-vis the cash resources
held by others, whose incomes were not apparently legitimated by any
higher virtue or authority. In short, parent-teacher scenarios instantiated
competing regimes of value: struggles between differently situated actors
and interests to define what was most important, what kind of price could
be set on things, services, and persons, and on what basis (Appadurai 1986,
14–15; Keane 2001, 65; Graeber 2001, 88). Though teachers were already
willing (or compelled) to offer their services to other individuals for cash,
it was the suggestion that wealthy parents might be able, with that cash, to
dictate coercively the terms of the exchange—what their money would buy,
where, and when—that was most upsetting and struggled against.

Being poorer than their students was at times a source of considerable
embarrassment. "When you are wearing the same outfit all year, . . ." one
teacher said, "you want something new. Looking noticeably worse than the
students is somehow unpleasant." Teacher Lena remembered how her
young students had noticed things she did not have, asking questions such
as, "You don't have a watch?" with the implication that they were shocked
she could not afford one (although, she explained to me, this was not strictly
true; she had already lost or broken a few watches, and could not afford to
keep buying them). Another uncomfortable incident had arisen when uniform jackets were being made for the children in her class. A parent helping to organize the making of uniforms had said to her, "Why don't we have
a jacket made for you, too? It will be all of 300 rubles." "*All of* 300 rubles,"

Lena repeated in the retelling, for this had been particularly offensive to her: the implication that her appearance was poor as well as the calling to attention of the fact that she would have difficulty affording improvements.

A young teacher and active English tutor, Anya, explained that she made sure to "look after herself" very carefully so that she would be attractive in every detail—hair, nails, makeup, clothes—when she went to others' homes to give lessons, because she had noticed that her employers liked it. But she also told of a more blatant and offensive example of this sort of judgment of teachers according to their attractiveness. A student's mother, herself displeased about the incident, had told Anya about a comment her daughter had made about another teacher at Anya's school. "Mama," the girl had said, "how can I respect my teacher if she has a run in her stocking?" In another context, the run might have been treated as a form of unculturedness. But though meticulous Anya would scarcely have been caught dead with a run in her own stocking, the tone in which she recounted the girl's judgment suggested that it had been interpreted as an illustration of the cold, precocious materialism of a new generation of young people who might well discount a well-intentioned elder on the basis of her impoverished wardrobe.

When speaking directly about the status of teachers in Russian society, teachers pointed to a conflict between, on one hand, the social or cultural value that they felt was attached to their profession and, on the other, the lack of recognition of that value implied to them by the very fact that their wages were so low. Some emphasized the respect many of their compatriots continued to attach to education and pointed to the fact that education was needed for such currently prestigious careers as law; or they might self-consciously say, as did Elizaveta, that although *she* thought it to be a worthwhile profession respected by many, others "consider that a teacher is a loser [*bezudachnik*]. Things haven't worked out for her, it doesn't have any potential, it's poorly paid." Nastia argued that everyone in Russia was worrying about their own problems, not concerning themselves about teachers' status; but "we feel bad on our own, because our work isn't valued. . . . If I received decent money, I'd work better."

If, in this framework, it was not acknowledged that money could ever *impart* social value, then it *did* serve at least implicitly as an indicator to self and others that such value was present and had been properly recognized. The issue at stake between teachers and affluent families was one of contested status and appropriate compensation—or more accurately, contestation and uncertainty about the very grounds for status and the significance of material compensation in the first place. From the teachers' perspective, at least, their relations with pupils' parents informed and made more pressing ongoing deliberations about their own contributions to society, reflecting larger discourses about "culture" and social value that to some extent still echo Soviet norms and ideologies. The image of the New Russian served as another prism through which these values and defensive stances were refracted.

Bandits in Raspberry-Colored Jackets: Examining Discourses about New Russians

"They have money, so they think they can do anything they want [*pozvoliat vse*]." So commented a Saint Petersburg art teacher in the fall of 1998. That day, I was talking with a group of his colleagues over tea about what they thought of the New Russians.[7] They were characterized by both money and stupidity, one teacher had said, whereas yet another colleague offered that they were involved in "speculation," which had been illegal (under socialism) and has since become legal. "They have their own fashions. We laugh at them all—they aren't worth envying," one of them went on, as the listening teachers murmured their agreement. New Russians were not simply wealthy, someone clarified, for wealthy, smart businessmen did exist. Rather, the New Russians were people who were "limited"; security guards (*okhrana*), for example, or people who wore not black jackets but green or raspberry-colored ones. These commentaries were representative of the characterizations of New Russians I heard over the course of my year in Saint Petersburg: their imputed lack of intelligence, "culture," and education; their immodest and conspicuous taste, often represented by the brightly colored (especially "raspberry-colored" or maroon) jackets they were said to favor; and their lack of proper respect for others.

The last word of the conversation that day—and perhaps its most telling moment—came a bit later, when an elderly teacher entered the room and was invited to sit down with us for tea. Someone told her that I had been asking about the New Russians; how would she define them? Her answer: "I would say, not ours" (*Ia by skazala, ne nashi*—that is, not "our sort" or "our people"). The remaining teachers commented in agreement, finding this last definition the most concise and accurate one offered so far.

---

7. A version of the analysis on New Russian discourses found in this section and the following one appears in Patico 2000.

Clearly, in defining these others, the teachers were also articulating the social standards to which they felt *they* adhered, highlighting concerns that were salient in their own daily lives. A nouveau riche class consisting of entrepreneurs (including former state apparatchiki and mafia players) as well some educated professionals undoubtedly had arisen quickly in post-Soviet Russia. They will be discussed here, however, not as they "really were" but rather in terms of how they figured in teachers' narrations of socioeconomic change and injustice. Indeed, as Caroline Humphrey (2002, 178) has observed, the terminology of New Russianness "refers to a new mentality and an aspirational status rather than to a defined social group . . . [and] is primarily used from outside." By distancing themselves from the behavior and choices they described as characteristically "New Russian," teachers were also constructing an idea of their own social value and uprightness.

Such stereotypes were mirrored and coproduced by the media. For example, in 1998–99 the local periodical *Petersburg Express* (*Peterburg-Ekspress*)[8] featured stories about New Russians, including, notably, one on their problem children.[9] According to the local therapists cited in the story, these teenagers and preteens were not only spoiled by their wealth but also received little parental attention (aside from occasional disciplining, often described as physical in nature). As a result, the children had negative relations with schoolmates, were rather cruel to others as well as emotionally needy, and had not learned basic life lessons such as how to make true friends (as opposed to trying to "buy" them). As the *Petersburg Express* story read, "A new class has appeared here—people who have made and continue to make money. They raised their children in carefree luxury, and are horrified at how they have turned out." These observations were well in line with problems cited by the teachers regarding their own pupils, including wealthy parents' lack of attention to children's upbringing.

Another issue of the same periodical, published just a few weeks after the August 17 crisis set in, emphasized the differential effects of the crisis, comparing and contrasting the situation of the wealthy with that of the poorer general population. For example, one article in the issue listed prices

---

8. Although this publication covers a variety of "serious" stories of political and social interest, it leans toward the sensational. Also, in contrast to other publications such as women's magazines that address related issues (consumer styles, raising children, morality and relationships), the *Petersburg Express* sides fairly clearly with relatively poor Saint Petersburgians, whereas those other magazines conjure the image of a more prosperous urban woman, single or married.

9. "Novye Russkie Otsy i ikh Dety," *Peterburg-Ekspress,* June 9, 1999.

of basic goods and described how they climbed over the first few weeks of crisis, making suggestions to readers expecting the worst about how to stock up on necessary staple items.[10] A central photo depicted a man hugging to himself a pile of groceries—basic items such as a box of pasta, a bottle of vegetable oil, and a can of Nescafé coffee—and the headline read: "My Riches." An accompanying article pointed out that the wealthy, too, were buying things up as fast as they could, in anticipation of rising prices and shortages; but they were buying different goods, such as cellular phones and other electronics. The paper's front page featured a photo of a tall, glamorous-looking woman, heavily made up and wearing a long fur coat, carrying a bag of groceries in one arm. The same products were visible as those pictured in the article described above: pasta, oil, coffee. The headline read: "The Rich Are Crying Too" (*Bogatye tozhe plachut*).[11] The "poor" rich girl in her fur coat apparently would cry over having to settle for the same mundane groceries that other Russians were already trying to hoard before those, too, disappeared or became too expensive.

Some of the most vivid and frequent representations of New Russians were those expressed in widely told jokes or *anekdoty:*

> Two New Russians meet and one draws attention to his new tie, which he has recently purchased for $300 [specific prices vary in each telling]. His friend admonishes him: you fool! You could have bought it around the corner for $500!

> Two old acquaintances meet, one a New Russian. He complains that he has many problems: he was in a car accident and has to drive an awful car; his wife has gone off to Hawaii; he has divorced her and must pay a lot of alimony; and so on. When the companion finally gets a chance to speak about his own circumstances, he says, "Well, things are really bad, I haven't eaten in three days," and the New Russian replies: "Oh that is very bad—you should make yourself."

> A New Russian checks in to a Western hotel. He wants to order room service for his companion and himself to his room, #222, for tea. Eager to show off his knowledge of English, he tells the clerk: "Tea and tea and two two two."

10. "Spasaisia, kto mozhet," *Peterburg-Ekspress,* September 9, 1998.

11. Note that this is a reference to the Mexican soap opera that was a runaway success in Russia in the early 1990s, called in Russia *Bogatye tozhe Plachut* (The Rich Also Cry).

As the three *anekdoty* illustrate, in the New Russian stereotype material flamboyance was presented as an index of less concrete but still observable qualities including a lack of education, putting on of airs, and obliviousness to the problems of the rest of society. In jokes these connections could be clear, exaggerated, humorous, and unequivocal.

But such lore also informed and reflected everyday observations, as when, in the course of a conversation about New Russians, Liza told me about one she had seen who had been "straight out of an *anekdot*." In this case, Liza had seen little that directly indicated the New Russian's behavior or attitude toward others; rather, she described his laughably archetypical appearance. A Mercedes 600 stopped on the street. This was the first sign that a typical New Russian had appeared on the scene, for the Mercedes 600 was the car to which those in Saint Petersburg most commonly referred in everyday conversations about the wealthy and their consumption; that particular model seemed to serve as a kind of vehicular uniform for all those who could afford such expenditures. Next, one of the car's windows came down and a man's hand poked out, adorned by a thick gold bracelet. Liza demonstrated its thickness for emphasis, holding her thumb and forefinger an inch or two apart. Soon more of the man became visible. He had a shaved head, also considered typical for New Russians or "bandits." Liza noted that he did not have on a jacket (or blazer, *pidzhak*—recall the raspberry or maroon jackets cited above), for it was hot outside, but he had on a shirt that exposed a very hairy chest and large gold chain necklace. He was listening to loud music. Everyone standing around had taken notice of the man. She explained that this had happened in the suburban town of Dunai, where her family had a dacha. The location made the occurrence particularly funny, for it was not a prestigious place—everyone rode around on bicycles there, Liza observed, so the Mercedes was noticeable. "If it had been Zelenogorsk or Solneshko [where there were more luxurious homes being built and, presumably, flashier residents]," she said, "it would have been more understandable. . . ."[12]

In addition to being flashy, uneducated, and insensitive, New Russians were assumed—at least in their most classic profile—to have links to the criminal as well as business worlds. A Saint Petersburg market research journal (Bezgodov and Sokolov 1999) reported the results of a survey in which respondents had been asked to complete the statement: "To be suc-

12. For an excellent discussion of the aesthetics and significance of New Russian "cottages" (*kottedzhy*), see Humphrey 2002.

cessful in business in Russia, it is necessary to . . ." Among the most common answers were "break the law" (14.2 percent) and "violate moral norms" (10.9 percent).[13] Ivan, an English teacher in his mid-forties, gave his opinion:

> Nowadays many New Russians are just bandits with primitive thinking, guns in their pockets, and raspberry-colored coats. . . . Of course, not all New Russians are bandits or stupid people. I think there are many clever people among them. But still, I think they are very closely connected to the mafia, because it's hard to operate without it [and run a profitable business].[14]

Anya told about a New Russian couple whose child she tutored in English, and whose wealth derived from sources that she described as somewhat mysterious. The family was, she emphasized, very wealthy, and an illustration of this was the fact that they had bought an apartment in the building across from Anya's (an expensive area) and it had not even been difficult for them—it was not as though they had been saving up and had spent everything they had, she surmised. The apartment boasted a Jacuzzi and a warmed floor, common luxuries among wealthy New Russians, according to Anya. She was not sure what the profession of the husband was, because "such people usually do not say how they earn their money"; but she had gotten the impression that he might be a security guard (*okhrana,* one of the professions associated with "New Russianness"; see Volkov 2001). The young wife did not work; her schedule consisted of nothing more than aerobics, tanning, massages, and parties, as far as Anya could see. She had also had operations to alter her nose and enlarge her bust. Report-

---

13. The only more popular answers were "money, start-up capital" (16.6 percent) and "connection, acquaintances, patronage/protection [*pokrovitel'stvo*]." Other responses included: 9.7 percent, have a mind, creative abilities; 7.6 percent, knowledge, habits (*navyki*), experience; 6.7 percent, change life in Russian society; 5 percent, adjust, *krutit'sia'*; 4.7 percent, work; 3.5 percent, strength, boldness, energy; 2.7 percent, honesty, decency (*poriadochnost'*); 2.7 percent, desire, will, determination (*tseleustremlennost'*); 2.3 percent, power, patronage / protection of power; 2 percent, cleverness; 1.8 percent, commit a crime; and 1.3 percent, luck/success (*udacha*).

14. There seems to be much truth to this, to the extent that protection services do appear to be indispensable in the conduct of business in Russia, as discussed in chapter 2. What I am particularly interested in here is not the strict veracity or falsehood of the claim so much as how such commentary is worked into broader frameworks concerning the morality of business and of capitalist market relations in general.

ing all this, Anya's face suggested a mixture of mild disgust and incredulity. "She is like a Barbie doll," Anya summarized, "which is actually exactly what she looks like, with the same silly expression!"

Yet the "New Russian" was not always so derogated and one-dimensional in daily conversations and reflections. Sometimes my interlocutors sought to clarify the usage of the term, insisting that there was more than one type of New Russian, or that the term was overapplied in popular usage and carried too many unwarranted assumptions. One English teacher in her early forties, Nadezhda, explained that she disapproved of the term because it was used to describe people of high material position, even very high, but with a negative connotation, referring to bandits, mafia members, or thieves. But, she argued, some of the wealthy are decent (good, principled) people (*poriadochnye liudi*). Teacher Ivan noted that he had met some New Russian parents in the course of evaluating their children's English for the purposes of school admission decisions. They were a very nice couple, whom he could not imagine behaving badly on the street. (The comment was offered in contrast to the more immediate case of a man he had seen moments before on the street, who was talking on a cellphone and had gestured rudely at a woman—a more stereotypical and expected vision of New Russian wealth.)

On another occasion, Ivan's wife Larisa and daughter Vera told of a similarly surprising encounter: When their car, an aged domestic hand-me-down from Larisa's father, broke down several minutes away from home, a New Russian in an expensive foreign car had stopped to help. Ultimately he towed them home, refusing any monetary compensation. Everyone on the street had stopped and laughed to see the luxury car towing a shabby Soviet one. The most surprising thing about the episode for Larisa and her daughter was the selfless gallantry of the New Russian, who had helped them in a moment of need and expected nothing in return. This did not change their opinion that he was definitely a "New Russian"; Vera noted, for example, that he had "the fingers," imitating the hand gesture attributed to New Russians: forefinger and pinky raised, remaining fingers and thumb folded down. (Saint Petersburg dwellers often gestured this way when referring to New Russians; and though I never noticed anyone motioning this way in public and unselfconsciously, my friends said that this was an authentic habit of New Russians and that it derived from prison jargon, referring to the presumed link between New Russian wealth and illicit activity.)

More rarely, New Russians were characterized in ways that cast their material success fairly positively in terms of their ability to adapt to new conditions. Katya, a teacher of about thirty, commented that before, New Russians had been thought of in terms of a certain stereotype: shaved heads (*bridlok*), red jacket, "fingers like this." . . . But now, she thought, it was understood that there were some *intelligentnye* people who had something in their heads and had also become wealthy:

> JP: Do you call people who are [both] wealthy and *intelligentnye* New Russians?
> K: I think so, yes. Because they can adjust [*sposobtsvovat'*] and earn money here now—in the new Russia.

Music teacher Liliia spoke similarly of the New Russians while throwing into question the position of less economically successful professionals such as teachers—what were the reasons for their being left behind?

> Well of course, the market must be a market, but simply we, our country hadn't gotten used to the market before that, we never had private property, we only had state property. And we simply didn't know how, didn't know. When the market appeared, those who were able to be resourceful [shrewd] turned out to be the "New Russians." And we, who can't be shrewd, who haven't been taught, we ended up worse than everyone. So maybe it was—it simply came into our lives very abruptly, and because of that it began so negatively. If it had been gradual, if the people had learned how to hold private property, and not just state property, then, maybe, it would have been softer and simpler. Because it was like an avalanche, this market fell on us, and whoever could came up to the surface, and those who couldn't stayed below. Unfortunately, it was exactly the intelligentsia, all the teachers, all the scholarly workers even, who were left there. We couldn't, we have no . . . no property at all, of our own.

Given the ambivalence that some expressed about what "being able to survive" really meant, it does not follow that Liliia's evaluation was unambivalently positive toward New Russians or deprecating of her own relative position. These kinds of comments do suggest, however, that wealthier Russians were seen (by some) to have "progressed"—and not only materially—where teachers and other professionals had not.

In short, there was some disagreement, or at least ambiguity, as to how "New Russian" was best defined and evaluated—that is, about how often people "straight out of an *anekdot*" actually appeared in reality. Critical applications of the epithet "New Russian" and the meanings attached to the term varied according to context. Ivan, for example, had acknowledged that some New Russians he had met seemed to be good (perhaps even cultured) individuals, even though as a general rule he was disposed to expect the opposite.

Far from detracting from the potency of the New Russian trope, such qualifications help to expose what is really operative in its application. In using the label and revising its meaning, they addressed the question of how inextricable from one another the aspects considered most typical of New Russians—wealth, criminality, tastelessness, condescension—really were. Was an *intelligentnyi,* or relatively intellectual and cultured person, who had become a successful businessman truly a New Russian? Was it possible to gain much material wealth without engaging in the morally suspect, often criminal activity usually assumed of New Russians? Precisely *who* should be called a New Russian was not always clear in everyday applications of the term. Below, dwelling on my conversations with one of the families I knew best (and who were, incidentally, among those having the most financial difficulty over the course of my year in Saint Petersburg), I suggest that their disagreements and uncertainty about what or who constituted a New Russian are best understood in terms of their ambivalence about their own positions in late-1990s Saint Petersburg, and in relation to the connections they understood to exist between material prosperity, moral value, and their own future possibilities.

The N. Family

The N. family lived in a formerly communal apartment in the Petrograd Side area of Saint Petersburg. Ivan and Larisa, both in their early forties, had lived there since their marriage about twenty years ago; but only recently (just before the financial crisis of August 1998 and after their neighbor in the apartment had died) had they finally been able to buy the last room of their four-room apartment. Their children, a fourteen-year-old boy and sixteen-year-old girl, attended the same English-language specialization school where both parents worked. Ivan was an English teacher and translator by education, who had worked in other capacities before coming to work at this school several years ago. Larisa was an engineer who had come to work at the same school after jobs in her specialization had dried up. She taught "Public Safety" and other courses and held class teacher respe bilities. Though their salaries were low—especially after the ruble depreci-ation of August 1998—they were stable and paid on time. Also, the fact that their school was a very good one with high-quality English instruction gave Ivan and Larisa an incentive to continue working there; for though it was technically a public school, entrance was not exactly open, and Ivan had told the administration that he had two children whom he would like to bring with him before he accepted the job. Their daughter Vera graduated with dis-tinction in the spring of 1999, but their son Misha had one year left before he would take the comprehensive exams that were the condition for contin-uation into the tenth grade; and because he was not an exemplary student, his parents felt that at least one of them must remain there on the faculty to ensure his admittance. Though many English teachers at the school earned extra money through private tutoring (often significantly more, in fact, than their official salaries), Ivan attracted few such students. As the financial cri-sis dragged on, with only meager salary raises that did not keep up with in-flation, the material situation of the N. family worsened.

One evening in the winter of 1998–99, Ivan had recounted a recent ob-servation at the local market at which he and his family shopped. As Ivan looked on, a man approached a merchant who was selling a type of quite expensive fish. The man was a New Russian. He asked to buy all the fish the merchant had, and then he inquired whether it was possible to buy the very crate in which all the fish were displayed there. The merchant agreed, and the man took the fish away to his car. Ivan appeared to present this as a striking example of the excessive luxury of the New Russian, who could af-ford to buy so many fish for his own consumption (to be cooked, probably, by his wife). (As noted above, in addition to their wealth, a consistent at-tribute of New Russians as they appear in popular jokes is their tendency not only to consume with abandon but also to prefer spending as much as possible on any particular product.) Ivan's wife Larisa, however, suggested that perhaps the man worked at a cafe or restaurant, which would explain the bulk of his purchase. No, Ivan said, it obviously was not that kind of person. Rather, it was someone who, say, worked at a bank; it was visible from the kind of face he had. I asked him how he could see this, concretely; Larisa remarked that she did not know how he could either. The man was well shaven, Ivan said, and looked like he did some kind of relatively in-tellectual work. More tellingly, Ivan cited his clothes: He was not wearing a raspberry-colored jacket but a black raincoat. "And not one of Chinese manufacture, like the one I have," Ivan went on, but a very good one.

The tasteless New Russian restaurateur, the prosperous and "intellectual" banker, the financially struggling and well-educated English teacher Ivan—their differences and possibilities were represented most strikingly by the quality and style of their jackets. The relatively tasteful and pricey coat of the fish buyer, the flashy jacket of the (absent) flamboyantly prosperous New Russian, the cheaper quality outerwear available to speaker Ivan (who recognized better taste when he saw it): These jackets indexed economic standings as well as much more complex social identities and degrees of "culture."

Larisa called upon similar criteria of profession, wealth, and material display in identifying a New Russian on another occasion, but she and Ivan differed somewhat in their determinations of whether the term was being appropriately applied. Their daughter Vera had started dating in the past year, and one of her boyfriends had come to the apartment to meet the family. His father was a wealthy pilot, Larisa explained to me over tea one night. He had an expensive foreign car, she went on, and when his son, Vera's boyfriend, had come to visit them, he had brought a "gentleman's set": sausage [*kolbasa*], champagne, bananas, and chocolate. But when Larisa then called the boy's father a "rich New Russian," Ivan took issue; a New Russian, he said, is a banker or a businessman. He (the boyfriend's father) was a pilot, which, Ivan claimed, just happened to be a profession in which people had earned a lot of money in recent years. Larisa did not contest this argument; and though the label "New Russian" was usually construed pejoratively, I knew from a previous conversation that the boyfriend had made a favorable enough impression on her. His family's undeniable prosperity, as concretized by the expensive foreign car and the gentleman's set, seemed to be enough of a reason for her, in this case at least, to call the boy's father a New Russian, though her husband disagreed.[15]

In a third and final example, the family argued about an alleged New Russian even closer to their family. Daughter Vera spoke happily of how her Aunt Masha was planning to take her along to England the next time

15. It is significant that the "New Russian" as a stereotype was practically always represented as a man (this is discussed further in chapter 5; see also Oushakine 1999). This may be related to the fact that being a New Russian had to do not only with wealth but also with particular activities (including crime) and displays (raspberry jackets, shaved heads, heavy gold jewelry) that were associated more with men than with women, as well as clearly differentiating New Russian men from other Russian men. An exception is found in the story here of Ivan's description of his cousin, a successful businesswoman, as a New Russian.

she went. Turning to me, Ivan asked: Have I told you about my cousin who is a New Russian? He reminded me of this relative, a Moscow doctor who had established a pharmaceutical company with colleagues a few years ago and was now starting a second company. Vera quickly objected to her father's choice of words; he should not call Aunt Masha a New Russian, she insisted, because that meant someone who was daft (*tupoi*) and had a lot of money, while Aunt Masha was smart and had made money through her hard work and efforts. Besides, Vera and her mother pointed out, Masha and her husband owned just a Zhiguli (a Russian rather than an imported car). This time it was Ivan who did not protest but let this objection to the attribution of New Russian identity stand.

In these stories, wealth, business, criminality, stupidity, and extravagance were persistently interlinked—but not inextricably so. Acknowledgment that wealth and material success did not *necessarily* imply moral transgression and lack of culture coexisted with "New Russianness" as a pejorative and persuasive, if somewhat vague, characterization of social difference. From one perspective, the N. family more or less agreed that New Russians were wealthy, sometimes but not necessarily businessmen and bankers, sometimes but not necessarily stupid and/or immoral. Yet it is significant that they found it worthwhile to identify New Russians justly. For labeling this way involved a certain degree of denigration and distancing, and thus was debated with particular care when specific individuals (including, but clearly not only, those known personally to the family) were implicated. In the course of these discussions, family members highlighted particular elements of the loosely agreed-upon constellation of New Russian traits and deemphasized others. In the process, they were exploring the nature of the links between wealth, labor, and honesty, among other aspects of social life.

Thus recognition, or rather articulation, of New Russianness constituted a sort of ongoing social question that was never quite decided. In its most archetypal expression, the New Russian was clearly an object for ridicule and derision: the raspberry-clad, dimwitted bandit of so many anecdotes. The teachers of whom I spoke in the beginning of this section claimed that such people were "not worth envying." Yet was Ivan's cousin a New Russian? Was she to be admired and/or envied, or did her success automatically make her morally questionable? And what of the fish buyer in the black raincoat, pegged by Ivan as a New Russian and a banker? Was their wealth in and of itself, or their involvement in commerce, enough to set them firmly into a different category of persons, one into which the N. family never imagined they could fall? Ivan, in his "raincoat of Chinese manufacture," had the cultural capital of high education, knowledge of English, modesty, and good manners on his side. However, the connections his family envisioned between material capital and the *lack* of such cultural capital, crystallized in their contested New Russian sightings, were rather uneasy and inconclusive. They pointed to the family members' ambivalence as they assessed their own places in society, identifying semipersuasive reasons for their current material disadvantage and looking into an equally uncertain future.

By the fall of 1999, Larisa's status at the school was declining. Most of her previous courses and responsibilities had been taken away from her. Though she had been told the previous spring by the administration that these activities simply were no longer going to be conducted at the school, a new employee appeared to fulfill those roles in the fall. Meanwhile, Larisa had been assigned a new set of classes with which she had little experience, as well as fewer hours, both of which reduced her salary considerably. She felt that she was being pushed out of the school and resented how the matter had been handled. Over the summer, she had looked for a new job, but she had not found a more attractive option. Ivan took on extra work that fall, teaching several hours a week at a second school and giving lectures at the state university. He had also done some translating work over the vacation. Yet by the middle of October, Ivan still had not received any payment for most of these new jobs.

Now Larisa had a new idea for a job scheme, formulated with a friend and former colleague who was similarly unsatisfied with his work situation. They had realized that the key was to identify an unfilled niche in the market that would draw on their specific qualifications, and they had several friends who were all teachers with various areas of expertise. What if they were to create an after-school day care group, where children would be given decent homemade food, there could be clubs (circles, *kruzhki*) such as drama and music, and the teachers would see that they completed their homework, with Ivan providing English tutoring, and so on? Nothing of this sort existed, Larisa said, and there was a need for it because those who worked at banks, for example, worked until about 8 o'clock at night. Of course they would need a space right away, and finding the capital to start would obviously be a problem; but they could get some children of New Russians, and she thought it might even be possible to go directly to a firm and offer the service to their employees, setting things up right on the premises. Ivan had heard this idea before, and he listened with some interest; but in the end he dismissed it, saying again that he did not believe that it was possible to get into business honestly. I had heard statements similar in spirit from Larisa, more than once in the previous year of our acquaintance; she had spoken of the "spiritual rules" (*dukhovnye pravila*) that were inevitably overstepped by anyone who had acquired significant wealth. But she did not echo the thought this night. Instead, she and I briefly discussed the idea that by working through another firm, one might be able to avoid direct involvement with criminal protection, falling under the firm's "*krysha*" or protective "roof" instead of acquiring one's own.

New Russian Discourses as Interrogations of Value

Everyday references to New Russians informed speakers' evaluations of the moral content of particular lifestyles and life paths. Larisa and Ivan's discussion of a prospective job plan was part of this greater, ongoing conversation about what morally acceptable and personally worthwhile paths might, after all, lie before them. . . . Or might not, as when Larisa's new idea was challenged by Ivan in one more application of the "business equals dishonesty" formula that was part of the logic of New Russianness. In other words, constructions of social difference such as the insistent but unstable category of the materially rich and morally bankrupt New Russian were part of the framework whereby people would continue to contextualize, legitimate, and sometimes question their own positions and trajectories.

As such, the image of the New Russian constituted a critique of contemporary society even as it undercut that very critique. Ridiculously unsophisticated criminals were reaping the profits to be had in contemporary Russia, went the narrative, while more educated, tasteful citizens were not granted such access—at least, not if they were to remain so cultured. As Anna Krylova (1999, 261–62) has stated in reference to New Russian *anekdoty*, "The post-Soviet *shutnik* [joke teller] implicitly counterpoises his/her civilized behavior, moderate spending habits, and erudition in history, geography, literature, theater, and music to the new beneficiaries of the post-Soviet economy" and "implicitly [offers himself] as much more deserving of the benefits of the new society." The discrepancy between qualifications and rewards was posited as a systemic problem. At the same time, the indeterminacy of the New Russian category—or perhaps, more accurately, its extremity in its most classic and condensed form, which limited its applicability in describing daily realities and specific individuals with whom one might actually identify or sympathize—corresponded to the possibility of considering more seriously how teachers really *might* be individually accountable for their own circumstances.

For, in any case, *kul'turnost'*, performed in part through material displays that required economic resources, was a keenly sensed and embodied matter of personal propriety and morality—generalized social critiques notwithstanding. Calling attention to the dysfunctions of power that might have been able to explain undeserved inequalities hardly dulled the immediacy of the experience of lack. In the often biting tone of teachers' stories about New Russians, one could also hear the anxiety provoked by the speakers' own uncertain situations.

The most basic and persistent logic of value that emerged from the teachers' stories about New Russians was one that posited worthy, cultured individuals as the proper beneficiaries of higher standards of living. The logic is persistent but also flexible, so that if one holiday party conversation, as described in chapter 1, yielded the conclusion that Mercedeses were undesirable by virtue of their association with those who could currently afford them, another might well vociferously criticize the conditions that kept worthy subjects from claiming their Mercedes and other just deserts. But they also fielded doubts about the questionable worth—after all?—of Mercedes-less subjects.

who's to say?

Chapter 4

Consumer Dilemmas and the State of Russian Civilization

Elizaveta and I were standing in the middle of Sytnyi Rynok, one of Saint Petersburg's outdoor marketplaces where rows upon rows of stalls and small tables display products from bread and fresh produce to pet food, mosquito repellants, and woolen slippers. As we walked through the aisles comparing the nearly identical wares of several different stalls that sold canned goods, Elizaveta had stopped and intently pointed out a shelf stacked with fish conserves. These looked like the kind she needed in order to make a salad for an upcoming teachers' gathering. Yet the label was unfamiliar, not the red one she remembered. New companies both Russian and foreign were starting up all the time, she explained, and buying untested products could be a mistake. For example, she said, pointing out a jar of mayonnaise marked *"provensal,"* there used to be a mayonnaise with this varietal name that was good. Then a new one appeared, also called *"provensal"* but made by a different producer, and it was awful. This particular day, Elizaveta was concerned not only that the mayonnaise be unspoiled and generally of good quality, but also that it have the proper texture for holding together the fish salad she planned to prepare.

She stopped again to examine the variety of mayonnaises at a stall. One of the cans read "new" across the top. "When it says 'new,'" Elizaveta warned, "that's dangerous too." Something else caught her eye, and she pointed out another can—red this time—and said *there,* this was the familiar kind of fish she needed. The label showed that these were from a known and reliable Russian factory. Meanwhile, the search for mayonnaise continued. "Calve," a Dutch brand, was good but twice as expensive, she explained as we walked. After several more minutes of scouting around and

— Seems like a commentator of USSR quality

101

comparing prices, Elizaveta was finished with her shopping but flustered. "I hate this running around for the sake of saving one ruble!"

Elizaveta was motivated to save every ruble she could due to the fact that her teaching and tutoring salaries were being stretched to support an un-employed, depressed husband as well as two daughters. Though her situation was particular, her struggle to establish dependable criteria that would allow her to identify commodities representing an optimal combination of quality, prestige, and affordability was a shared, and in some ways novel, dilemma for Russians in the late 1990s. The economic transformations of the past decade had ended Soviet shortages and made available an array of diverse consumer products, some locally produced and others imported from abroad. This influx had provoked much careful examination of labels and experimentation with previously unfamiliar goods. But while foreign products often aroused special curiosity, their appeal was not self-evident nor guaranteed; nor was getting a taste of "America" or the "West" neces-sarily the main "point" of their consumption. Rather, as my shopping trip with Elizaveta hinted, a range of anxieties underlay the most mundane de-cisions, including concerns about food safety, quality, and deceptive mar-keting. And these concerns about the material qualities and economic value of commodities were, likewise, closely connected with concerns about the comparative valuation of consuming *subjects*—here in an explicitly global frame.

Visits to the market were, indeed, charged episodes in which individuals analyzed and strove to ameliorate their own material standards of living— especially as they imagined these to compare with a range of others', at home and abroad. Consumers connected their understandings of large-scale issues of global political economy with more personal and immanent ques-tions about the well-being and social status of their own families. As we shall see, ideals of "civilization" were central to these discussions, transposing the local and national deliberation over culture and values described in chap-ter 3 into a conversation about which populations of the world lived better and worse, who deserved to live better, and who was being shortchanged. In other words, in everyday provisioning, logics of value were writ global.

Looking back to the early 1990s, teachers and other friends in Saint Petersburg told me of the initial rush there had been to try all the new im-ports possible, especially all kinds of food products. These included brand-name items that quickly became famous, such as Snickers candy bars and Folgers coffee. But there were also fruits and vegetables they had not been able to purchase before at all, such as bananas, and even ones which they had never before seen, such as kiwi. There were imported versions of more familiar goods such as cheeses, albeit in completely new packaging and much greater variety. Shortly—some say within just a few months—the novelty wore off, as consumers gained experience and compared imports, often unfavorably, with more familiar, locally produced goods, which were generally also less expensive. Indeed, domestic foodstuffs were considered by many to be, on the whole, healthier, fresher and tastier than foreign counterparts. Most recently, in the context of the post–August 1998 crisis, many food items, especially but not only imported ones, had become much less accessible due to swiftly rising prices.[1] Some said that going to stores could be like going on an excursion to a museum: lots of things to gawk at, but nothing to buy for oneself.

Nonetheless, certain categories of imported goods as well as particular countries of origin remained especially desirable and were generally considered to be higher in quality and more attractive in style than domestic variants. These included the products of countries that were grouped together in conversation as "Western" or European, whereas the specific goods in question might have originated from Western Europe, Scandinavia, or the United States. Other prominent exporting countries, including China and Turkey, tended to be assessed more derisively. Domestic production yielded mixed reactions, largely depending on what kind of item was under consideration. At play in all these evaluations were what Cook and Crang (1996) define as "geographical knowledges," that is, local understandings of the origins and paths taken by commodities through the global economy. These discourses are "based in the cultural meanings of places and spaces" and operate "through the deployment of various constructed (and of course, contestable) . . . [knowledges] about where . . . foods, and other cultural objects and actors associated with them, come

1. According to Russian newspaper accounts (including the *Saint Petersburg Times*), the financial crisis in the fall of 1998 brought mixed results in terms of the imports/domestic issue. In some cases, it was suggested, domestic products began to move much more quickly, because their price relative to imported goods fell dramatically. This was not necessarily the case, however, if the domestic producer relied on imported raw materials or equipment. Also, one magazine noted that the Russian public had gotten used to higher quality, and that it would not switch to cheaper goods (likely to be domestic) unless they were really of good quality. There was, however, a proliferation of certain domestic products and new offerings by local companies and factories such as Saint Petersburg's Petmol following the 1998 crisis. By 2003, when I returned to Saint Petersburg, the increase in domestic food products found in most shops and the decreased availability of imported ones was noticeable; see chapter 7.

from and in what settings they can and should be situated, encountered and used" (p. 132).

Such geographical knowledges were used to contextualize not only commodities but also consumers themselves, as their shopping experiences informed their senses of where they were situated in a perceived global hierarchy of privilege, "civilization," and deservingness. If, as Comaroff and Comaroff (2001) and others have suggested, subjects in late capitalism imagine themselves primarily as members of a global community of fellow consumers, that membership is not—in Russia, in particular—unproblematic. This is the case not only because access to the knowledge and commodities through which people signal such affinity is inequitable but also because that "global community" of consumers is crosscut in local imaginations by persistent discourses of nationhood, development, and race, as this chapter demonstrates. The imagined community of global consumers was not understood as the "deep horizontal comradeship" of Anderson's (1991) nation-state, but rather was deeply riven by various kinds of hierarchical distinctions and essentialized identities.

Although the narratives presented here pertain to a broad range of shopping concerns and commodities, including clothing, electronics, and home furnishings, the most detailed attention is devoted to teachers' commentaries on food—not so much because of the special place food products might reasonably be assigned as the most intimately consumed of consumables, nor because they seem to provoke more nationalistic consumer sentiment than do other commodity categories, but because the finely grained particularities of decisionmaking about food (including, notably, the problem of food's perishability) both complicate and clarify the basic logics, assumptions, and motivations according to which Russianness, Europeanness, and other categories of identity and value were being defined in all kinds of consumer situations.

The Relevance of Origins: Constructing Russia and Europe in the Consumer Marketplace

By contrast with the state system of shops at which most (legal) purchases were made during the Soviet era, by the late 1990s there was a broader variety of privately owned shops, kiosks, and boutiques from which Saint Petersburg consumers could choose. These choices represented shoppers' efforts to strike the appropriate balance between price, quality, and convenience. Most teachers regularly went to a few shops that were on their way home, either on their walk between school and home or near the metro station they regularly used. One teacher, Liliia, described a rare ideal: a very good shop in the village where her summer dacha was located, where the owners took special care to advise their customers, worked long hours, and had reasonable prices. For these reasons it felt like "*svoi*," or one's "own" store, Liliia said, though she had no such *svoi* stores in the city; nor, she felt, were there likely to be any in the bigger, less personal urban environment of Saint Petersburg. But as they followed established daily routes, shoppers had fair ideas of the range of offerings and prices of the nearby options.

Many of the teachers lived and worked in the Petrograd Side area of Saint Petersburg, which is desirable for its prerevolutionary architecture, proximity to the city center, and relative quiet. They were frequent customers of the district's outdoor marketplace, Sytnyi Rynok. Here, rows of tables and stalls—often replicating nearly exactly the same selection of goods many times over—sold produce, packaged foods, and other household products (see figures 4.1 and 4.2). Prices for many goods were lower there than in most shops, and it was convenient because just about everything a family needed on a weekly basis could be found there: canned foods, breads and pastries, fruit and vegetables, meat and fish, cheese and other dairy products, cleaning supplies, toilet paper, batteries, a small selection of clothing and shoes, and so on. Shopping could also be more cumbersome at the *rynok* than in regular shops, for one needed to inspect the differing prices being charged for the same kinds of produce or meat, or even identical packaged goods, at rows upon rows of tables and stalls. In an adjacent and overcrowded pavilion, merchants—mostly "southerners" and "blacks" (as Saint Petersburgians call the sellers from southern Russia and other former Soviet republics, assumed to be recognizable by their darker skin)—asked passersby what they needed and offered samples of their tomatoes, apricots, and other produce. Their insistent calls annoyed some shoppers. In regular stores, a barely masked indifference that was reminiscent of the Soviet shopping experience was still common among salespeople, although some higher-end boutiques featured smiling and solicitous service.

Although consumers looked for good deals, surprisingly cheap goods aroused suspicions of poor quality. For example, one might wonder whether the individual peddlers who stood outside of *rynki* (plural) were trying to sell foodstuffs that had not passed proper food safety inspections. As one teacher remarked, "Each time we guess whether it's good or bad." Yet consumers looked for certain clues that made their guesses far from random.

Figure 4.1. Women stand at the gates of Sytnyi Rynok selling flowers, shopping bags, and other wares, 1999. Photograph by the author.

Figure 4.2. Stalls at the outdoor *rynok,* 1999. Photograph by the author.

Apart from anyone's specific evaluation of a particular product and its relative merits, it was a fact of daily life in late-1990s Saint Petersburg that the country (and in the case of domestic products, city or region) of a commodity's origin or manufacture served as the most common reference point in discussion of that product. For instance, I was witness to the following three episodes:

> Facing a kiosk that sells a variety of domestic and imported ice cream cones and other frozen confections, two acquaintances converse: "What kind would you like?" "—Russian (*rossiiskoe*), probably."

> A woman tells of having tried a new flavor and brand of ice cream at the home of an old friend who now lived abroad but was visiting Saint Petersburg. "I liked it so much. . . . [It was] our Soviet [ice cream], . . . but so tasty. . . . I even said to myself, 'Well jeez!' [*Nu nado zhe*]."

> A few friends have purchased some potato chips and beer and are eating them while chatting at one's apartment. Everyone agrees that the chips are good, and no one has tried this kind before. "Interesting," one of them muses, "is this made here?" (Literally, "Is this of our manufacture?" "*Eto nashego proizvodstva?*")

In the first scenario, a woman is disposed toward choosing "Russian" ice cream (somewhat different in taste and usually less expensive than imports), stating this as her first preference rather than referring to a flavor, brand, or other characteristic. A second woman takes note that a tasty new ice cream, one she has not seen or eaten before, is in fact a domestic product. She seems pleased (and somewhat surprised) to discover this fact. Finally, a group of friends trying a new potato chip (modeled after imported brands, but with the unusual addition of mushroom flavoring—a rather local touch) wonder before anything else—such as committing to memory the brand name or examining the ingredients—whether the chips have been made in "their" factories.

The terms in which these questions were discussed are significant. *Rossi-iskoe* (Russian)[2] and the rather anachronistic *sovetskoe*[3] (Soviet) were heard

---

2. Note that "Russian" here refers not to ethnic Russianness (as the adjective *russkii* refers to nationality in the sense of a group with common history, culture, language, etc.) but to the Russian nation-state (the adjective *rossiiskii* might modify, e.g., the state, the army, citizenship, or any kind of national institution).

3. In fact, exactly what the informant meant in calling the ice cream "*sovetskoe*" is

less often in this context than the more proprietary though vague *nashe* ("ours") and *otechestvennoe,* which I translate as "domestic," but which could be rendered as "native" and derives literally from "fatherland." In the way the teachers used it, this "fatherland" was so familiar that it was rather value neutral; that is, they would use the term without seeming to care particularly about supporting domestic production as an act of patriotism (Patico 2001b; cf. Caldwell 2002).

Ambiguous though their political shadings may have been, such descriptors undoubtedly had roots in the Soviet past, for citizens of Soviet Russia (perhaps especially Muscovites, who were at the political and economic center of the empire, and secondarily Saint Petersburg residents) were enjoined to identify with the activities of the state, and in particular to conceive of state-produced foodstuffs and other consumer items as *nashi,* "ours" (Humphrey 1995). "At some level," Humphrey writes, "people did make this identification, while simultaneously realising this to be part of the gigantic deception [*obman*] of the Soviet regime" (p. 43). In the Khrushchev era, state-sponsored images portrayed comfortable Soviet consumer lifestyles that were in fact unattainable for the Soviet public—or, with time, attainable but only for the middle class and with very little available variety. According to these public discourses, the USSR was at the forefront of world development in every sphere; yet occasional, disorienting glimpses from television and foreign visitors suggested that this might not be so. Meanwhile, Soviet people employed various semi-legal and illegal strategies to obtain scarce goods, even as attitudes toward direct involvement in "speculative" black market activity were ambivalent. Amid the rapid market expansions of 1993 Moscow, according to Humphrey, consuming Western goods ceased to signify resistance against power, and consuming *nashi* ("ours") became a new sort of political statement (Boym 1994, 64–65; Humphrey 1995). Ideological tensions were reflected in Muscovites' evaluations of newly available

---

somewhat unclear. She could have been referring to local or domestic (Russian) production, using the older, familiar term "Soviet" to firmly distinguish this item from "Western" or European imports. She might also have meant that the product was not from Russia but rather from Belarus, Ukraine, or another former Soviet republic. In such a case, the product might still qualify as "ours" as compared to "imports" (i.e., goods from further abroad, at least in symbolic/political terms); but perhaps it would not be possible to call such an item "domestic" (literally, "fatherland"). She clearly was *not* using "Soviet" as a designation of a long-familiar *type* of ice cream, because the point of her comment was that its interesting flavor and tastiness made her surprised to find that it was "Soviet."

foods: Tightly packaged products from abroad were described as "doubt-ful" and "likely to cause illness" (Humphrey 1995, 54–64).

Such skepticism persisted into the late 1990s, though previously unfamiliar forms of packaging had become more customary and were being emulated by local firms and factories. Concerns about health and quality, as well as standards of tastiness or (especially for nonfood items) style, were often expressed in terms of the categories of imports versus domestic goods. Yet preferences for the domestic or the imported (particularly "Western") did not apply equally to all kinds of goods, and orientation toward Russian products was rarely, among the teachers, presented as an ideological matter of performing one's patriotic duty. Similarly, no one with whom I discussed these questions seemed very inclined to buy *only* imported goods, even if they could have afforded the expense. Rather, a more multivalent set of criteria was brought to bear. The geographical origins of commodities were noted as part of people's overall assessments of quality; they informed expectations as to which goods could be relied upon for quality, flavor, freshness, or durability. However, more complex associations accounted for consumers' choices of particular goods and evaluations of the market situation in general.

The disposition to highlight geographical origin was reflected and reinforced by how goods were presented in shops. Fruit in an open-air stand, meat at a butcher's counter, cheese in a dairy shop, boxes of tea, detergent, and items of clothing—all bore labels and prominent signs announcing the country or the Russian city from whence the item had come. This was not the same situation as in the United States, where garments might have small tags inside stating in tiny letters "Made in Taiwan." Nor was it a matter of finding the small print that provides such information on bottles of cleaning fluid or mass-produced food products, as they are packaged in the United States. Rather, prominently visible tags, placed behind glass countertops or attached directly to goods, often handwritten in pen or magic marker, indicated both price and country. The tag on a sweater hanging in a *rynok* might proclaim to passersby "700 rubles, wool, Korea"; a sign at a cheese counter would announce, "80 rubles/kg, Estonia" (see figure 4.3).

Origins were thus consistently available to consumers' awareness, even where consumers claimed they did not determine choices as much as price and other factors. Shoppers were acutely cognizant of the fact that, in contrast to the previous decade, goods were flowing into Russia and Saint Petersburg from around the world, and from certain places in particular. Finnish instant cereals, German yogurts, and Dutch fruit lined some shops'

Figure 4.3. Cheeses on display at the *rynok* are labeled with varietal name, price by kilogram, and country of origin, 1999. Photograph by the author.

shelves, while outdoor market stalls displayed clothing such as leather jackets from Turkey, China, and Korea (in most cases, the country of provenance was indicated merely as "Korea," rather than as "North Korea" or "South Korea").[4] When a teacher came to my home one evening in winter wearing what he described as the classic Russian hat—made of fur, with ear flaps—he noted jocularly that this particular one was made in Korea: "I think the Koreans are sewing especially for us!" Boutiques had descriptive names that drew attention to geographical origins, such as "Clothing from Italy" or "Goods from India." Countries were held to be relatively predictable indicators of quality and other characteristics, as revealed in comments such as "As a rule, German coffees are good"; "I know good chocolate comes from Lithuania and Estonia"; and "I like only Finnish muesli and, I think, Dutch. . . ." Interestingly, in the last example the speaker described these muesli as "Finnish," but when I asked whether she was referring to various Finnish brands or just to one company or *firma,* she stated that they were all

4. Caroline Humphrey affirms that shuttlers are bringing goods into Russia from South Korea, as well as from Singapore, Turkey, and elsewhere (2002, 89). However, in this discussion I retain teachers' chosen label for the origin of these goods: "Korea."

made by one manufacturer. Though the opinion she offered may have been formulated this way as a response to my own interest in imported versus domestic goods, the general tendency to name specific products and groups of products according to their country of origin rather than brand name suggests that origin was generally understood to be the most meaningful way to sort commodities and to predict their quality (compare to Vann 2003, 2005).[5]

Branded (i.e., name-brand) or *firmennye* goods were sometimes elided, as a category, with high-end Western products—even though there *were* local name brands, some of them well known and frequently mentioned as high quality. In fact, *firmennye* products also existed in the Soviet Union, though all goods were state produced. Catriona Kelly (1998a, 224) notes that Soviet-era advertisements "alerted customers to new Soviet wonder products that had just come on the market, and to the virtues of established ones (especially *dostatochnye tovary*, goods not in short supply, or *firmennye tovary*, 'branded goods,' i.e., goods made and/or sold by the elite state companies that were often the descendents of former private ones)." In this light, it makes sense that expensive, elite products with high name recognition (such as Adidas) should be seen as *firmennye*, while ordinary domestic products generally were not— even though these less expensive and distinctive post-Soviet Russian commodities carried name brands, strictly speaking. When I asked Maria, an English teacher in her early forties, whether there were any things that she preferred to buy only imported or only domestic, she responded by contrasting *nashi* goods not with imports, but with *firmennye* products. When it came to food, she explained, she was not too picky, because *firmennye* products were expensive. She did not mind buying Chinese cutlets, for example; "even if it's Chinese—whatever, somehow I don't care that much" (*khot' ona i kitaiskaia—Bog s nim, ia kak-to ne ochen'*). Here the *firmy* (companies) stood for well-known multinational, American, or European names, such as the Adidas sportswear this teacher's teenage daughter favored and that Maria said

---

5. Somewhat similarly, Elizabeth Vann (2003), working among consumers in Vietnam, found that Ho Chi Minh City residents downplayed the significance of brand names as predictors of quality, looking carefully instead at the countries in which commodities had been physically produced. Goods whose countries of production and of design/branding coincided were considered "source" goods and inherently of better quality than those whose production had been outsourced (e.g., from the United States to Vietnam). Middle-class consumers were "guided by the assumption that successful production must be marked by unity; that is, the unity of people, place, raw materials, and knowledge . . . [an] ideal model of production . . . imagined largely in organic terms [in which] these relationships are thought to be natural, and their integration naturally harmonious" (p. 234).

she bought for her when she could. In fact, Maria went on to say that dressing well was another matter: "It's good quality, it's prestigious. It's name brands [*firmy*]." Teachers and their teenage students alike named designer labels such as Calvin Klein when it came to discussing fashionable clothing that was, for most people, prohibitively expensive. Brand names certainly also were named in conversations about specific goods people liked (or disliked) and/or recommended, whether imported (Nescafé coffee) or domestic (Smak frozen meat dumplings).

In response to more general questions about preferences and shopping strategies, however, geographical origins were often key elements of the answers, potentially eliding differences among various product lines manufactured in the same country. Discussions of clothing fairly unequivocally posited Western European items as high quality and stylish, while Turkish, Korean, and Chinese garments were seen as more likely to be shoddily made (see also Humphrey 1999). One day, I visited a fabric store with Olga because she needed to buy some material with which a friend would sew her a pair of pants. She looked at other fabrics, too, talking about the possibility of choosing something for a future skirt or blouse. I pulled out one bolt of fabric and showed it to her, because it looked similar to another in which she had expressed interest but was less expensive. Olga said that she liked the one I had chosen but pointed out that it was Korean. Though it looked nice in the store, Olga surmised, it might not hold up well when washed. Over tea a few moments later, she told me about the new sweater she was wearing, which she had bought recently at the nearby Sytnyi Rynok. It had not been cheap, she explained: "700 rubles, and it's Korea!" Olga felt the sweater had been expensive given that it was made in Korea, but she had risked purchasing the sweater anyway because it had suited her in color, fit, and style.

Anya, a twenty-five-year-old teacher who took great care in her dress, makeup, and jewelry and loved to spend the money she earned working multiple jobs on new wardrobe accoutrements, was especially vocal in this regard. She often commented that she had a penchant for Italian clothing and shoes, although they were generally expensive. In the midst of shopping for a new suede coat for the winter, she explained that she would have to forgo expensive Italian coats for another she had found that was "Turkish, but good" and not so pricey. On another occasion, we walked to our area's main commercial street to shop for a leather skirt she was hoping to buy. Although she would need to see how the models available at various shops fit and decide which was cut most flatteringly, she had already learned that they were all roughly the same price. Meanwhile, some were English and German, others Indian and Turkish. If the prices were comparable, she reasoned, "Why would I want to buy some Indian trash [*drian'*]?" In the end, she did buy an Indian one, for it suited her best in all other ways and because an impartial saleswoman at a different shop had assured her that Indian leather was fine. But Anya did not do so without a good deal of fretting and debating (Patico 2001b).

The importance of origin was affirmed and reinforced not only in private conversations but also in more public ways: in interactions with and advice drawn from salespeople, and by association with the kind of surroundings in which the products were typically sold: a crowded outdoor marketplace or *rynok* versus more elaborately decorated shops with well-dressed salesgirls. One evening in the fall of 1999, Nastia, a relatively affluent teacher and mother of two, was looking for new clothes she could wear to work, maybe a sweater or a skirt. First, we looked in a *veshchovaia iarmarka* (a marketplace that sells "things," *veshchi*—e.g., clothes, shoes, and perfume—as opposed to food and other perishable items) near her home. Because she did not find anything quite to her liking there, we ended up at a much more expensive shop across the street that featured clothing from Italy and elsewhere abroad. Though Nastia was not sure that she could justify the expense of the $150 to $200 outfits she was trying on, she liked them so much that she commented to the saleswoman that she would not want to go back anymore to the *iarmarka* for clothes shopping. When the saleswoman suggested that there also was not much difference in price between the two, Nastia (quite rightly) contradicted her: "What are you talking about, of course it is quite significant." The saleswoman recouped: "Well, and for that, it's not from Turkey" (*za to ne Turtsiia*).

The interaction had reproduced an argument that neither woman would question: Nastia had much preferred the style and quality of these more expensive garments, and it seemed obvious to her as well as the saleswoman that this difference could be attributed to the difference in country of origin and not to the particular manufacturer. In fact, not all clothes carried brand labels, and this was especially true of those sold at *rynki,* which might have only an exterior, pinned-on label reading "Russia" or "Korea" and the price. In any case, shoppers were quite comfortable taking geographical origins as primary indicators of quality and value.

The significance of this is that judgments about particular goods contributed to the construction of a more broadly conceived status hierarchy of the countries or regions from whence they came, a hierarchy that ranked production standards and perceived standards of living in those locales as well as the relative civilization and sophistication of their populations. The very materiality of an object such as an Italian- or Turkish-made leather coat was infused by consumers' knowledge of Italy's and Turkey's places in this hierarchy (as in Nastia's understanding that the dresses lay better on her body because they were not from Turkey, and Anya's inclination to question what *looked* like a nice skirt because of its Indian origin). In turn, these judgments reinforced the self-evident quality of such a hierarchization.

The connection between material culture and regional standards of living was epitomized by the custom of referring to putatively European-style home renovations—indicating not necessarily a specific aesthetic style but also high-quality, imported appliances, plumbing, and other durable and decorative elements—as "Eurostandard." The *idea* of a European standard, if not the exact terminology, has a long history in Russia, of which Westernizing efforts such as Peter the Great's offer notable evidence. Reference to Peter also reminds one that the sense of connection and attraction to Europe may be specially salient for people living in Saint Petersburg as opposed to other Russian cities, including Moscow (cf. Caldwell 2002). In any case, the opposition of Europe or the West (as civilized) to Asia or the East (as backward) has been an enduring one, taking on new significance in changing contexts of the twentieth century (Bassin 1999; Gleason 1999). In terms of material culture and standards of living, the USSR's stated goal was to catch up with and surpass the West; as Humphrey reminds, Soviet citizens only partly believed that this had come to pass. As a rule, consumers were eager to obtain clothing and other goods from Western and even Eastern Europe, whose products generally were considered to be more durable and stylish than Soviet ones.

In the late 1990s, Russians referred to the "European standard" as a way of distinguishing among the many goods from around the world that were readily available in shops and marketplaces. When they cited this "standard," they situated below Europe both Russian goods (many of which were apparently held in higher regard before the opening of the market "enlightened" everyone) and the products of Asia and areas marginal to Europe—Turkey as well as "Korea" and China. Furthermore, they suggested that the "European" was not merely a fashion, preference, or type of cachet but also a *standard* of quality, sophistication, and sometimes propriety, as when one woman (a former teacher now working for a British foundation in Saint Petersburg) laughed self-consciously that she regularly read *Cosmopolitan* articles about appropriate office attire in an effort to "pay attention to [obey] European standards" (*prislushivat'sia k evropeiskim standartam*). Conversely, non-European things were not just less attractive or efficient but also in a fundamental sense *substandard.* In short, the category of European, like that of "Western," exceeded its ostensibly geographic significance.

Thus, Germany and Sweden were more European than postsocialist Poland or Bulgaria, countries whose production and living standards may or may not be thought of as better than Russia's but in any case were seen as not of a kind with those of Western Europe. This was illustrated when an acquaintance who had traveled to Italy commented on how tasty the Orbit chewing gum there was compared to the Orbit available in Saint Petersburg. She concluded good-naturedly that "our Orbit must be made in Poland!"[6] Teacher Maria reminded me that when Russia was part of the Soviet Union, their "imports" had been goods from East Europe (in retrospect, she seemed to find East European goods a poor substitute for "real" imports). They had been eager to have them then, but now, "we don't [even] look at Bulgarian goods, because we know there is better." And when a friend of mine fretted over whether her American Internet correspondent would be willing to visit her in Saint Petersburg (she could not afford to meet him elsewhere in Europe, as he had initially proposed), she reasoned that "maybe this is not Europe like some places" (i.e., "maybe this is not *as* European as other places," *mozhet byt' eto ne takaia Evropa*), but there were plenty of pleasant things for a Western tourist to see and do.

Nastia, a teacher who had grown up in Tallinn, Estonia (though ethnically Russian and a resident of Russia since university), compared the populations of Estonia, Russia, and also Britain, which she had recently visited. A continuum of traits emerged, with Estonia as an intermediary point between, on one end, Brits' politeness, high material standards of living, and a tendency toward practicality and narrowly defined interests (one's own family home, car, yard), and on the other end, Russians' relative vulgarity (especially in their public manners) and poor work ethic but greater attention to the "spiritual" side of life and to warm interpersonal relations. Nastia saw traits to admire and to criticize on both ends of this cultural continuum, which serves as a reminder that aspirations to achieve the Eurostandard in consumption are not equivalent to slavish admiration of all

6. Orbit is a product of the Chicago-based Wrigley Company. According to the company's Web site, it operates fourteen factories around the world, including four in Europe. In addition, it opened a new plant in Novgorod (Northwest Russia, about 140 kilometers from Saint Petersburg) in June 1999, hoping that local production would make it less vulnerable to the effects of fluctuations in the ruble's value (*Saint Petersburg Times,* June 29, 1999). The conversation recounted above took place during the same year, in September 1999.

that is European, Western, and "over there." Yet such contrastive conversations did affirm the status of Russia (along with the rest of the former socialist bloc in Eastern Europe) and even Saint Petersburg—the traditional "window to Europe"—as neither Europe proper nor totally other to it, in cultural sophistication as in material production and consumption.

And of course, acquisition of Eurostandard sophistication reflected on the consumer herself. As I walked home with Ivan from school one day, he pointed out the window frames as we walked by apartment buildings both shabby and newly renovated. One could easily ascertain, he explained, where wealthy New Russians (nouveaux riches) lived, because theirs were the apartments with the Eurostandard windows with double-paned glass and substantial white frames. Regular people had the usual thinner-looking wooden frames with peeling paint. Yet approval of the person did not follow directly from good windows; New Russians themselves were not considered to be more sophisticated by virtue of their attainment of these goods, and this was connected with the morally questionable ways in which they were understood to have acquired their wealth as well as the perceived lack of education, manners, and taste that rendered them inappropriate subjects for such consumption. As seen in chapter 3, the proper correlation of cultural sophistication with routine consumption of high-quality material goods was illustrated in the breach in teachers' critiques of New Russians, who were said to flaunt expensive things in such an unseemly way. By contrast, images of a Western middle class, as seen in chapter 2, offered more appealing pictures of comfort, respectability, and normalcy—if tempered at times by negative connotations such as the "narrow interests" Nastia mentioned.

Although consumer goods and their qualities played an important role in the imagination of a global hierarchy of lifestyles and privileges (and vice versa), then, they did not stand as simple metonyms of East and West, nor were East and West equated with negative or positive value in simplistic or univocal ways. Rather, as the rest of this chapter explores further, they figured centrally in people's working theories about *relationships* of inequality among populations of consumers and producers. Though many imported products—especially "European" ones—were held in high regard, those found to be low in quality conveyed additional messages about the political-economic power relations that underlay commodity flows. Food shopping brought these conflicts to the fore.[7]

---

7. A version of this chapter's analysis of food and globalization is found in Patico 2003. On the themes of globalization and consumerism discussed in this chapter more generally, see also Patico 2001b.

The Stale, the Contaminated, and the Dumped:
Detecting Food Quality

Many kinds of imported commodities were admired and desired in Saint Petersburg. But in conversations about food, people were at least as likely to discuss the merits of "fatherland" or "our" production over European, American, or other choices. An analogous situation prevailed in television and billboard advertising: Though furniture, cigarette, and electronics manufacturers drew attention to the Europeanness of their products, food companies —including some based outside Russia[8]—chose to focus on recognizably Slavic and Russian themes, such as the imperial balls and Pushkin-esque duels portrayed in Rossiia chocolate commercials and the scenes of simple and hearty village life that sold "Sweet Mila" milk. Why should Russian history and culture have been referenced in association with food, in particular?

One explanation some social scientists might offer is that people are comfortable with that which is most familiar, and that food preferences are socialized relatively early in life and experienced at a particularly sensual, visceral, subconscious level (Rozin 1998). According to this line of thinking, it is simply more difficult for people to change food habits than other kinds of practice, and this provides a possible explanation for their rejection of imported foods. Without question, food and cuisine are powerful vehicles for nostalgia, especially in the face of globalizing food practices and the perceived threats transnational corporations pose to local traditions (Leitch 2000).

Yet this does not provide an adequate explanation of why domestic foods were favored in the particular context of postcommunist Russia. For one thing, as noted above, though some truly new imported items were available in Saint Petersburg in the 1990s (some of which already had become mundane and expected parts of life, e.g., bananas or packaged yogurts), many of the goods I will discuss here were not, strictly speaking, new to the local diet. Rather, it was the availability of imported versions of these foods—including produce, cheeses, sausages, and so on from places as far away as the United States, Britain, the Netherlands, and China—that was new. These products could, of course, differ in taste or appearance from previously common Soviet counterparts as well as contemporary Russian products. But more important is the fact that these differences were sometimes taken up by consumers and given further kinds of significance.

8. E.g., in 1998–99 a frequently run television commercial for Twix candy bars (a Mars product) included a prominent reference to the Russian cultural icon Alexander Pushkin, and Cadbury named a line of candy bars after historic Russian towns.

Domestic foods often were described in Saint Petersburg as, quite simply, tastier than imports. In that sense, one teacher asserted that he was "on the side of domestic" foods, though he claimed not to espouse the view that "*nash produkt*" ("our food product") should be bought for its own sake. "If our analogue [to an imported product] is good, I'll buy it; but if not, why bother with patriotism?" This attitude was rather typical among the teachers, in that they did not discuss buying domestic as the right thing to do for the national economy or to protect the integrity of national identity. This might seem somewhat surprising given that production—a previous source of Soviet pride—often carried for teachers and others a positive moral significance and suggested a sense of integrity and "real work" that commercial trade did not. On a few occasions, I heard informants rue the fact that it seemed as though everyone was buying and selling—commerce having an air of superficiality and falsity here—while no one in Russia was *producing* anything. This was not a healthy economic development, they suggested, believing that Russia was never going to have a really strong economy this way.[9] But in their own consumption as they described and enacted it, they were looking out for their own daily interests, protecting the health of their families, sticking with what they found tasted good, and seeking out the highest-quality things they could reasonably afford.

Looking further for explanations of why food might constitute a special case, some would argue that it has a special symbolic significance as opposed to other consumer items insofar as it is taken directly into the body. Mary Douglas (1992b, 115, 116) asserts that the permeability of the body makes it available for use as a representation for society and its anxiety-ridden boundaries: "The idea of society is a powerful image; . . . it has external boundaries, margins, internal structure." Likewise, "The body is a model which can stand for any bounded system. Its boundaries can represent any boundaries which are threatened or precarious." Applying this logic, it would seem that foods brought into the Russian "body" from outside its national borders serve as particularly powerful symbols for more general social fears, perhaps regarding the compromising effects of foreign

9. It is indeed the case that in the early post-Soviet years, given high rates of inflation and a politically unstable environment, Russian entrepreneurs were drawn more to circulation and middleman activities than to production, which required more capital outlay (Silverman and Yanowitch 2000, 116). By 2003, teachers in Saint Petersburg spoke approvingly of the fact that some formerly closed local factories had reopened and that local industry generally was getting back on its feet, which meant more jobs and more locally manufactured commodities in shops.

economic and political penetration on national integrity. Here imported foods would not only stand for a feared foreign domination but would, in fact, represent that domination metonymically; for one of the most concrete and direct ways through which Russian citizens experience the new position of their country in the global political economy is in their roles as consumers. Conversely, some particular products such as yogurts were specifically noted to be better in their imported versions. Also favored were imported (French, American) wines and cognacs, which most people could seldom afford. These beverages were marked clearly as luxury items rather than everyday family foods, which might suggest that they were less threatening than other imports precisely because they were less integrated into daily consumption patterns.[10]

Yet all these universalizing, symbolic explanations are of limited use in making sense of the particular ways in which Saint Petersburgians were approaching food issues at the turn of the twenty-first century. More pertinent were consumers' specific dissatisfactions with the political and economic transformations of the preceding decade and how these were instantiated in questions of food choice. The teachers expressed their concerns less in the language of purity and pollution, or of borders and boundaries (cf. Berdahl 1999), than through images of local and global socioeconomic inequality and hierarchy. That is, loyalty to Russia was not at issue so much as a set of more dynamic power relations was being conceptualized. In everyday life, this framework pointed less to the inherent superiority, desirability, or comfort of Russian products than to ideas about the paths domestic and imported goods followed before arriving at Saint Petersburg's markets.

Thus my interlocutors spoke not (or not merely) of sympathy for the "domestic" but also of the advantages of relatively local produce, milk from the nearby Petmol plant, and chocolate from the Krupskaia factory in Saint Petersburg. Apples and other types of produce that came from nearby cooperative farms might not look as attractive as the shiny, flawless fruits that came from abroad, but they had more taste (it was said) and were assumed to be fresher. One did not know exactly when and how an imported, packaged roll-up cake (*rulet*) had been made (these were nonetheless quite popular for a time), whereas local bakery stands carried breads and sweets that one knew (or assumed) had been baked in Saint Petersburg the day before.

---

10. The fact that they were clearly set apart from more mundane, predominantly domestic goods such as bread and potatoes also rendered them more appropriate for the services to which they were put as presents and in celebrations; see chapter 6.

Domestic goods, too, especially cheap items specially transported to Saint Petersburg, could fall under suspicion or derision, as a teacher told me about one not very tasty but inexpensive sausage on sale in the city. "It seems," he said, "that the town of X doesn't know how to make tasty *kolbasa*—so they have to sell it cheaply in Saint Petersburg." Another teacher remembered friends having gotten sick after eating Ecuadorian bananas, and others had their own stories and warnings about food poisoning.

There were particular things to watch out for—in any food products, but especially in imports. A crucial question was that of expiration dates. For instance, when several teachers discussed groceries to be purchased for a teachers' party, one was delegated to buy packaged torts. "Should I get those ones, those imported ones?" she asked. Her superior cried, "Only don't get those! They're expired!" A male teacher, Dima, noted that when the imports had started pouring in to Russia, "the West" had sent its expired goods that had not been eaten at home. Another man theorized that the reason why goods were so cheap at the market in Sennaia Ploshchad', reputed as one of the cheapest shopping areas in the city, was that foods were sold there past their expiration dates. Though a shopper could, of course, examine the expiration date to avoid problems, false expiration labels notoriously were pasted over earlier, authentic ones. The evidence I observed of this problem was primarily apocryphal, based on informants' fears and often seeming to derive from word-of-mouth warnings more than their personal experience.[11] But on one occasion in 1999, I was sold a bag of locally baked *prianiki,* spice cookies, that turned out to be hard as rocks. Liza and I laughed over our tea at this mishap, until the sobering thought came to us that someone else might have spent her last kopecks on the same batch of petrified cookies.

In general I encountered few problems, except for one night when my husband became quite ill. Our landlords were convinced that the hot dogs he had eaten earlier that day were to blame. In friendly conversation, we were often warned to be careful about where we bought fresh meat and sausage and to be selective in choosing frozen meat products such as *pelmeni* (a popular dish similar to meat ravioli or dumplings) that could be con-

11. On the question of imports in general, the British beef scandal got press in Russia, as did the European Coca-Cola contamination while I was there in 1999—though I never heard anyone discussing the latter. Newspaper articles I found in 1998–99 addressed potential dangers in local/domestic products more than imports, including a health-threatening bacteria affecting bread, radioactive berries growing in particular regions, and other problems. See Virkunen and Mironenko 1999; Leont'eva 1999; *S.-P. Vedemosti* 1999; and Virkunen 1998.

taminated.[12] Sometimes they recommended particular brands and, quite commonly, named local sausage factories deemed to be either safe or questionable—though my various acquaintances' judgments on these matters were often inconsistent with one another.

Some shoppers were conscious of avoiding consumption of harmful food preservatives. Again, imports were particularly, though not exclusively, implicated, because of the technological complexity of vacuum-packed and other packaged foods as well as the fact of their having been transported long distances. Prime suspects included imported (and now also many domestic) *polufabrikaty* (literally, "half-made" or half-assembled) food products, such as frozen cutlets, *pelmeni,* and soup mixes. "Long-lasting meat seems like a bad idea," one woman commented, saying that she tried to avoid buying them too often. Another, Liliia, called the use of preservatives (in *polufabrikaty*) "unnatural," and said that up until a few years ago they had not been used in Russia—or, perhaps more likely, she corrected herself, they had been used but people had not known about them. Nowadays, even local producers such as the long-established, widely trusted Petmol dairy plant used preservatives; for it was logical to conclude, as one teacher observed, that the long shelf-life milk sold in Parmalat cartons had been somehow altered. A number of chemicals deemed especially harmful (the names of which start with "E" and are completed by identifying numbers) were enumerated in newspapers and magazines in the middle to late 1990s.[13]

In the course of an interview with Elizaveta, my questions about how she chose what to buy from the range of goods now available in shops led to

12. According to Yuri Ignatjev (1996) of the Consumers Society of Saint Petersburg, as of 1996 the State Committee of Sanitation and Epidemiological Surveillance (SES) was responsible for setting parameters for food safety analyses, but these were inadequate. "For example, currently, only three types of hormones are included in MBD [the national Medical-Biological Demands and Sanitary Standards created in 1989]. . . . These do not reflect the hormones used in the veterinary world, and, considering that St. Petersburg imports more than 70 percent of its meat, such omission is critical. The recent beef scandal in Europe stirred great concern in Russia, but the list of hormones for analysis and control remained unchanged. Similarly, MBD controls only three antibiotics in meat, while 15 are monitored in the United States. . . . Despite these deficiencies, . . . in 1995 a total of 730 tons of food products were rejected in St. Petersburg, or more than four times the amount in 1994. Fifty-eight percent . . . were meat products, 13 percent were beverages including milk, and 9.5 percent were vegetables. Twelve percent of all meat products in 1995 were rejected mostly because they exceeded parameters for several toxic chemicals, and 5.4 percent breached microbiological safety standards, often the result of unsatisfactory storage and transport conditions" (p. 5).

13. E.g., *Ona,* December 1998, 122–24.

her description of the potential dangers of buying imported foodstuffs. She mentioned various warnings she had heard either through the media or from acquaintances about allergenic food additives and preservatives found mainly in imported products. A student of hers had become quite ill and had been out of school for some time, Elizaveta recounted, and as it turned out, the source of the girl's illness had been an allergy to imported foods. When I asked later for more details, such as whether the allergy had been to particular brands or ingredients, she said she did not know—she simply knew that the hospital's diagnosis had been "imported foods." Elizaveta clarified, however, that the goods Russia received from the United States, as far as she knew, were not necessarily the best of what that country had to offer to its own citizens. She told the story of a former student who had spent some time studying in the United States and had come back glowing with health. No, it was specifically these imports that were the problem.

Regardless of whether any or all the particular suspicions detailed above were legitimate (and it seems that at least some were), these concerns clearly reflected and informed understandings of the global political economy and schema of value. One needed to watch out, Elizaveta suggested, for goods sent to Russia for sale when their expiration dates had already passed (such that they could no longer be sold in the home country), as well as products that represented the lower end of another country's production from the very beginning. These practical consumer decisions drew upon and, in turn, informed understandings of Russia's and one's own positioning among a world of other manufacturers and, of particular importance, consumers. One wanted, Elizaveta implied, to be careful not to purchase other countries' cast-offs, the goods foreign producers considered unfit for at least some of their own compatriots. Thus suspicion of imported products had become part of a particular interpretation of the power relations between local consumer markets and those abroad.

Similar suspicious were aroused, in some, by the "second-hand" clothing shops that now could be found in Saint Petersburg (and were called "*sekhond-khend*," syllables directly transliterated into Russian and otherwise meaningless to those who do not know English). Anya, a discerning shopper often willing to pay high prices for what she saw as fashionable and high-quality clothing, told me that one could sometimes find good things there; but Veronika suggested that there was something offensive about *sekhond-khend*. She asked me whether we had "second-hand" in America and whether I knew from whence the clothes came. When I said that I thought they were usually contributed to American shops by local people, she retorted that "we know exactly where they come from"—from Europe. In other words, the items for sale in Saint Petersburg second-hand stores were the things Europeans no longer wanted. In the case of foods, these suspicions served as guidelines for choice in a market where unaccustomed variety could be overwhelming, miscalculation could threaten health, and reliable information was scarce; for consumers generally assumed that labels and even brands could not necessarily be trusted to provide assurance of consistency. A bottle of vodka might actually contain water, vinegar, or something more lethal, and a jar of Nescafé might or might not contain tasty coffee (people had observed that there were actually a variety of *producing* countries and the country of origin was said to affect quality greatly).

Some information was available to local consumers in the mass media (print, television, and radio), though buyers often depended more on hearsay. Newspapers and women's magazines published comparisons of commonly used products such as mayonnaise and vegetable oil and guidelines for identifying fresh, safe products.[14] *Domashnii Ochag,* the Russian version of *Good Housekeeping,* featured information about home appliances such as washing machines (October 1998) and kitchen tools (November 1998). Catalogs on sale at newspaper kiosks around the city listed goods from foodstuffs to electronics to real estate, including data on manufacturers and local prices. Free advertising papers such as *Tsentr Plus* and *Ekstra Balt* printed small ads that give businesses' phone numbers and locations. The free papers came unsolicited to private residences and, according to the Saint Petersburg market research journal *Teleskop* (1999–93), were among the most frequently read periodicals in the city as of 1999. Both free periodicals and, from time to time, other daily and weekly newspapers such as the somewhat sensational and populist *Peterburg-Ekspress,* reported on comparative prices for staple items at the city's *rynki.*[15]

Shoppers were most likely to consult this range of publications when deciding on major purchases such as home appliances, in order to compare not only prices but also specific features and guarantees. And it was primarily for such sizable family purchases that they reported eliciting the advice and experience of colleagues and friends (e.g., about what television they

14. See *Burda Woman* 1999; *Krestianka* 1999; Fedorov 1999; *Sankt-Peterburgskie Vedemosti* 1999.

15. This was true, at least, in 1998 and 1999, and may have been more widespread at that particular moment due to the special problems of the crisis period. More recently (as of 2003), *Peterburgskoe Kachestvo* ("Petersburg Quality") published such information for consumers both in a regularly printed paper periodical and online.

had and how it had performed).[16] In contrast to the late Soviet and earliest post-Soviet years of shortage, such information exchange about relatively small, mundane purchases was no longer necessary on a daily basis because everything was readily available in shops. Instead, trial and error suggested which products were safe, while visits to friends' homes might provide the opportunity to try something new to oneself but already tested by another who could be trusted. Finally, salespeople were sometimes asked for advice about which products were worth buying. This was not exactly a disinterested source of information, as people acknowledged; still, some said, when the salesperson herself offered that one product was fresher than another, it was safe to assume (or at least, one wanted to believe) that she was telling the truth. After discussing these issues with teachers, I began eliciting such advice more frequently in shops myself. I was urged more than once to buy something other than what I had originally ordered because, the salesperson told me, the product I had chosen was not very tasty.

Their advice was not always dependable, of course. Oksana recounted buying a loaf of bread one day; she was told by the saleswoman that the loaf was fresh, but when she felt it, it did not feel fresh—it was hard. When she questioned the woman further, Oksana was told that this was "last night's" bread. Recounting the event, she indignantly complained that if the store had received the bread the night before, who knew when it had actually been baked? Probably during the previous day, meaning that this was really day-old bread that the woman was trying to pass off as fresh! Some women believed that shopping at the same establishments on a regular basis led to slightly more favorable treatment, in that a salesperson was less likely to drive away a faithful customer by selling her substandard goods and might therefore steer her toward fresher, tastier choices. As a last resort, contact information for local bureaus of consumer affairs was posted on the walls of many shops. If shoppers purchased stale, health-threatening, or otherwise unsatisfactory goods and were refused refunds, they could contact these authorities. However, those I asked about this course of action said that they knew little about the process and had never gone through it—despite the fact that they had had occasion, citing cases of food poisoning and other problems. They assumed that what little might come of it would not be worth the trouble.[17]

16. On the cultural significance attached to these large appliance purchases, see Shevchenko 2002b.
17. For a description of some of the problems the Consumers' Society of Saint

In sum, a variety of priorities and perceived pitfalls came into play as Saint Petersburg consumers decided on food purchases for themselves and their families. The divide between imported and domestic products played an important role, but the origin of an object did not stand alone as a sign of value or lack thereof. Rather, it was interwoven with other standards and suspicions that informed choices and helped to reduce the threatening unpredictability of commodities on the market. In this way, individuals' renderings of their own well-being and material satisfaction—or lack thereof—sometimes fit into a scheme of international development and difference that stretched far beyond the realm of their everyday experience but made a particular kind of sense of it. Every stale import and food-poisoned child reflected on the state of things with one and one's country, and consumers sought to make the best choices possible under the circumstances.

"Russian Exotica"

In all kinds of contexts, people in Saint Petersburg would tell me—sometimes with a smile or laugh—that Russia was "behind" the United States and Western Europe. Often the situations that prompted these comments were not ones I could anticipate. "Of course, we are ten years behind in everything," a friend told me when I explained that it seemed to me that Mary Kay cosmetics (which she had seen and about which she had had asked my opinion) had been more popular in the United States about a decade ago. "Here everything is simpler [*U nas vse po-proshche*]," a university professor told me when I likened her plant, which I did not recognize by appearance or name, to wheat grass I had seen in America. Hers, it turned out, was oat grass; wheat grass, she explained, "is a more expensive [plant] culture," and thus she deemed my familiarity with it a reflection of

---

Petersburg attempts to address, see Ignatjev 1996: "Some things haven't changed since the collapse of the Soviet Union. The safety of the food supply, for example, is still an open question and the main food safety and quality guidelines in modern Russia are the same 'Medical-Biological Demands and Sanitary Standards' (MBD) created in 1989 by the State Committee of Sanitation and Epidemiological Surveillance (SES) of the former USSR. And GOSTs, special government standards, are still applied by the former Soviet State Committee of Standards to evaluate the toxicological and microbiological safety of raw materials and food products." Further details are provided about pesticides and antibiotics banned by Russian law and steps being taken in Saint Petersburg to address the deficiencies in current regulations.

American sophistication. Other teachers surmised that Americans (unlike Russians) did not have to iron their clothes. "There hasn't been a special machine created to do it?" one woman checked, seeming incredulous when I told her that that particular form of drudgery had not been escaped in the United States. And on a national television show, a bachelor who liked to spend all his time traveling to exotic places around the world discussed how difficult it was to find a wife who would be willing to share this lifestyle. His next planned journey would take him to see how a "Stone Age" tribe in Africa lived. Russian girls were used to civilization and were not interested in that kind of life, the young man regretted. In response, the host of the show proclaimed that "if you want to see the Stone Age, you can stay here!"

Clearly, material culture in contemporary Russia was being conceived in relational ways; for the most part, Russian technology and commodity culture was understood to be less advanced than Western Europe's and America's. Conversely, such assessments were often stated with notes of irony, poking fun at Western as well as Russian life, at times pointedly so. Material advancement was sometimes believed to be accompanied by the reduced capability of individuals to do anything for themselves. For example, when Anna showed me her recently renovated kitchen and spoke of the particular kind of paint that had been needed for the ceiling, I (a longtime renter at the time with little home renovation experience myself) was not sure to what she was referring. Anna subsequently realized that as an American, I probably would not know such things, because we "do not do such work ourselves." Then, over the course of the afternoon, I helped her prepare lunch. When I said that I was slow at peeling potatoes, she drew another conclusion—not that potatoes are less frequently prepared and consumed in the United States as compared with Russia (which I subsequently offered in my own defense) but that we probably bought potatoes in some other, semiprocessed form, so that my lack of exposure to raw, unpeeled potatoes would explain my lack of skill. The general logic perhaps was expressed most concisely by the electrician who was my neighbor in Saint Petersburg, when he observed my relative lack of ingenuity in addressing a problem with my electronic equipment: "Civilization has spoiled you."[18]

18. Related stereotypes I heard specifically in reference to Americans included that we were childlike, naive, and followed rules unquestioningly. However, people at times associated me with "the West" in general, as, e.g., when Dima talked about sausages that had been sold locally that were Danish and German and probably "among the cheapest you have [there]." Of various "Western" countries more generally, it was said that life was much calmer than in Russia, where people run around from job to job; that one did

Ivan told a humorous story that he said had been in the news several years earlier. A group of Russians had traveled to Hungary, and at their hotel they (among other Hungarian guests) had been served fish with mayonnaise. Subsequently, the Hungarians had all become dreadfully ill and gone to the hospital, while the Russians were all fine. Ivan explained that the Russians were used to eating fish that was not very fresh, and that this explained their greater resistance. That is, long-term exposure to low-quality food had made them heartier than their Hungarian counterparts (interestingly, another postsocialist population), who by contrast were presented as living in relatively easy conditions. Such humorous, ambiguous evaluations of Russian life took part in a kind of "cultural intimacy" (Herzfeld 1996, 3): "The recognition of those aspects of a cultural identity that are considered a source of external embarrassment but that nevertheless provide insiders with their assurance of common sociality." Poor living standards over the long term were transformed into a source of national pride (albeit a dubious one) and endurance, along the lines of "whatever doesn't kill us makes us stronger."

Hence there were acknowledged downsides to "civilization," and conversely, some worth to be found in the skills and ingenuity that came from the experience of living in more difficult conditions. Still, the (national) self-denigration implied in such comments and the value placed on Western lifestyles should be taken seriously insofar as these discussions were often infused with the sense that well-developed material culture was integral to and an indicator of a normal, "civilized" society. Two events that took place in English classes in which I participated provide examples of how matters of technological development were explicitly (if often humorously) framed as "civilizational" issues and understood to reflect generalized cultural differences.

In the first case, I was helping a friend by speaking with her middle school English class on the topic of New York City. After I had pointed out notable

---

not have to worry so much there about everyday life (*byt*) because there were more conveniences; that housewives were thrifty and careful, cutting out coupons and not so harried as their Russian counterparts; but also that people were more focused on narrow, more strictly material interests (their own houses and cars), whereas Russians liked to spend time discussing the philosophical side of life. Regarding this last definition of Russian identity, see Pesman (2000) on the Russian *dusha* or "soul," which is conceptualized in terms of generosity, spiritual sensitivity, and sweeping emotions (among other associations). This soul or "soulfulness" (*dushevnost'*) is occasionally framed in opposition to "civilization," as when one of Pesman's informants noted that "civilization" (in this case, observance of polite manners) can sometimes constrain and thus negatively effect *dusha* (pp. 21, 89).

sites on a map and told the children a bit about the city's history and high-lights, they were to ask me questions in English. A boy's hand went up. "Are there any castles in New York?" I explained that no, there are not, adding that there are many big buildings, but no castles, because castles were built mainly in earlier centuries and New York is young compared with most European cities. The teacher asked the kids whether they had understood, quizzing them: So why aren't there any castles in New York? With no answer forthcoming, she prompted: What kind of city is New York? She had to answer her own question, recalling that the city was young, modern. . . . In a stage whisper, one of the boys added to his classmate, "Civilized [*tsi-vilitsovannyi*]."

On another occasion, a more serious and collected high school girl taking an oral English exam had to respond to the statement that "civilization is breaking out all over the world" (the question really referred to civilization "breaking up," but she misunderstood the idiom). In her answer, she asserted that "civilization" was comprised of technology and "polite relations among people," including the ability to make contracts and to depend on others. The girl judged that civilization was not flourishing in Russia, for though it was trying to emulate the West, such "polite relations" were not prevalent. In more sober conversations as well as jokes, then, Russia was portrayed as less "civilized" and sophisticated, in technology and material culture as well as social relations—for better or for worse.

Low-quality goods reflected directly on the position and character of Russia vis-à-vis a world of other nations and markets. Nastia recounted that her daughter had gotten some kind of rash due to consuming a cheap drink mix, and she surmised that the dyes used in such products were to blame. She had drawn the conclusion that one could not go for these cheaper versions but had to buy decent, dependable brands like Fanta. Nastia said that there were chewing gums, too, from China that were not healthy—better to buy Orbit. She noted with frustration and some disdain that "all 'normal' countries have already refused them" (i.e., low-quality, unhealthy imports from Asia). Though Nastia's comments indicted the nation as a whole for its "abnormality," such discourse generally veered away from discussion of the state regulations and monitoring standards that were apparently ineffective in ensuring reasonable food quality and safety (though a few women mentioned that onsite inspections of fresh dairy products and meats at the *rynki* provided some insurance against contaminated foods).

Instead, these commentaries placed more emphasis on relationships within the aforementioned hierarchy of development and civilization, with the significant result that consumers and their ways of life were implicated in all this. That is, though the teachers did not seem to understand themselves as holding any power or influence through which to ameliorate these problems—such decisions were out of their hands—"abnormal" conditions reflected on the overall sophistication and developmental level, both cultural and economic, of a people. On this note, teacher Maria told me that she was in favor of the market and held little nostalgia for the socialist economy, but that she would prefer a "civilized" capitalism rather than the "wild" one Russia had now. It would be nice, Maria said, to jump straight ahead to the "civilized" version. She had gained some perspective about what this meant on a visit to Germany; there, she had seen that there were beggars on the streets, but even they were dressed nicely! By contrast, Maria said, the kind of poverty you see in Russia could probably be observed only "somewhere in Africa, in a weakly developed [i.e., developing] country." For "in other normal, civilized countries, everyone receives unemployment." Such disparaging comments intermingled judgments about political economy and cultural status, casting Russia and the standard of living enjoyed by its citizens as substandard (not Eurostandard) and even exotic.

Consider the following story: Tatiana, a retired schoolteacher, had something new to show off when I visited her in September 1998. She smiled broadly as she led me through her apartment to show off the newly installed windows in her bedroom and living room. They were indeed impressive compared to the frames that could be seen on most apartment buildings in the city, with their peeling paint and thin wooden frames. She was especially satisfied with herself for having succeeded in purchasing these so-called Eurostandard fixtures because if she had waited just a few more weeks, the crash of the ruble that began on August 17 would have dashed her hopes of acquiring such windows anytime soon. As she pointed out all the details of their manufacture, she explained that there had had not been enough money to buy new windows for the kitchen. She added with a laugh that they would leave these old ones for the purpose of "excursions," calling the windows a form of local "exotica" that might especially interest the foreign exchange students she frequently hosted.

In a variety of analogous contexts, the term "exotica" was offered up, always with a smile or laugh—but, it seemed, as part of an actual apology to me about material environments with which the speakers thought I would be uncomfortable. Of course, the fact that such comments were occasioned by the presence of an American ethnographer does not make them any less illuminating of how the teachers perceived their own positions in society and in the world through the lens of comparative consumer possibilities. A makeshift door handle, crafted from a stick; a broken-down, messy house (the hostess was inviting us to visit even though it was not in very presentable shape—we could visit it as "exotica"); a traditional-style oven at the family dacha—all these were placed in the category of "Russian exotica." The first time I met Maria, she asked me why I had chosen to come to Russia: "For something different, wild?"

Interestingly, when my acquaintances alluded to Russian exotica or similarly disparaged local standards, they occasionally referred not only to the material but also to the physical and natural environment, apologetically indicating that rustic rural environs—which *they* enjoyed for relaxation— might be quite literally too uncivilized for my comfort. In such instances, they seemed almost to suggest that the place I was from was so "civilized" that we had banished dirt and had built everything to "Eurostandard." For example, when my husband and I visited a forest park in a historic suburban town, our young host warned us that it was an unkempt "Russian forest," and perhaps not what we were used to or would like. His mother, he explained, had been to a forest in Germany, and it had been nicely kept with neat paths. As we crossed a muddy creek over a wooden plank, he called over his shoulder that it was a "Russian bridge."[19] During a dacha visit with a friend's family, her mother, having recommended I clean the dirt out of my sneaker soles with a stick, asked while watching me do it: "Are you sorry you came to this dirt/dirtiness [*griaz*]?" (They were more concerned about the state of my shoes than I was; indeed, I was continually amazed by how clean most local women managed to keep their shoes in those dusty

19. Klaus Mehnert (1962), a German news correspondent (who lived in Moscow for the first eight years of his life and later returned professionally), presents a somewhat similar example of apology for rusticness or lack of sophistication in countryside. Here the apology is a reference not to exotica but to lack of culture/culturedness (see chapter 3) in a Siberian village, 1956: "Twice a day, day after day, this man, with a disabled leg, had to make his way through this river of slush to and from work—a distance of nearly seven miles daily. The road, he said apologetically, was not very *kul'turno*, and it would be nice to have it paved. But the present plan contained no provision for it, and nobody knew whether it would ever be done" (p. 37). Along rather similar lines but with a different assignment of blame, a young woman who worked with my husband at a local English school was surprised when he likened nearby roadwork, which had been going on for months and made getting to the closest metro on foot rather messy and cumbersome, to similar construction debacles in the United States: "But it is so civilized there!" The woman had been complaining about how long these projects often take in Saint Petersburg, citing the laziness of local workers; she did not think such a scenario could take place in the United States.

streets, and I felt ashamed of the mess mine always were by comparison.) As in the young boy's response about New York's lack of castles, urban modernization carried a morally loaded association with civilized cultural sophistication, such that people imagined a visitor from Western civilization might be discomfited by the rustic "dirt" that Russian urban dwellers themselves found refreshing.

During the same dacha vacation mentioned above, my husband and I accompanied our friends for some relaxation by a lake not far from their cottage. As we laid towels on the sand and settled down for some sunning, our hosts commented on the glass bottles and other rubbish that littered the beach. The couple laughed and were casually apologetic about the mess, describing it as a typically Russian kind of disorder. A moment later, however, Misha gave the observation a positive valence: He said that he felt comfortable there, in Russia, amid the broken and strewn bottles. He had traveled extensively with the navy and had found that Western places could be *too* clean, *too* perfectly kept, making him feel constrained and ill at ease. On a related note, Dale Pesman observed in Omsk, Siberia, that a [positively valued] "simplicity, linked to imagery of the village, could also entail notions of 'primitive' and 'uncivilized.' Post-Soviets of all classes could be playfully delighted to crown themselves . . . superior, natural savages, and to claim . . . to be naturally creative and in contact with national feeling, to be folk, the people [*narod*]; in short, 'normal'" (Pesman 2000, 194).

Still, references to "exotica" were "self-peripheralizing" (Liechty 1995, 186), drawing attention to a perceived primitiveness of Russian lifestyles that was contrasted to a different standard of value and sophistication. This was in the context of a recent shift in urban Russians' "global contrastive awareness," whereby they had realized several years prior, as teacher Nadezhda explained, that there had been all kind of things used and consumed around the world about which most people living in the Soviet Union had had little concrete idea. This newly understood contrast and realization of their previous ignorance was, in her words, "offensive" (*obidno*). Further, "exotica" can be read as a model of inferiority and difference not only organized in geographical space but also incorporating a temporal element; these were things understood to be on their way into the past.[20] The circumstances described as "exotica" were not considered to be permanent conditions; nor were they held to describe the full reality of Russian life. Speakers distanced themselves from exotica by joking about it, affirming

20. Elena Zdravomyslova, personal communication.

that they were cosmopolitan enough to have an idea of what they were missing, while declaring that they were not worthy of their degraded material positions in the world. The following story suggests such a reading.

"Living Like White People"

In May 1999, I invited a group of teachers to celebrate my birthday, and toasts to the birthday person are traditional at such gatherings. In a toast to me one teacher, Larisa, said that perhaps at some time in the future the situation here in Russia would be better than it was now, so that I would want to come back not to work but *"prosto tak,"* just to visit. Another guest, a teacher's husband and former naval officer who had sailed around the world, commented that it really was not so bad here in Russia; there were places where life was much worse. "Where?" Larisa asked challengingly. Africa, he argued, China. . . . Larisa looked at him, nodded, smiled, and said, to the amusement of the other guests: "Yes, if we were only blacker, it would be just like Africa here!"

Like references to "Russian exotica," the joke presented a very critical commentary on the current state of things in Russia. No concrete parallels were drawn between lives in the two locales, but Larisa made the point that living conditions were so poor in Russia that they could be compared with those of blacks in Africa, who were made to stand for the most primitive lifestyle of all. Meanwhile, the fact that the remark was humorous drew attention to the cultural distance or difference of sophistication normally assumed to exist, nonetheless, between the two places and their populations. Indeed, on another occasion, the same naval officer and his friend affirmed this distance in a comforting way, once again highlighting the distance between Africans and Russians—though unsatisfactory local conditions were the grounds for the comparison. Recalling his experiences in Africa and looking around my kitchen, the sailor said that if he lived in this small space with his entire family in Africa, he would think he was well off. After he described, with distaste, the condition of the homes there, how crowded they were, and how people were urinating in the hallway, his friend smiled, saying, "Compared to Africa we feel good about how we live!"

Conversely, two jokes directly comparing Russian everyday life to European standards assessed the former negatively (and more unequivocally than the Hungarian fish anecdote cited above):

Oh, why did Peter the Great defeat Sweden? Otherwise, we'd be living like Swedes today!

And:

—I am going to sign up to fight in Kosovo.
—Why?
—To become a NATO prisoner of war and live like a human being!

In poking fun at the poverty seen to prevail in Russia by comparison with Europe, these jokes suggested, however seriously, that material standards of living were ultimately more important than ideological patriotism—and more nurturing of "humanity."

As they evaluated their material lives, then, these urbanites compared their own conditions, or own "civilization," with others', in such a way that technological advancement, cultural standards such as cleanliness, and characteristics of persons including race were understood as interrelated, that is, as different aspects of cultural complexes that could be described in geographical or national shorthands (Russia vs. Europe or Africa). The same logic was reflected in an advertisement for the World Class sports club in Moscow that ran in *Domashnii Ochag* in November 1998. The ad featured five photographs of brightly decorated individuals: three "natives" adorned with face paint, headdresses, and other ornaments; a woman who appeared to be a Japanese geisha, in white face makeup with pink cheeks and lips and wearing a bejeweled headdress; and last, what appeared to be a European or American sports fan, a Caucasian man wearing a red and white crepe paper wig and red and white face paint. The slogan beneath the photos stated, "There are many ways to improve your image, BUT. . . . Only World Class sports club will lead you on the true road to perfection." In the ad, a call to personal development of a sort (aerobics, personal training) that had become newly popular in the 1990s (and reflected trends that had emerged earlier in America and Europe) is contrasted with more exotic efforts at "image improvement" that are portrayed as misguided and further from World Class "perfection." The need for personal improvement through exercise is argued by contrasting this worthy endeavor with representations of low civilizational development (and, in the case of the sports fan, of undignified folly).[21]

21. On a bleaker note, the September 1998 issue of *Argumenty i Fakty* (vol. 39), 988, featured the following cover graphic: The words "Masks of the Peoples of the World"

Calling up racialized images of low quality of life and lack of dignity, people sometimes referred to the elusive privilege of "living like a white person [*belyi chelovek*]," as when Tatiana showed me the new, substantial lock of the front door of her apartment building ("we are now living like white people") and another woman explained that she had lately been escaping the watchful eyes of disapproving school administrators by coming home during her free periods to drink coffee in peace in her own home, "like a white person." A Russian professional journal, *Nutrition and Society,* featured an article on a newly opened Moscow restaurant called Russian Bistro that served traditional Russian foods in a fast-food style.[22] The article was titled "Will We Snack Like 'White People'?" The restaurant was said to "correspond fully with the European standard": "Walls covered with pink marble harmonized with impeccable round white tables and high stools, and a wooden staircase leads upstairs." The idea behind the restaurant, the article continued, was to combine "filling and native Russian cuisine" with "European cleanliness and comfort." The author concluded that along with good prices and quality, people valued "feeling like a white person." A satisfied customer was quoted: "I am passing through Moscow, and ran around the city all day and got hungry. And here for 15 thousand [rubles] I ate my fill and felt like a white person."

As Fikes and Lemon (2002, 507) have described, "white person" in this usage means to post-Soviet subjects "not only a 'pale complexioned and/or biologically European person,' but also a 'person enjoying civil rights' or 'a normal life,' as opposed to the usual suffering of bureaucratic constraints in a crumbling Soviet infrastructure." Fikes and Lemon link such discourse to "decades of Soviet reportage on racism in the United States, [which] meant that Soviets were aware of competing pragmatic deployments [of] racializing terms in the West" (ibid.). Though official Soviet ideology linked racism with capitalist exploitation and proclaimed it to be a Western evil foreign to the USSR, and "meta-terms such as *race* were only just entering broad circulation" in the 1990s, Lemon observes that racist discursive practices were not themselves new to Russia (2002, 57). For while "'race' was

appeared above a montage of photos: a grinning native of unidentified origin in face paint and head dress, a (Venetian?) festival mask, a (Southeast Asian?) wooden figure, and others. In the foreground, a male figure with the word "Russia" on a patch on his chest holds a bomb and a grenade. He is wearing a black knit ski mask, and he appears to stand for the Russian contribution to world exotica. This is a grim commentary on the Moscow bombings of that fall, positing terrorism as a primary basis of Russian cultural distinctiveness.

22. *Pitanie i Obshchestvo* 1 (1996): 8–10.

not a relevant category in either Soviet or post-Soviet social life because the relevant *terms* in official and academic use were not race but *natsional'nost'* or *narodnost'* [both of which translate roughly as 'nationality' in English]" (ibid.),

> racial logic lives not only in the terms that refer to things but in the various ways people use language to *index relations* in specific contexts. . . . Race, as an organic metaphor, is not only about bodies . . . but about a particular connection *among* bodies, bodies whose substance is bound over time, unmixed with other bodies' substance. . . . [It] is "not essentially about skin color," though it often is . . . *anything* isolated as difference can be made to signal some ostensibly essential nature connecting generations. (Lemon 2002, 58; emphasis in original)

In the Soviet context, such racial logic could be seen in discriminatory discourses concerning Roma ("Gypsies"), Jews, and indigenous peoples not considered to be ethnically Russian; and it was part of how the groupness of nationalities both "small" (e.g., the nomadic peoples of the Siberian Far East) and "large" (Russian, Armenian, Uzbek, and so on) was generally understood (see Lemon 2000; Slezkine 1994b; Grant 1995). In post-Soviet Saint Petersburg, it was also a language for sorting through global shifts in consumer hierarchies, for thinking about comparative standards of living, and for expressing the shame associated with unfulfilled desires.

Indeed, the jokes and apologies performed to me by teachers and their friends used "whiteness" and "Africa" (as opposed to "blackness," which referred to darker-skinned or "swarthy" people more generally and was often used to talk about people from southern Russia and non-Russian former Soviet republics, not only those of presumed African descent) to index differential amounts of technological and cultural sophistication, material wealth, and convenience as well as dignity and full humanity. Elizaveta made explicit the historical connection between racialized ways of talking about consumer privilege and the Cold War context of Soviet reportage about U.S. racism. Recall her story of the girl with an allergy to "imported foods": In the same conversation, she explained to me that high-quality imports were fine but expensive. Those of poor quality, she went on, people said were "for Negroes." I asked her to explain: was this an expression that people used—"goods for Negroes?" Yes, she said, it was, for the association went back to Soviet propaganda and its reports that giving blacks low quality, even harmful foods had been one mode of intentional, systematic racism in the United States.[23] She added that Russia had become a "Third World country," thus calling upon both racial and developmental categories to invoke a sense of Russian loss and inferiority. Teacher Kseniia similarly complained that "Europe 'throws goods out' here, as to the Third World," a problem that she said she had seen discussed in Russian newspapers.

This interpretation of the relationship whereby Europe "throws things out" to Russian consumers has a very relevant history. In common parlance of the Soviet era, it was the state that "threw out" goods to the shops for people to buy. Caroline Humphrey (1995, 47) explains the significance of this slang:

> In Soviet times there used to be an underlying sense that for the most part goods were not really bought by choice, but allocated. . . . Thus, even though the Soviet consumer formally engaged in buying—went to a shop, decided what to purchase, and paid money for it—the ways people talked about this reveal that at some level they realised that they were at the receiving end of a state-planned system of distribution. "What are they giving [*daiut*] in GUM [a central Moscow department store] today?" people would ask. In slang "they" threw out [*vybrosili*] or chucked out [*vykydivali*] goods to people in stores. This was recognition that shops and markets were lower-priority parts of the same system as the specially distributed packages of luxuries to officials and the nameless, closely curtained buildings that contained foreign-currency stores.

That a teacher should describe the trade relations among Europe, Russia, and the developing world using the same notion of "throwing out" suggests much about how she has experienced and interpreted the presence of low-quality imports in Saint Petersburg stores.

The analogy attested to the fact that while in the Soviet era, consumers were differentially positioned vis-à-vis channels of authority, influence and privileges that were controlled and apportioned by "them"—that is, the state —European economic powers were a new "them," along with the ridiculed and mythologized local nouveaux riches. But the position of the European *consumer*—by contrast with that of the New Russian—appeared overwhelmingly (if not unambiguously) as both enviable and normal.

---

23. Regarding the significance of the "Negro" in Russian and Soviet society and history, see Blakely 1986.

In short, comparisons of Russian lifestyles—about which many were especially bitter in the context of the post-August 1998 financial crisis—to "African" conditions dramatized the degradation involved in financial hardship and in the related difficulty of avoiding low-quality, potentially harmful commodities. People used racially inflected terms of development and civilization both to decry and to laugh about some of the things they found most stressful and humiliating about post-Soviet life. Though the continent of Africa held special power as a condensed representation of lack of status, power, and sophistication, it was through a similar logic that low-quality imports from Asia, the United States, and elsewhere reflected badly upon Russian life vis-à-vis global standards. Questions of power and privilege were key elements in the imagination of lives lived around the world, and these matters were often very present in the minds of consumers as they confronted choices in the marketplace.

Civilization, One Purchase at a Time

> Desires for Western goods were not spurred by a yen for assimilation or basic cultural change, but rather people saw Western goods as posing a series of questions about their standing with ancestral powers and other spiritual forces, causing them to search for reasons why they were less well favoured by the powers of the universe than whites appeared to be.
>
> —Chris Gosden and Chantal Knowles (2001, 7),
> on cargo cults in Melanesia

Like the cargo cults of another time and place, post-Soviet consumer practices are the product of a shifting awareness of the world outside Russia, responding to the changing power structures of the post–Cold War era. Though this process was prompted by Russia's recent integration into the global consumer market, the logics according to which commodity flows were conceptualized and made meaningful derived in part from the assumptions and discourses of Soviet life. If, even in the late 1990s, commodities from around the world made sense to some people in terms of their "allocation" to Russians, the connection between a population's *own* worth and the material conditions in which they live becomes all the more distinct; for it would seem that a new seat of authority—not just an invisible hand of the market—had consciously assigned and released these goods to them, assessing citizens' places in a global hierarchy of merit and priorities.

Now these teachers, for whom economic upheavals of the 1990s had arguably brought more anxieties than freedoms, had reason to fear that they were being judged in a similar fashion. Though they desired and felt they deserved to live at "the European standard," the local economy was developing such that this was seldom possible for schoolteachers and many others. That they might, then, be grouped (by themselves, or by Westerners as the teachers imagined them) along with Africans and "Negroes" as uncivilized people living at a very low material standard was an uncomfortable realization, defused and refuted through humorous acknowledgement of that positioning. The status of a "Third World country" receiving others' unwanted castoffs was not one those in Saint Petersburg seemed to have expected they would occupy, nor did they want to believe they merited such treatment.

For—echoing the logic of *kul'turnost'* described in chapter 3—internally civilized subjects were felt to deserve, and in a properly ordered world would be held recognizable by, their appropriately civilized consumption. If the trope of culturedness evoked Soviet norms of propriety and was used to critique post-Soviet class developments and crass nouveau riche materialism, notions of civilization more directly articulated the anxieties attending globalization and desires for greater access to expensive consumer commodities from the West. But in both cases, shifting measures of value and authority were being interrogated as unsettling questions were raised about why an ostensibly deserving public was not receiving its legitimate rewards (Patico 2005).

In another context of recent neoliberal marketization and social transformation, 1990s China, Louisa Schein (1999) observes a similarity between contemporary consumers and the cargo cultists of anthropological fame. She draws a distinction between the groups, however, in attributing to her Chinese informants an "imagined cosmopolitanism" that framed "cosmopolitan space as one of community," prompted by

> a longing for horizontality, for eradicating the differentials of power and wealth that otherwise amount to exclusions. . . . The [cargo] cults were much more concerned with indigenization, with bringing what Europeans had home; by contrast the Chinese imagining of cosmopolitanism is about surmounting the spatial constraint of locality, about entering the global scene by means that deny geographic immobilities. For Chinese consumers, then, attaining a kind of worldliness becomes an end in itself, replacing the material measure that cargoists sought. . . . It is a kind

of subjectivity that refuses the politics of difference, of disparate communities, of the historical positioning of Chinese mainlanders in inferior ranked positions in a global order. (Schein 1999, 360–62)

In the case of Russian schoolteachers, speakers were not denying a politics of difference so much as they were affirming its existence, reinstating and materializing it with each consumer judgment. Russia was "behind the West," to be "white" was more respectable than to be "African," and it went almost without saying that Turkish garments could only be of lower quality and less stylish than Italian ones. What consumers resisted, though, was how their current economic capacities seemed to align them more with the developing than with the developed world. As members of a Soviet middle class still dependent on a now floundering set of state institutions, they framed their situation as that of "white people" subjected to "African" conditions.

This kind of talk seemed to make a case for teachers' own essential "whiteness" while also expressing a great deal of uncertainty about their membership in that category of privilege. On one hand, consumption was indeed, as Vann has argued for postsocialist Vietnam and Russia, a matter of "collectivity and sociality . . . [understood as] a social act that binds citizens to nations through processes of production and consumption" (Vann 2005, 484).[24] Yet "civilization" was also, to some extent, negotiable through personal practice—meaning that the burden lay on individual citizens to maintain and nurture rather than let slip their own status in a global hierarchy of consumers. For women who had come of age in a world of scarcities, consumer choice itself presented a sort of dilemma and a skill to be cultivated; and doing it well held out some promise that one might at least be slowing the plunge of one's own family into the "Third World."

24. Vann (2005) compares the emphasis of Vietnamese consumers on "source" production with findings by Caldwell (2002), Humphrey (1995), and Patico (2001b) regarding post-Soviet Russian attitudes toward domestic and foreign commodities. Though there are important differences between Vietnam and Russia and across all the studies, Vann concludes that across the board, this research shows that while postsocialist consumers may be embracing certain aspects of a "neoliberal understanding of the market and of themselves" insofar as "they link consumption practices with their construction of personhood," they do so in ways that are "informed less by a sense of personal, autonomous identity than by one of collectivity and sociality" and refashion "the neoliberalist project to reflect more local concerns" (p. 484).

Chapter 5

Femininity and the Work and Leisure of Consumption

> In post-perestroika Russia, as before, the world of hair salons, makeup, and body presentation remains for many a form of alternate existence, a parallel world. Life is brutally difficult for thousands of women, who cannot frequent a beauty salon every week, and so continue their old habit of painstakingly saving money so as to visit "their own" hairdresser. The only difference, perhaps, is that in today's uncertain conditions such forays vouchsafe less joy than in the past, even though they may smack of what a bygone era elevated to the status of "forbidden pleasures."
>
> —Nadezhda Azhgikhina and Helena Goscilo (1996, 117)

If post-Soviet consumption takes much of its meaning from the relative newness of being able to indulge—however selectively—in formerly "forbidden pleasures," the contemporary meaning of those pleasures can only be fully understood by looking at how consumption fits into the broader range of activities and identifications through which individuals define one another as successful, valuable, and morally upright persons. For the Saint Petersburg teachers, a key mode of talking about these identities was through the morally laden, gendered dichotomy of work versus leisure or idleness. As we have seen, many teachers' narratives dwelt upon the social usefulness of their own professional labor while decrying what they interpreted as the vacuity or even social violence of nouveau riche entrepreneurship. Yet they also—as illustrated in stories such as Olga's humiliating encounter with a cosmetologist and Elizaveta's rueful reading of a home goods catalogue that portrayed her distant but inevitable "future"—regretted how little time and few resources they had to keep up with current consumer trends and to civilize themselves as they saw fit, whether through

140

wardrobe improvements or trips to edifying museums. In this sense, they clearly valued New Russians' capacity to consume, if not their stylistic or professional choices; and their own inability to consume as they felt they should could be a source of stress or shame. In this chapter, I devote closer attention to how teachers—particularly women, as most of the teachers were—framed issues of social usefulness, deservingness, and self-improvement in the context of constructions of femininity, practices of self-adornment, and the keeping of the home. Against a backdrop of jarring changes in systems of social support and distribution of wealth, these gendered framings of work, leisure, and consumption were part of the teachers' ongoing efforts to define and redefine the moral significance of their own and others' professional, personal, and consumer choices.

These judgments came to the fore when conversations in 1998–99 turned to New Russian women. If teachers identified New Russian men by their conspicuous consumption and ridiculed them for it, they attributed similarly conspicuous, frivolous consumption to those men's stay-at-home wives. Yet, as we shall see, they impugned women in less humorous, much more ambivalent tones that expressed yet more sharply the speakers' anxieties about their *own* places in post-Soviet life. When it came to the achievement of social usefulness through public labor—*and* to performance of femininity through acts of consumption and domesticity, which for these speakers were equally important ingredients of female personhood—what the teachers perceived as a suitably middle-class and modest kind of self-perfection was more often than not defined in the breach. The deliberation over logics of value is observed in this chapter, then, as a deliberation about why the "wrong" kind of woman seemed to have gained greatest access to the resources it took to be attractively feminine and a good homemaker in contemporary Russia.

Some theoretical and historical contextualization of the meanings attached to the "domestic" in Russia and elsewhere is a necessary background to these contemporary narratives. Perhaps the single most important insight gained from long-standing debates in feminist anthropology about the public/domestic divide has been the recognition that both the content and the status of these categories must be understood as culturally specific as well as historically variable (e.g., Rosaldo 1974; Ortner 1974; Rogers 1975, 1978; Yanagisako 1987; Collier, Rosaldo, and Yanagisako 1997).[1] Susan

---

1. Terminology itself can be problematic: As Sylvia Yanagisako (1987, 111) has pointed out, indiscriminate application across cultural contexts of the domestic/public framework can be misleading because it is a mixed metaphor: "a socio-spatial metaphor

Gal and Gail Kligman have noted that even within the context of one country or group, the dichotomy can be applied quite variously. Examining the evolution of public/private discourses in socialist and postsocialist East Europe, Gal and Kligman (2000, 41, 50–51) describe these as shifting, "fractal" frames that refer to "nested interdependencies of work, time, and materials" and of "production, consumption, and reproduction," such that "everyday public and private distinctions—whether of activities, spaces, or social groups—are subject to reframings and subdivisions in which some part of the public is redefined as private, and vice versa." Gal (2002) takes this point a step further, usefully identifying "public/private" as an indexical ideological apparatus through which actors continually redefine and discursively reorganize social reality in the shifting contexts of everyday life, rather than as a straightforward or innocent description of social organization.[2]

Postcolonial parallels can be useful for thinking about discourses of gender and domesticity in contexts of rapid socioeconomic and political change. Scholars of colonialism and postcoloniality such as Chatterjee (1989), Chakrabarty (1997), Abu-Lughod (1990), and Ong (1987, 1990) have shown how contestations of women's virtue and debates about their proper obligations to family and society are frequently part of the language in which nationalist and modernist agendas are articulated. In such situations, state and popular discourses—ranging from debates about women's veiling to generational disagreements about the propriety of lacy lingerie, and including both arguments for women's education into "modernity" and insistence on their roles as the keepers of "traditional culture"—call up notions of gendered "space" that is not primarily physical in nature but also demarcates social categories and moral boundaries (what von Bruck 1997

---

of authority [mixed] with a labor-specialization metaphor of differentiated functions." In other words, the generic domestic-public concept might obfuscate the actual organization of roles, values and power relations observable in a given setting; greater specificity may be found in the configurations in which concerns over space, labor, and authority are articulated.

2. "Public and private will have different specific definitions in different historical periods and social formations. But once a definition is established, the semiotic logic forms a scaffolding for possibilities of embedding and thus for change, creativity, and argument. In these nested dichotomies, there is always some skewing or redefinition at every iteration. Furthermore, redefinitions that create a public inside a private or a private inside a public can be momentary and ephemeral. . . . Or they can be made lasting and coercive, fixing and forcing such distinctions, binding social actors through arrangements such as legal regulations and other forms of ritualization and institutionalization" (Gal 2002, 85).

calls "sociomoral space"). Discursive spaces such as "the traditional home" are not only highly gendered but simultaneously imply other modes of inclusion and exclusion, including nationhood and class, that are linked with ideals of respectability and moral legitimacy.

For Saint Petersburg teachers in the late 1990s, the moral significance attached to the domestic hearth and the cared-for female body were connected with differently inflected visions of post-Soviet transformation: its most welcome versus its most deplorable aspects, the freedoms as well as the losses it encompassed. Hence discussions about women's sources of personal satisfaction in and out of the home became ways of talking about the desirability and difficulties associated with market capitalism, and vice versa. Images of New Russian women condensed these deliberations and put a sharper point on the ambivalent nature of teachers' desires—which included being feminine in ways that seemed possible only through the consumer marketplace (and for those with significant resources) and yet reaffirmed the importance of other loci of social and professional value for the achievement of full personhood.

Work, Home, and Gender in the Soviet Era

The purposeful reconfiguration of public and private relationships was a key goal of the Communist Revolution in Russia, even if the resulting social structures diverged significantly from the original design. Scholars widely agree that the socialist states of Eastern Europe, the USSR, and China made significant progress in achieving their stated socialist revolutionary goals of bringing women into public workforces and providing for social welfare (see, e.g., Molyneux 1981 and Moore 1988). They also concur, however, that a gendered division of labor persisted in the wage workforce, that women's salaries were significantly lower than men's, and that the presence of women in highest echelons of leadership and power was rare (e.g., Einhorn 1993, 1995; Kligman 1994; Clements 1991).

This state of affairs, though it resonates in many ways with the lives of women and men in industrial societies around the world, might seem surprising in that it emerged in the USSR, a nation that purposefully brought the vast majority of its women into the paid labor force and declared a war against domestic drudgery and the bourgeois subjugation of wives by their husbands. In fact, the contradiction can be easily explained in terms of the relatively constrained commitment ultimately made by the Soviet state to transforming traditional gender relations, and in light of the informal activities and popular discourses through which citizens both resisted and colluded with the regime's intentions.

Verdery (1994, 232) nicely summarizes the overall effect of socialism on gender relations in the USSR and Eastern Europe:

> Socialism visibly reconfigured male and female household roles. One might say that it broke open the nuclear family, socialized significant elements of reproduction even while leaving women responsible for the rest, and usurped certain patriarchal functions and responsibilities, thereby altering the relation between gendered "domestic" and "public" spheres familiar from nineteenth-century capitalism.

Revolutionary plans to relieve women from burdensome domestic work through full socialization of child care, laundry, and cooking spurred designs for new communal living arrangements and associated services in the 1920s (Andrusz 1980). Faced with pressing housing shortages and limited means, however, the Soviet state backed away from responsibility for the functions served by nuclear families, ultimately emphasizing the continued importance of the family for social stability and economic growth. In fact, maintenance of the "domestic hearth," maligned as a repository of bourgeois values and female oppression in revolutionary years, became a value in and of itself in the 1930s. "Coziness" (*uiut*) and hygiene were now associated with the well-being of the community; socialist housewives were held responsible for this well-being, for making their husbands more "cultured," and for thereby bolstering male labor productivity (Buchli 1999, 56, 84; Ashwin 2000, 13). (In the sense used here, "culturedness" could refer to aspects of proper behavior relevant at work or at home, such as tidiness and promptness, into which husbands could be inculcated by wives; see Kelly 1999b.)

Though urban women continued to work, efforts to mobilize them into joining the labor force were relaxed, and the women's councils that had been devoted to this goal were dissolved (Khotkina 1994, 89). This change in orientation seems to have been brought about, at least in part, by a reduction in the need for female labor given an influx of unskilled workers from the countryside to the cities (ibid.). Similarly, women took up more "men's jobs" (e.g., heavy industrial labor) during later periods when male labor was scarce, notably World War II. Yet even in the early years of Communist revolutionary fervor and great demand for workers, there had never been any discussion of encouraging men to help with the domestic work traditionally performed by women—only of women's moving "out" into the public sphere (Buchli 1999, 26). At the same time, men were granted the majority of leadership roles in the public "building of communism" (Ashwin 2000, 1). Furthermore, the role of motherhood was retained as one deemed natural and vital for women; it even came to be emphasized by officialdom (alongside labor force participation) as among women's most fundamental obligations, for which they received support and recompense from the state in the form of social services (child care resources, maternity leave, etc.) (ibid.). Still, the lion's share of responsibility for child care, food preparation, grocery shopping, and housework as well as household budget organization remained on women's shoulders (Einhorn 1993; Kligman 1994; Baranskaya 1989). This basic social contract was in effect until the fall of the Soviet Union, if with periodic shifts of ideological emphasis.

For example, in the second half of the twentieth century, promises were made to citizens not about better social services that might have relieved the burden of domestic labor but rather about better *commodities,* presented as indicators of a rising standard of living in the USSR (Andrusz 1980; Dunham 1976). In the 1970s, mass media publications such as *Literaturnaia Gazeta* began to acknowledge the dissatisfaction of many women with their husbands' lack of participation in household work, printing selected articles and letters to the editor that railed against men's capricious demands and dependence on their wives (Holt 1980, 42). However, in the midst of what was being decried as a "demographic crisis," academic (pedagogical and psychological) publications of the 1960s, followed by mass media in the 1970s and 1980s and finally by school curricula, expressed concern over high divorce rates and low birthrates. The latter were reported to be too low in the European republics of the USSR to sustain their current population levels; and the preservation and strengthening of "natural" gender role differentiation was said to be part of the solution. Sociologists blamed working women's alleged neglect of their families for social problems such as divorce, youth deviance, and alcoholism in the last decades of socialism, leaving little question as to women's special responsibility for the care of the home and family (Moore 1988, 145; Pilkington 1996a, 1996b, 1996c).

Housing was scarce and separate apartments for new young families were often impossible to acquire, and consequently grandparents often shared living quarters with the younger generation. Thus working mothers were not necessarily left to manage on their own; but their mothers and other older female relatives were at least as likely to be heavily involved as husbands, a situation that continues today. Because the retirement age was relatively low, women pensioners in many cases performed unpaid household labor and provided child care for their sons' and daughters' children (Verdery 1994, 231). Many urban dwellers had to share communal apartments with other individuals and families with whom they shared no previous relation. These residents were often of quite different classes and backgrounds, and their placement there was decided by the local Housing Committee.

Thus, though the nuclear family was not dismantled as the basic unit of social and economic organization, a less radical form of communal living did become common in the Soviet Union. People generally resented it, for it translated not into less work for women but rather into less control for families over resources in the living space (including cooking facilities and bathrooms). Svetlana Boym recalls how this arrangement played out in the late Soviet period:

> *Kommunalka* ["communal apartment"]—a term of endearment and deprecation—. . . consisted of all-purpose rooms (living rooms, bedrooms, and studies became a "decadent luxury") integrated with "places of communal use," a euphemistic expression for shared bathroom, corridor, and kitchen, spaces where hung schedules of communal duties and where endless complaints were exchanged among the fellow neighbors. (Boym 1994, 123–24)

Separate families allotted among themselves individual stove burners for the private use of each and argued over whose dirty pots had been left in the sink. As Boym vividly describes, there was little sense of privacy in this "private" sphere, except for those "flimsy partitions," both physical and social, that residents erected between themselves.

From the 1920s, living in a "separate" (single-family) apartment was a sign of privilege; by the 1950s, this privilege became somewhat more common, as the construction of new housing on the outskirts of cities enabled more citizens to live in separate (still state-owned) apartments (Boym 1994, 125; and see Andrusz 1980). During perestroika in the 1980s, an official goal was set to provide all nuclear families with their own apartments by 2000, which was one effort among others to address the problems of low birthrates and high divorce rates (Attwood 1990, 6). In Saint Petersburg in the late 1990s and early 2000s, some families continued to live in communal dwellings, whereas many former *kommunalki* had been privatized, renovated into huge apartments for the wealthy or, as in the case of one teacher's family, purchased room by room as other residents departed or died. As in the past, however, newly married couples were likely to live with whoever of their parents enjoyed roomier quarters, because few were able to purchase apartments straightaway and buying on credit was usually impossible.

Particularly for those in the USSR who did not have to share communal apartments, the home—especially the kitchen—has been described as an important locus of friendly, intellectually engaging, open interaction for both men and women, uninhibited by the ideologies and restrictions regnant in public life (Boym 1994, 148; Temkina 1996; similar observations have been made of Eastern European socialist settings, as in Gal 1994, 278). The intelligentsia gathered in each other's kitchens, especially in Moscow, where separate apartments were more common than in Leningrad:

The kitchen became a kind of an informal salon for the culture of the 1960s, of the thaw generation. The most important issues were discussed in the overcrowded kitchen, where people "really talked," flirted, and occasionally ate. . . . It was a company of friends, unofficial though not antiofficial; in this collective the bonds of affection and friendship constituted its ideology. (Boym 1994, 147–48)

Feminist research of the early 1990s, conducted by scholars native to postsocialist countries as well as foreign observers, suggested that "the family itself was an ersatz public sphere, representing the anti-state and freedom" (Funk 1993, 223). Home life was constructed as separate from the realm of the state—ideologically as well as spatially—though not necessarily isolated from another kind of extrafamilial realm of ideas and debate. Socializing in domestic spaces represented a kind of "free time" devoted to meaningful social interaction and prized in those terms.

It must not be forgotten that such "domestic" activity encompassed illegal and semi-legal economic activities. Economic life and exchange relations under socialism were inextricably linked to the maintenance of a range of social relationships, because consumer networks drew on a range of affiliations including kin- and friendship-based ties. Thus Verdery suggests that in socialist Eastern Europe, "the space in which both men and women realized pride and self-respect increasingly came to be the domestic rather than the public sphere, as they expressed their resistance to socialism through family-based income-generating activities (the so-called 'second economy')" (Verdery 1994, 232). In connection with this, sociologists have argued that women's "double burden" had a certain positive effect for them. According to Anna Temkina (1996), domestic duties, including consumption-related tasks, had their own particular kinds of personal rewards, because organizing the household in conditions of deficit called for special skills, creativity, and frequent communication with others. Temkina suggests that women's engagement and effectiveness in these practices gave them a sense of self-respect and importance generally denied to men; and because these activities were often conducted at the workplace, women experienced there, too, a special kind of self-realization and satisfaction in social contact—quite aside from whatever their official job descriptions might have suggested (see also Gray 1989; Temkina and Rotkirch 1997).[3]

In any case, the discourse of the "home" clearly gained new significance as it began to be publicly acknowledged that perestroika was ushering in new market conditions, including new measures of financial accountability in industries and enterprises, that would bring unprecedented levels of unemployment.[4] The idea that women should perform their domestic roles more devotedly and to the exclusion of other involvements often was advanced in the context of nationalist equations of "home" with the nation, such that women's behaviors were linked symbolically to the moral strength and political integrity of the population as a whole. In the 1990s, much feminist scholarship viewed this insistence on the reestablishment of "traditional" gender roles as a contributing force in the growing marginalization of women from postsocialist political leadership, governance, and other (public) sites of power throughout the region (Pilkington 1996c; Temkina 1996; Zdravomyslova 1996; Verdery 1994; Kligman 1994; Einhorn 1993; Funk and Mueller 1993; Temkina and Rotkirch 1997; Ule and Rener 1996).

Meanwhile, most women, in Saint Petersburg as throughout Russia, continued to work out of financial necessity—or at least would have liked to be earning salaries (Ashwin and Bowers 1997, 25). According to many commentators and statistics of the early 1990s, post-Soviet women have constituted a majority of the involuntarily unemployed. Other data suggest, however, that there may not be much of a gender gap; 1998 government (Goskomstat) statistics, based on indicators *other* than voluntary registra-

---

3. On the work experiences of Soviet and post-Soviet men, see Kukhterin 2000 and Kiblitskaya 2000a.

4. In this sense, emphasis on women's domestic callings can be interpreted as a move to protect men's jobs; see Attwood 1990, 10–11; Ashwin and Bowers 1997, 21; and Voronina 1994, 138.

tion on unemployment rolls (where women are strongly represented but that appear to reflect only a small number of those actually out of work), showed that 13.3 percent of women and 13.7 percent of men could be classified as unemployed (Ashwin 2000, 17–20, Ashwin and Bowers 1997, 22–23). Regardless, it does appear that women have absorbed many of the burdens resulting from the loss of social safety nets.[5] Despite the fact that the "private" or domestic sphere has been emphasized in post-Soviet public discourse (and earlier in "private," quotidian discourse and practice) as a primary site of satisfaction and social contribution for women, it should not be forgotten that the Soviet working woman's "contract" with the state (Temkina and Rotkirch 1997) brought her a measure of security (social services and permanent employment) as well as workplace camaraderie. The Soviet "collective" (*kollektiv*) was in many ways a more meaningful social unit than it is today, given Soviet-era employment stability and practices such as the direct allotment of consumer privileges according to membership in particular work collectives (see also Berdahl 1999). The partial loss of this locus of security and identity has been painfully felt by teachers—though it can also be experienced as a welcome sort of increase in individual freedom. According to statistics available as of the early to middle 1990s, less than 10 percent of Russian women would have chosen not to work outside the home if their husbands had earned sufficient wages to support the entire family (Waters 1993, cited by Einhorn 1995, 229). This preference was echoed by the teachers among whom I worked in Saint Petersburg at the end of that decade.

Meanwhile, some women have been eager to eschew salaried labor for domestic life, thereby exercising a choice that was not usually possible under socialism. In Saint Petersburg, sociologists found that new female roles based on a "traditional" division of labor (with women in the home, men in the workforce) were emerging in the 1990s as part of a new bourgeois gender norm. This model was observed primarily in wealthy families that could afford for husbands to be the sole breadwinners. These husbands often apportioned housekeeping allowances to their wives, a departure from the

5. E.g., Bridger, Kay, and Pinnick (1996, 59) report that Russian women have been first to cut back their own consumption in favor of providing adequate food and other provisions for children and husbands. As Temkina and Rotkirch (1997) note, whereas the Soviet state offered women medical care and day care in exchange for their wage work, this system has been partly replaced with women's dependence on family and friends for such services.

more widespread practice whereby wives oversaw family budgets (Zdravo-myslova 1996; Temkina and Rotkirch 1997). Such "bourgeois" arrangements were emerging alongside the growing (though not total) obsolescence of informal economic and networking activities that were so crucial to good family provisioning in the Soviet period.

It should be clear by this point that the nature of the "home" to which women were (perhaps) to return—the content of the responsibilities, privileges, and constraints associated with the domestic—was far from self-evident. The beginning of an answer about what kind of value people were finding there lies in the meanings they attached to women's work outside the home, to the new privilege enjoyed by a wealthy few to avoid such activities, and to the *other* activities with which those privileged women now (reputedly) filled their time. Teachers' ideals and frustrations, and the contrasts they set up between themselves and the "sit-at-home" wives of the nouveaux riches, were part of an overarching deliberation about the relative and interrelated significances of work, domesticity, and consumer activity as bases of selfhood and social worth. It must be noted that the descriptions of New Russian lifestyles that appear in this chapter, and likewise the tales of Russian men's failures, are presented not as "facts" but rather as discourses that help illuminate the *teachers'* perspectives on social change and inequality in Saint Petersburg.

"We Are All Bad Homemakers"

Approximately half of the sixteen or so female teachers mentioned by name (or rather, pseudonym) in this book were married, and most had either one or two children; all the others were divorced, most of them raising a child or children for whom they were the primary providers. Divorce is indeed common in Russia, but some teachers noted that there seemed to be a disproportionately large number of divorced women in their teachers' collective; this was at least partly explained by the fact that single women welcomed the stability of work at a school. Moreover, employment at a good school held a special attraction for those with children, for their children were usually accepted to study there without further ado. Whether married or unmarried, the teachers were more or less evenly divided between those who lived with only their own spouses and/or children (including some women who had moved to Saint Petersburg from provincial towns without their extended families) and those who lived (or were in daily, face-to-face contact) with their parents. Some still lived in communal apartments, alongside nonrelatives with whom they may or may not have maintained cordial relations. Others had been lucky enough to rent or buy separate apartments or to gain ownership of the communal flats they once shared with others; in one case, the family had managed over several years to purchase the additional rooms one by one as they had been vacated by the original tenants. One woman, a single mother and relative newcomer to Saint Petersburg, rented a room while she looked for a buyer for the apartment she had left in her provincial hometown.

Despite this range of family backgrounds and living situations, many common notes were struck in the teachers' depictions of post-Soviet home life and of their own and other women's—and men's—domestic roles. Shared moral imperatives emerged when they treated the question of what made a good *khoziaika,* for example. *Khoziaika* can be translated as "homemaker" as well as "hostess" and "landlady," and it may be closest to the English "mistress," in the old-fashioned sense of "female head of household." A good *khoziaika,* the teachers agreed, should take good care of her children; prepare tasty, home-cooked food; make sure the house is in order; decorate it nicely to make it cozy; keep the family well clothed; and when guests are coming, ensure, through her behavior as well as appearance, that the general atmosphere is a welcoming one of warmth and attractiveness. For the most part, the teachers treated these roles as legitimate, necessary, and specifically female—but also unattainable. They complained about how much more harried and hardworking they had become over the past several years of lower salaries and long work hours, such that they themselves were not very good *khoziaiki.*

For example, teacher Liliia's own descriptions of ideal roles for a household's *khoziaika* contrasted with the more minimal and harried tasks that she normally had time to fulfill. She described a "good *khoziaika*" as someone who could whip up tasty things for guests using whatever she had— definitely not by resorting to store-bought food. Such a woman was someone, in her view, who could set the table nicely and at the same time refrain from calling attention to her accomplishments. She admitted that she was not a good *khoziaika:*

I am a bad *khoziaika.* I'm always at work. A real *khoziaika* has to be at home, actually, then she is a good *khoziaika.* But for us it's impossible, since I have to combine work at home and work at work, and not just one job, so . . . of course it's necessary to be a good *khoziaika* in the sense that there is food at home and everyone is shod and fed. That's already a good *khoziaika*. But I guess now there aren't any good *khoziaiki* at all, real ones like that.

Liliia suggested that her failing was one shared by many Russian women for distinctly historical reasons:

> We don't have the conditions for it. It was beaten out of us. All those years *khoziaiki* weren't allowed to be *khoziaiki,* and we don't know how anymore. And not in one generation. My grandmother was a bad *khoziaika* too, and my mother also. She tries, does, but it doesn't come out, because there is no foundation for it, no *domovitost'* [thriftiness, quality of being a good housewife]. Because there clearly was never any home, either—a room in a communal apartment isn't a home [home/house—*dom*]. And there was never any money, nor the things that were wanted. So we were all bad *khoziaiki.*

Thus Liliia blamed communal living quarters and conditions of scarcity throughout the Soviet period for preventing several generations of women from fulfilling their obligations as *khoziaiki* to create pleasant and efficient home environments. Notably, she did not point primarily to women's participation in the workforce to explain these problems; rather, she suggested that the Soviet system's general economic weakness had prevented women from fully attaining their proper gender identities. Though being a good *khoziaika* seemed to be unachievable in contemporary Russia, Liliia referred to a normative notion of the *khoziaika* that nonetheless held power for her.

Her *khoziaika* embodied a version of female domesticity dependent upon private property. Detailing the continuing problems of urban life today, Liliia went on:

> Liliia: I can't say for Russia as a whole, but among those with whom I socialize—both colleagues and relatives—there are no good, real *khoziaiki,* because of the conditions. Although I have a relative who retired and moved to Pskov [a small, historic city in northwestern Russia], bought a home and really set up house, even though she is an urbanite. She started raising cows and everything, and she has a wonderful household there. She became a *khoziaika* and everything is good with her. But to do it she had to

completely rip her life apart. That is, she dropped everything here: her children—they were already grown up—her apartment —and left. . . . Otherwise it's impossible here.

JP: And what would be needed so that there would be good *khoziaiki* in the city?

Liliia: Normal living conditions. To feel that one is a *khoziaika*—that "this is mine and I live here." We don't have that. And the chance . . . to be able to renovate freely, clean everything up. Spend more time working on it. To not just run home to feed someone, get some sleep and again run off to work, but really have the time to take care of the home. There are no such possibilities. . . . Women are really all exhausted and spent, so it's almost impossible in our conditions.

Liliia's reference to proper housekeeping in the provincial city of Pskov reflects the fact that the classical *khoziaika* role (as well as that of the male *khoziain,* discussed below) is to some extent rooted in peasant life, for which the household and domestic environment hold an economic and social significance rather different and greater than that of the urban apartment. In response to my questions, however, women—as well as the few male teachers with whom I discussed the same issues—had no trouble generating descriptions of what *should* be possible to achieve as a *khoziaika,* even in the city, were it not for the various ills and "abnormalities" (compare with Fehervary 2002) that plagued contemporary Russian society.

Many teachers, like Liliia, not only recognized that ideal types were seldom personified in real life but also offered specific historical explanations for this disappointment. Whereas Liliia suggested that women throughout the Soviet period had been unable to carry out their gender-specific responsibilities very well, most others (if often more vague on this point) spoke instead about the problems of inflation and loss of job security that had followed quickly upon the dismantling of the Soviet system and affected both men and women. Like Liliia, many of the teachers said that they were bad *khoziaiki.* Home renovation projects such as the acquisition of new furniture, kitchen appliances, or fixtures and the installation of better wallpaper, tiling, or windows were incrementally pursued by some families but remained pipe dreams for others, especially in the aftermath of the 1998 financial crisis. And even the smaller, less-cash-intensive tasks of daily homemaking were difficult for working women to keep up, according to the teachers:

A good *khoziaika* is someone who runs the home well. How she does it—
that is to each to decide. [The ideal is when] the home is order, but this
is not the only goal of the woman; that at the same time she has a life beyond the kitchen. There is an ideal to aspire toward! (Nadezhda, divorced, two children)

[Q: What is a good *khoziaika?*] A clean house; lunch and breakfast;
clothes that are clean, good, well taken care of. It is hard to combine work
with being a good *khoziaika*. A working woman is not in the condition
[*sostoianie*] to do everything herself. (Liubov', married, one child)

[A good *khoziaika*] has to be a free person. I'm not saying that she
shouldn't work, probably everyone should. . . . But if she is really the
khoziaika of the house, her work must be limited: half a day, that's all. . . .
[She has to keep the home] clean, pretty, very cozy. I don't have time!
. . . Of course a good *khoziaika* will serve her guests tasty food. . . . But
[the hospitable *treatment* of guests] is more important. . . . Food isn't the
most important thing, but her inner comfort, which her guests must feel.
But all the same it requires time. If she comes home late, at 8 o'clock,
and the guests are coming at 9, how will she look? She won't even have
time to get herself together. Maybe that is unimportant too. . . . But I
know that how a *khoziaika* looks, as well as the home itself, is very important. (Lidia, divorced, two children)

When it came to defining the "standard" roles appropriate to male heads
of household, *khoziainy,* some teachers (including men) listed specifically
male domestic responsibilities: painting walls, nailing things in, laying
wire, and fixing broken household appliances. Others had trouble naming
any *particular* duties for men within the household at all, aside from the one
considered most vital in urban conditions: that of making money for the
family through outside labor. Unfortunately, this standard for men often appeared to be unrealistic and, indeed, was not very familiar in the everyday
lives of teachers. Whether due to divorce, physically or mentally ill husbands, or what the teachers described as simply unmotivated, depressed, or
childish spouses and boyfriends, many of the women were substantial, primary, or even sole providers for themselves and their children—paltry
teaching salaries notwithstanding.

What was often seen by the women as a general lack of motivation and
responsibility among Russian men was blamed on the morale-crushing economic upheaval of the last decade, said to be experienced differently by men

and women because of their divergent responsibilities and expectations. Again, Liliia:

> A woman has to worry more about the family, pay more attention, run around to stores more, seek out either, before, "deficit"[6] goods or else less expensive ones; while the man has to be more concerned with providing materially for the family. Well, the woman too, naturally; . . . well, it's different in different families. But that's how it's really supposed to be. In my family it's the opposite: I've taken care of most of the material providing. Well and housekeeping has been shared equally.

Speaking about men's domestic contributions, Liliia noted that in previous years, apartment renovations had been more financially feasible; it also seemed to her that husbands had taken more initiative in carrying out such projects. These days, everything seemed to be more difficult and discouraging. I asked Liliia what she thought of the idea, already expressed to me by several other women, that it was easier for women to adjust to post-Soviet economic upheavals than it was for men:

> Yes, I think so too, that yes, it's easier for a woman. Somehow just by virtue of her nature. Maybe, for example, it's all the same to me what I eat right now. Whatever is there, is there. This isn't the main thing for me; for me most important is feeding the kids. For a man, of course, it's more difficult in this sense, that he really does have to spend more time searching for work, and there's no extra work to find. For him it's harder, since they suffer this more emotionally than women, that is, they are more susceptible to stress than women; they suffer more, naturally. They have a small circle of concerns; women have more: children, work, and home. And for that reason, . . . when you're always doing something you don't suffer so much. When you work all the time, you just work, and naturally it's easier. But they have more time to think, to look, they are more susceptible.

As Liliia's explanation hints, the fact that men apparently had found these recent difficulties harder to bear than had women was partly seen as a matter of inherent, even biologically determined psychological differ-

---

6. The adjective *deficit* refers here to goods that were routinely absent from store shelves in the Soviet shortage economy.

ences between men and women. "Women are more *vynoslivye* [hardy, able to endure] than men," I frequently heard. "They learn a new job and go on," one teacher explained, while men become helpless when they lose their positions. "Oh Russian men," another woman exclaimed while considering the failures of a boyfriend she recently had been helping to support, "they are not *sostoiatel'nye* [well-off, well-grounded]!"

One woman, Nastia, was in a notably different and more enviable situation. She worked long hours as a teacher, private tutor, and advanced student of English but had a talented, hardworking husband by her side. Nastia once told me that a woman ideally should be at home taking care of her husband and children. Yet this female "destiny," as she described it, was at odds with her own desires. "It's terrible to be home all day cleaning dishes." Although Nastia also commented, in a moment of fatigue during a busy school day, that it must be nice to be a housewife, she quickly recalled that, "of course, there are bad points. You don't teach anyone anything, you just serve people." In fact, Nastia considered herself negligent toward her own teenage children, having tired in recent years of housekeeping and cooking. One winter evening, she and her husband Kolia recounted how she had stayed out late and gotten drunk at the teachers' New Year's party, which was shameful because her son was at home sick. Kolia concurred, if tolerantly, with Nastia's self-admonitions, telling me that the teenagers "barely know who their mother is." Kolia was busy with multiple jobs himself, but he also did most of the family's shopping; according to Nastia, he knew much better than she where each thing they needed, whether shampoo or champagne, could be found and at what price. Indeed, as one of Nastia's school colleagues put it, she "has a good husband. Whether she has cooked or not—it's all the same to him. He earns money, keeps track of it himself, goes shopping; . . . she doesn't go. And she trusts him in everything."

Shining examples like Kolia aside, the women criticized average men for what was cast as their general paralysis, while not holding them fully responsible for it. By contrast—but with a similar effect of questioning available paths to success today—New Russian men were derided for their more active but also immoral, illegitimate pursuit of prosperity, as seen in chapter 3. Women entered this stereotypical picture almost exclusively as *wives* or *girlfriends* being supported by New Russian males. Teachers sometimes, though much more occasionally, mentioned the independently affluent, professional working woman (married or unmarried) as another new, and possibly more appealing, social type on the local scene. Though such women exist in urban Russia, the "career woman" model has not been so dominant in the popular imagination as the stay-at-home "housewife" scenario, at least by the late 1990s (Temkina and Rotkirch 1997, 199). Neither model has been dominant in practice, but the latter has been noticeably present in public discourse (ibid., 202; see also Bruno 1997).[7]

Though Nastia stood out among her colleagues as a woman with a particularly admirable husband, she was far from alone in her conviction that husband or no husband, money or no money, the world of work and of purposeful social interaction was not one from which she wished to escape. Teachers' disparagements of wealthy wives' isolation from that world highlighted, in turn, socially valued work and personal consumer display as alternative, ideally complementary, but sometimes competing modes of post-Soviet personhood.

"Sitting in a Golden Cage . . ."

Would overworked, underpaid teachers have preferred to tend to their homes and families rather than have careers, given the choice? "No, no, no," said Liza, "to stay '*v forme*' [in shape] one has to be with people and have some intellectual life. . . . Sitting at home all day with the rags? No." Her colleagues concurred in viewing work as a crucial opportunity for social interaction and self-realization. Indeed, virtually every woman with whom I spoke about these issues said that if her financial position had allowed a different choice, she would have liked to work part time, maintaining that part of her life while also creating more time for care of her home, her children, and herself. A few mentioned having stayed home for a couple of years when their children were young—a time remembered as "not the best experience" by one, while another recalled having "gotten stupider" (*poglupela*) during this period.

7. As Serguei Oushakine (2001) and many others have discussed, another prominent female image in late Soviet and post-Soviet media and discourse has been that of the prostitute—especially, in the earliest years of marketization (late 1980s), the hard-currency prostitute (the "*interdevochka*" or "intergirl" made famous in a popular novel and film of the same name) who sells herself to foreign men. This model of materially privileged but morally degraded womanhood resonates, to a certain extent, with the stereotype described in this chapter of the New Russian wife who (putatively) trades any hope of a meaningful life for the comforts of marriage to a wealthy businessman or criminal.

Such comments might seem to suggest that the domestic *khoziaika* ideal described above was not, in fact, particularly compelling to these women, at least as an end in itself;[8] and indeed, as the rest of this chapter will illustrate, both professional qualifications and more individualized, "deceptively frivolous" (Abu-Lughod 1990) matters of grooming and self-display were probably closer to the fore of most women's concerns. What is significant nonetheless about the *khoziaika* ideal is that however fantastical it was and, perhaps, was even recognized to be, it did appear to hold a great deal of normative value for the teachers. Like Eurostandard apartments, it sometimes was imagined to be more norm than exception in the standard-setting West, as in one teacher's comment to me that because life was calmer and easier in the West housewives had time to clip coupons and go about their daily responsibilities in more efficient, less harried ways than she and her peers had ever enjoyed. Yet teachers did not see this role being fulfilled by practically *anyone* in their own country, even Russia's most obvious candidates: its new stay-at-home wives.

As the teachers constructed the issue, there could be two reasons behind a woman's not working outside her home: either she had lost her job and had not been able to find a new one—an unfortunate circumstance; or she was wealthy, supported by the activities of a financially successful man, and had made a voluntary choice not to be employed (or perhaps her husband had required that division of labor, a frequent occurrence according to a 1998 *Cosmopolitan* article). Women's magazines of the late 1990s portrayed marriage to a wealthy Russian man as a trade-off that was perhaps understandable but needed to be carefully considered; though they were obviously good providers, such husbands were alleged to be demanding and restrictive, inattentive emotionally, and likely unfaithful.[9] "Now there are more rich people, and more poor—a gap arose [*razryv stal*]," one teacher said. "The wives of the wealthy sit at home. Their mistresses too."

"Sitting at home" thus was often understood as a mark of material comfort and privilege, and the teachers did frequently come across women in that situation—particularly in the wealthier families of their pupils. It is telling that the phrase used was not "to stay at home" but to "sit" there: The words expressed criticism less of women's *exclusion* from public activities than about their *inactivity;* laziness and withdrawal from regular social interaction were cited as negative consequences of not working outside one's

8. I thank Mathilde Schmidt for this observation.
9. Orlinkova 1998; Rutman 1997. For more discussion, see Patico 2001a.

home. Tenth-grade students expressed similar sentiments when I raised the question in discussion groups. One girl said that she would prefer to work regardless of her future financial position, for otherwise she would be bored, "watching TV and sitting on the couch all day and becoming a fat, unpleasant woman." She further remarked that rich, nonworking women did aerobics, went shopping, and thought only of themselves. Nannies would take care of their children, for such mothers were concerned primarily about their own attractiveness.

The at-home wife and mother, then, was imagined as unpleasantly idle—or at least as lacking in any worthwhile pursuits or concerns beyond self-centered, superficial ones—and such laziness and isolation were understood to undermine one's fundamental personhood and social worth:

> To sit in a golden cage, have riches, . . . I was talking to a woman. Sometime, I think last year, I taught her child. Then the child entered this school. And she [the mother] was so well-groomed [*ukhozhennaia*]. She lives with a wealthy husband. She doesn't work. He forbids her. Well, the boy [her son], he's big already, in the fifth grade, [but] nonetheless. And she says: "I used to work. I was a person. But now? I don't feel like a person. Well yes, I have everything. But it doesn't make me happy. I envy you." And I laughed, "Let's change places!" Well and, . . . in short, we were just joking. But of course you get tired from such monotony and poverty. [Still,] I think that when you go out among people, it's easier all the same. (Maria)

In a particularly succinct expression of the belief that work outside the home was a necessary ingredient of full personhood, one girl declared that "I won't feel like a woman [if I stay home], but maybe like a dog or cat who eats and sleeps all day!"

This picture of the wife who "sits at home" consuming, neither drawing from nor meaningfully contributing to the social world around her, recalls the vicarious consumer of Thorstein Veblen's (1994) leisure class. Veblen argued at the turn of the twentieth century that in modern society, status is based upon comparative judgments of pecuniary ability, displayed in particular through waste of time or wealth. In his terms, house servants and wives serve as vicarious consumers of material wealth and of "nonproductive" time. That is, they display not only true idleness but also the evidences of time spent in ways that are not strictly "productive," such as training in manners and breeding, "quasi-artistic" accomplishments, and so on (Veblen

1994, 28–29). The time New Russian women were said to spend in grooming themselves, shopping, and going to aerobics classes seemed to qualify as such "non-productive," "vicarious" display of their husbands' financial success. Teachers expressed hostility toward so much unproductive and apparently antisocial consumption as such—yet in some cases, they expended considerable amounts of their own scanty money and time to maintaining attractive, feminine, manicured, well-groomed appearances. This apparent contradiction points up how unsettling state-employed professionals like teachers have found the idea that in post-Soviet Russia, enviable consumption does *not* seem to be organically linked to the possession of a respectable, collectively valued, and culturally legitimated identity, that is, one produced through socially useful work as they have understood and performed it.

Focusing more specifically on women's shifting relationships to the state, Temkina and Rotkirch (1997) have described a similar process in their contrast of the "Soviet gender contract" with the newly popular contracts of "housewife" and "sponsored woman" (unmarried but supported by a man). The late Soviet contract, Temkina and Rotkirch argue, can be seen as having both official and "shadow" aspects. The official continued to emphasize gender equality, women's wage work, and their roles as mothers, while at the more implicit level of popular experience positive value and opportunities for self-expression were found in gender difference and domesticity. Thus the Soviet shadow contract, "with its value of family sex appeal, consumer culture, and what is perceived as a Western consumerist, bourgeois life style," resonates closely with the post-Soviet "housewife" and, to some extent, the "sponsored woman" models of gender relations espoused by some (especially affluent youth) in Saint Petersburg by the 1990s (Temkina and Rotkirch 1997, 196). Given the continuities and discontinuities in gender ideologies and economic conditions that these developments represent, it is understandable that teachers should have approached them with ambivalence, for they had shared in some of those experiences that had made feminine domesticity and lifestyles perceived as "Western" so appealing; and at the same time, the partial decline of the old Soviet gender contract, whereby labor force participation dependably brought financial security and social status, had taken a heavy toll in their lives.

Yet additional economic and political ramifications of the collapse of state socialism must be brought to bear upon these contradictions. In the mid-1990s, Caroline Humphrey (1995) observed that the political significance of buying imported goods in Moscow had recently shifted. Though it had represented an act of resistance against the Soviet state before the breakup of the USSR, it signified no such resistance against the newest oppressing powers, the suddenly wealthy and deeply resented New Russians whose commerce helped bring those goods to local shops. For similar reasons, the political and social significance of "leisure" or nonwork time has been transformed in the former socialist bloc. Katherine Verdery (1996) has shown how under socialism, the Romanian state in effect limited citizens' free time (e.g., by making people stand in all kinds of lines), thereby preventing their energies from being applied toward other, politically inflammatory or personally profitable ends (though many people defiantly pursued the latter as far they could).[10] By the same token, scholars of Eastern Europe under late socialism observed that citizens quietly resisted the coercive power of the state and its bureaucratic structures precisely by extracting from workdays as much time for personal ends as possible (Konrad 1984, 201–4). In the 1990s and 2000s, by contrast, many people faced involuntary unemployment while others enjoyed private wealth and limitless leisure, free from previous state regulations limiting private commerce and enforcing universal state employment.

Thus leisure time has developed a different range of meanings than it had in the past. It no longer represents a form of popular appropriation of state-controlled resources but rather can be a conspicuously flaunted asset that sets apart certain private citizens from others. It is worth noting that teachers did not use a term equivalent to "leisure" in their own discussions; they talked about women who "sat at home." But the term "leisure" suitably resonates with Veblen's vision of modern capitalist society, which, though it leaves something to be desired as an explanation of consumer motivation, is similar in sensibility to the teachers' complaints. Indeed, teachers did not typically credit wealthy women with using their free time to take care of children or husbands, nor indeed to maintain *any* other meaningful social relationships. Nor were New Russians thought to go to the theater or ballet or to read fine literature—the kinds of activities teachers would include on their lists of the "cultured" and worthwhile activities for which they themselves had all too little time and cash. The urban apartments of the wealthy

---

10. Verdery (1996, 41) allows that the state's expropriation of citizens' free time was not necessarily designed as such, but rather came about as a combination of intended and unintended consequences of state actions and "structural properties of Romanian socialism as a social order sui generis." In particular, strict austerity policies instituted in Romania fostered an especially bitter sense of a struggle over resources between the state and the populace.

(not to mention their suburban homes; see Humphrey 2002) could be quite opulent according to local standards, but the days spent by wealthy wives within these spaces (or anywhere else, for that matter) were cast from outside as truly self-centered, empty time.

Intensive self-beautification was part of this emptiness. Like "sitting at home," feminine beauty—as pursued through the purchase and display of commodities such as clothing, cosmetics, and jewelry as well through the time-consuming cultivation and care of the body—itself appeared as a kind of conspicuous display of newly, differentially available resources.

". . . So Well Groomed"

By comparison with the 1990s, relatively little was readily available to Soviet women in the way of quality cosmetics and public information about skin care and makeup application.[11] Simplicity and lack of artifice characterized officially preferred aesthetics for women's appearance for many years.[12] But in spite of all the obstacles—or perhaps, more accurately, because of them—enhancing one's looks became an important means of self-expression for women (Azhgikhina and Goscilo 1996, 107). As with other consumer shortages, people found alternative solutions for acquiring desired products and "looks," such as cultivating relationships with hairdressers and tailors. Of the later Soviet and perestroika years, others have commented that "obtaining fashionable clothes was both incredibly difficult and incredibly important. . . . Looking good was a way of asserting control over oneself, and over life in a controlled and drab Soviet society" (Visson 1998, 133–34; see also Gray 1989, 160, 164).

The contemporary, post-Soviet stereotype of the archetypical staunch, serious Soviet working woman includes her drab, androgynous, severe phys-

---

11. This paucity should not be overdrawn, however; as with all shortages, people had strategies for locating and obtaining desired goods. Furthermore, in major cities such as Saint Petersburg, some high-end shops carried items such as cosmetics imported from France (Edna Andrews, personal communication).

12. See Attwood (1999, 130) for a discussion of how women's beauty was treated in Soviet women's magazines of the Stalin era, including how "conventional" beauty came to be encouraged in the press in the 1930s, after having been criticized in the 1920s. In the 1930s, women were supposed to be both beautiful and workers; the latter identity had previously been associated with more severe, androgynous approaches to dress and grooming.

ical appearance (Lipovskaya 1994, 124). In the mid-1990s, Irina Khaka-mada, a female politician frequently featured in women's magazines, told *Krest'ianka* (Peasant Woman) magazine that while she had found greater confidence and a sense of personal style as an adult, as a teenager she had not been pretty or well dressed.[13] Rather, she had been "awkward and scrawny, with a limp ponytail. Unrefined, uncomfortable with myself (lit-erally, "innerly constrained / un-free"). A purely Soviet product" (*uglo-vataia, toshchaia, s zhiden'kim khvostikom. Nesvetskaia, vnutrenne nesvo-bodnaia. Chisto sovetskii produkt*). Soviet women's magazines such as *Rabotnitsa* (Woman Worker) and *Zhurnal Mod* (Fashion Journal) offered suggestions as to the "newest" (usually very simple and practical) styles as well as patterns for sewing clothes for oneself. These magazines, along with guides to ethics and etiquette, placed greater emphasis than would post-Soviet publications on issues of cleanliness and neatness and on the impor-tance of choosing modest clothing appropriate to the social context and one's age. Such guidelines were often framed in terms of consideration for the feelings of others (clothing should not "cry out" for others' attention but should add to the pleasantness of the shared environment) and as indica-tions of one's own "inner culturedness."[14]

In the late 1980s and into the 1990s, such publications continued to en-courage "a sense of moderation" or measure (*chustvo mery*) and to insist on age and context appropriateness as important ingredients of "elegance." However, such relatively staid pronouncements began to appear alongside celebrations of *ekstravagantnost'* (extravagance), most frequently in youth fashion; *supermodnye* ("superfashionable") items from the runways of Eu-rope; and the cultivation of *imidzh* (image) for its own sake or to increase one's chances of success in business or personal life (see also Kelly 2001, 373–74). These trends became especially noticeable with the advent to the Russian market of Russian-language affiliates of *Good Housekeeping* (*Do-mashnii Ochag*) and *Cosmopolitan* (published under the same name in Moscow). The magazines' glossy pages presented an endless stream of commodities to the potential buyer (along with articles about male-female relationships, exotic travel destinations, novel career paths, etc.) and quickly eclipsed their Soviet predecessors in circulation and popularity.

13. January 1996, 20–21.
14. Sagatovskii 1982; "Domashnii Kaleidoskop," *Rabotnitsa*, February 1986, 8; "Khoziaiushka," *Krest'ianka*, September 1986, 1; *Krest'ianka*, July 1987, 27; "Do-mashnii Kaleidoskop," *Rabotnitsa*, January 1988, 8. For a more extensive analysis of advice literature throughout the Soviet era (and well before), see Kelly 2001.

Above all, "*zhenstvennost*'" (femininity) became the last word in women's dressing in the 1990s. Advertisements for cosmetics and hair care products from international firms such as L'Oréal began to fill the pages of *Rabotnitsa* and *Kresti'anka,* along with a great increase of articles describing how to apply makeup. Significantly, the text that introduced fashion photo spreads and beauty advice columns frequently included reminders of just how basic the desire to be beautiful was to female identity: "Concern about one's appearance is a characteristic of every woman, of any age and character" ("Khoziaiushka," *Krest'ianka,* January 1992, 7); "Is there a woman in the world who does not care about the appearance of her face?" (*Rabotnitsa,* October 1994, 31); "In all eras, women have used all their strength to try to 'perfect' their appearances" ("Khoziaiushka," *Krest'ianka,* August 1995, 12–13). Occasionally, the tone became almost admonishing: "A real woman must, no, is simply obligated [*obiazana*] to love pretty clothes" (*Rabotnitsa,* April 1995, 11–13).

Rebecca Kay (1997, 81–82) has argued that the public emphasis in the 1990s on "femininity" as a desirable goal (and I would add, as a "natural" and eternal element of womanhood, as seen in the magazines described above) is attributable to people's intention to reject or turn on their heads all the old official Soviet values. But as I have described, careful attention to female grooming had been important at the level of popular practice and even, to a certain extent, state-regulated media and literature far earlier. The post-Soviet difference is that these priorities have become more explicitly and publicly laudable as values in and of themselves, and that the means to satisfy these desires have become much more readily available. As a writer for *Rabotnitsa* reflected,

> Remember when identical, unsightly [*neprigliadnye*] dresses and suits lay on our counters? How much time much energy and time we expended in search of decent clothes. . . . Now we, *like all normal people,* choose clothing *according to our* [financial] *possibilities and tastes.* (*Rabotnitsa,* September 1996, 12–15; emphasis added)

By the late 1990s, a wide range of items had become available to women in Saint Petersburg, from 50-cent, locally produced skin creams to $50 examples of the latest European age-defying technology.[15]

---

15. This is not to suggest that $50 imported treatments are always better than 50-cent local ones. A few women did comment that some of these local brands were very good and/or better formulated for local women's skin; and certainly most were wary of

In this context, beauty products, though still widely valued and desired, played a somewhat shifted role in women's conceptualizations of femininity. Consumer "gains" such as the appearance of better cosmetics in local shops themselves held ambiguous implications for individual women, becoming loci for the articulation and contestation of both social distinction and ideals of womanhood. For in the newly "free" and uncertain market environment of inflation, high prices, and low salaries, these items were, like leisure time, both more and less accessible to women than they had been in the Soviet past.

Thirty-five-year-old Olga consoled herself that despite the fact that she did not have much money for new clothes and makeup, she thought she was "still a woman in her soul." In chapter 3, I described Olga's encounter with a cosmetologist who told her she looked too "provincial"; Olga had surmised that it might have something to do with her "loud teacher's voice." Popular films and passing comments made by teachers and others depicted the archetypical teacher as a domineering, unfashionable, and/or eccentric kind of woman. Many of my friends and acquaintances, though they complained of having insufficient funds for various wanted items, did manage to maintain supplies of beauty products. Some, whether by virtue of slightly better financial situations or personal priorities, visited tanning salons, went to cosmetologists for facials, or attended aerobics classes on evenings and weekends. In fact, the great care Russian women take with their appearances was repeatedly offered to me as a characteristic that distinguished them from European and American women, who were perceived to be far more indifferent toward their looks and pragmatic about their dress. This was true despite the fact that many of the most desirable products used in beautification—French or Scandinavian cosmetics, clothing of Italian leather, advice from *Cosmopolitan,* and so on—were themselves strongly associated with the West. Whether based upon travel abroad or contact with English teachers, exchange students, and tourists from Western Europe and the United States, the general conclusion was that most women there bore little *personal* interest, not to mention success, in matters of style.

Conversely, whether accurate or not, the teachers' assumptions that wealthy, exceedingly well-groomed women also tended to be unintelligent and bored (and married to morally compromised men) mitigated the dissatisfaction and self-reproach teachers expressed when they considered their

---

being "duped" by expensive items that might not turn out to be of accordingly high quality. Still, my impression was that expensive European cosmetics were attractive to many.

own lack of consumer privilege. If too little attention to physical appearance reflected rather poorly on a person, so did too much. Affluent, expensively dressed and coifed women were said not to fulfill the teachers' own visions of what ideal, productive, and thus legitimate or defensible lives would be like; to quote Maria, they were "well groomed" but sitting in "golden cages."

However, it would be wrong to dismiss the teachers' reprovals as nothing more than bitter attempts to make themselves feel better. These discourses bespeak something more: the persistence of a key logic of value, however idealized, whereby one's social (public) contribution was supposed to be a primary basis of one's identity, reflected and perceived in part through material goods. The cultivation of feminine attractiveness—much like other "cultured" projects of self-improvement—had the potential to effect a morally valid kind of "self-civilization" (chapter 3). This potential was betrayed by the excesses and failures of *pointlessly* privileged women. The archetypical New Russian wife may not have been directly implicated in her male counterpart's crimes or other unsavory behavior; but she was no more worthy, in teachers' eyes at least, of recognition as a worthwhile social actor, because she was usually deemed to lack the personal fulfillment and social involvement that an occupation gives one. Hence, widely available, expensive cosmetics and services could be afforded only by apparently undeserving women.

Liliia spoke once more to these conflicts as she continued to explain why there were "no good *khoziaiki*" in Russia:

L: Women are really all exhausted and spent, so it's almost impossible in our conditions. Well, maybe there are those who are buying themselves big private houses [*osobniaki*]—rich New Russians—but I think she is also not a *khoziaika*. They don't concern themselves with [spend time on, *zanimat'sia*] that.

JP: And what do they concern themselves with?

L: Well, I don't think that the wife of some New Russian is herself a *khoziaika*. Probably she won't wash the floors, set up the whole living quarters. She'll hire someone, she'll buy it. She's not going to choose potatoes at the *rynok* [market] herself, no. So all the same she's not a *khoziaika,* she is an owner [*vladelitsa*], but not a *khoziaika*. She doesn't know how to do it. That's what I think. Actually I haven't come into contact with them, but I think it's so.

"Ownership" and material resources were not enough to make a woman a true *khoziaika* with all its affective as well as practical connotations. Liliia had succinctly identified the key tension running through so many of the women's commentaries, for while working long hours for scanty wages often seemed to be the bane of teachers' existences, these burdens were also part of how they distinguished themselves in a positive way from those other women whose lives were so enviably easy.

In this light, more was at stake for individual women than the need, for propriety's sake, to strike a modest balance between the extremes of careless inattention and garish extravagance. These material objectifications of womanhood and refinement spoke directly to the broad questions Russians needed to address as one social contract gave way to another, still socially and morally ambiguous, set of choices and subject positions. In the end, ideal identities were seen as elusive not only because individuals were recognized as imperfect but also because contemporary circumstances appeared to dictate against the "right" kind of woman playing the "right" kind of role in family and society. Such a woman would have considerable access to material resources and yet not be reducible to these. Wealth and self-adornment would express and confirm that person's worth but would not be the basis of it.

Contradictions of Consumer Femininity

If New Russian women's presumed grooming, aerobics, and so on were sometimes dismissed as frivolous, excessive, or tacky, they also pointed to a newly cementing kind of normative femininity that the teachers found persuasive, if impossible. More consumer-oriented than ever, this femininity was inevitably dependent upon financial success and material privilege, and thus it was open to interpretation as illegitimate or at least morally ambiguous. This clearly was not to say, however, that the clothing and cosmetics that "a bygone era elevated to the status of 'forbidden pleasures'" (Azhgikhina and Goscilo 1996, 117) no longer called out to teachers, and undoubtedly to many others, as among the primary means through which to create themselves as attractive, feminine, and respectable subjects. Meanwhile, no one seemed to be disputing that a significant amount of free time and affluence were indeed necessary to achieve real success in this, or to become a proficient *khoziaika*. In short, women were caught up in desires and conditions for their fulfillment that were frequently contradictory. Consumer display was key to a broadly desirable if idealized kind of womanhood, and yet in the present social universe it could also be understood as emblematic of a *lack* of personal integrity and satisfaction.

Such contradictions were sometimes discussed as social problems, as in Liliia's feeling that there were "no good *khoziaiki*," which resonated closely with the teachers' idea that the country suffered from a "lack of culture." On the face of it, both statements were generalized critiques of the postsocialist state of things. Yet when interrogated, they revealed more situated indictments: Why were the rewards of society, such as material comforts and leisure time, being enjoyed by people who did not deserve them and indeed were often ignorant as to how to use them? At other moments, the same contradictions could be experienced more as personal failings and troubling reasons for self-reprobation. Indeed, their pressure was felt keenly by women such as Olga, the teacher who hoped that she was "still a woman in her soul" despite not having much money for nice clothes and cosmetics. The teachers' critical commentaries about New Russian women did not only display the stereotypes teachers held of these social others (with whom they had some contact in the schools and on city streets, but with whom they were less likely to share much personal sympathy or close knowledge). They also demonstrated how seemingly trivial items, from panty hose to skin creams, enabled women to experience—or if lacked, kept them from experiencing—themselves as having fully realized their potential identities not only as respectably middle class but also as successfully feminine. In this, we can see how teachers experienced their relative material impoverishment as an assault on their very personhood, in an intimate and embodied way.

Thus, teachers' critiques of New Russian women revealed not only post-Soviet class tensions, nor just the ambivalent ideals of womanhood to which they felt beholden. Encompassing all these concerns, critiques of New Russian women were particular versions of that profound, more widespread, and continuing process through which post-Soviet people were defending, rejecting, and ultimately reconceptualizing the possible and hoped-for relationships among capitalist markets, state institutions, and a differentiated citizenry. Ironically enough, as this process continues, many women are likely to draw upon the resources to be found in places like *Cosmopolitan* and *Home Hearth*—images of commodified femininity and leisurely domesticity that were distasteful when embodied by New Russians yet held significant appeal when *not* perceived to constrain meaningful social participation and full personhood. Perhaps they will yet be reworked into less contradictory—if not necessarily more equitable or liberating—sociomoral categories for capitalist Russia.

Chapter 6

"Signs of Attention": Gifts and the Recognition of Social Worlds

One morning in May, I stopped in to the classroom of my friend Anya, who had told me that she would have a free period and that we could spend a little time together then. Three bouquets of flowers stood in vases on her desk. Knowing that flowers were among the things commonly given to teachers by students' parents and that the end of the school year—a gift-worthy occasion—was approaching, I asked Anya whether these bouquets had been such gifts. Yes, she had even been surprised to receive so many nice ones, and she pointed out some pink roses that were particularly pretty and fragrant. For March 8, International Women's Day, there had been even more! Anya had received a good number of presents for her birthday, too, because each of her classes had presented gifts as groups, while some individual children also brought their own presents, if only a simple *svetochik,* one bud.

Anya brought down a can of coffee from a shelf. There was just enough for one cup for each of us left in the can, Anya said, as she heated up water using an immersion heater that she kept there for the purpose. From a bag sitting on a chair near her desk, she extracted a box of chocolate. I saw that there were at least three boxes of candy there. Had these also been given to her? I asked. Of course, Anya replied, and went on to say that she very much enjoyed receiving these presents. It was something she never bought for herself, and when you refuse yourself something . . .

We drank our coffee and chatted, and while I was there two young girls came to the door. One of them was holding a white plastic bag, which she presented to Anya. Looking inside, the teacher turned back to her student, saying "You know what I like!" She gave the pupil a hug, told her that she was a good girl, and encouraged them both to have a good summer. The girls left, and when Anya came back to the child's desk where we had been sitting together, she pulled a can of Nescafé Gold coffee out of the white bag. It was quite a small jar, but "Gold," we both knew, was better and more expensive than regular Nescafé. And now we could drink a second cup.

Sociability and Exchange

Spending time together in conversation around a table and food—even if just a cup of coffee at a school desk—is a key aspect of sociability and of the sustenance of friendly relations in Saint Petersburg. This activity usually takes place in someone's home; but at workplaces and even at school, classrooms and immersion heaters can stand in for dining rooms and kitchens as locales for relatively private relaxation and socializing. More public areas for informal interaction at school included the teachers' room, or *uchitel'skaia;* the dining hall, where teachers sometimes snacked or ate lunch along with students; and, at one school, the *kurilka,* or smoking area—in this case, a dank back staircase where many teachers took breaks while classes were changing. Though the cafeterias served tea, some preferred to drink cups of tea or coffee at their desks between classes, alone or with friends. One might take the chance to catch up with a close colleague, or might, as at one of the schools in which I worked, gather with a "micro-collective" or clique of friends who floated in when they were free and the electric teapot was on. This meant keeping one's own store of coffee or tea stowed in a desk, and colleagues could take turns in replenishing a joint supply. Given the teachers' low salaries and the high prices seen in stores in late 1998 and 1999, this represented no small expense.[1] The expense was offset by the fact that teachers often received cans of coffee and boxes of tea from children and parents before major holidays. Accompaniments such as small pastries and cakes could be purchased from the cafeteria, and chocolate was nice to have, too. Gift boxes of candy or bars of chocolate

1. In May 1999, one moderately priced store sold a 95-gram can of Nescafé Classic for 50 rubles; the same size of Nescafé Gold sold at about 110 rubles. Prices varied somewhat at different markets, and larger-sized cans could be more economical, if one had enough cash on hand: 200-gram jars of Nescafé Classic could be seen for under 90 rubles, and of Gold for 190 rubles. By September 1999, 50-gram containers of Nescafé Classic sold for 40 to 50 rubles at some markets. Compare these prices to the school salaries teachers received—about 1,000 rubles per month.

with prettily decorated wrappers often appeared as gifts from class pupils or tutees.

Such exchanges—like the rituals of tea and coffee drinking to which they often contributed—were affirmations of good feeling among teachers and between teachers and students; but they did such work within the larger context of the shifting pragmatic and moral concerns associated with marketization. Since consumer goods that once were scarce and difficult to obtain had become readily available in urban Russia to those with enough cash in hand, while money as well as time were becoming ever scarcer resources, the contextual significance of giving and receiving—as well as the relationships that were created and recognized thereby—could be particularly unstable and anxiety-provoking. New financial concerns constrained opportunities and shaped conventions for friendly socializing, and the social networks once activated to obtain desirable commodities in the Soviet shortage economy were proving no longer much needed or advantageous.

Yet certain forms of networking, exchanges of "favors," and gift giving have continued to be practiced in institutional and private arenas where privileged access and variable qualities of service are at stake. In addition to addressing important concerns such as health care emergencies or a child's acceptance into a good school, there are all kinds of occasions when people present one another with small tokens such as boxes of chocolate and bottles of alcohol such as cognac. Some of these are intended as extra thanks to individuals who are understood be doing—more or less—what they are supposed to do as part of their job anyway. Others are part of more explicitly orchestrated exchanges of special favors and services. Thus, despite the fact that many of these strategies derive from the repertoires Soviet citizens developed to deal with the shortage economy, they remain as elements of expected behavior in friendships as well as less intimate relations, and they are used to deal with resources that are still limited—if constrained in different ways now than in the past. As Caldwell (2004, 33) points out, these exchanges are forms of "making do" that represent collective efforts through which people "graft social relations onto economic interests," ensuring their own material survival through the nurturing of strategic and meaningful stores of social capital.

In this chapter, I do not focus on such exchange relations as means of survival, however, particularly because they played a less central role in teachers' day-to-day provisioning than they appear to have for the often more acutely impoverished and elderly Russians interviewed by Melissa

Caldwell in Moscow. Nor am I directly interested in how people maximize "capital"—whether economic or social—through such relationships, though their pragmatic aspect can hardly be denied. Rather, I ask how such relations produced and expressed logics of value in the late 1990s by considering several questions more explicitly: What was the place of personalistic exchange in a more market-oriented economy? How did such gifting practices help define social relationships and categories, and in what senses did state-employed professionals still find these exchange-based identities persuasive and necessary? Because measures of socioeconomic status were in flux along with the assigned values of commodities and conditions of access to them, it makes sense to return, at last, to a classic question in the anthropology of "value" by examining the interrelation of subjectivities and material things as these become manifest in practices and ideologies of exchange.

A key issue in anthropological theories of the gift is that of "misrecognition." The concept as described by Mauss (1967) and elaborated by Bourdieu (1977, 1996) suggests that in gift exchange, transactors uphold the "sincere fiction" that their offerings are based upon purely disinterested and affective motives; they hide from themselves and others the "true" nature of their strategic and deeply interested investments of time, care, and material resources—investments that, given standard of norms of reciprocity, invariably "pay off" in the long run. Indeed, for Bourdieu, such collective misrecognition is key to the operation of gift economies; it is what sentimentalizes and cements the social relationships formed thereby and ensures their maintenance over time ("as if" for the sake of "pure" friendship). The ethnographer of Russia Dale Pesman argues, in response, that this version of things is unnecessarily cynical and does some violence to the subjective experience of such ritual. Instead, based upon her observations in a Siberian city in the early 1990s, she suggests that "when possible, exchange was not only discussed but *experienced* in terms of friendship and help . . . through spirited chains of 'help,' one might occasionally lose track of for what one owed whom and what one was owed. New friendships were born" (Pesman 2000, 131, 137). Practices that sometimes looked like bribery, such as setting bottles of alcohol in front of people in order to gain access to goods and services, could at other moments open the possibility of real camaraderie, resulting "in hours of *sitting* together and the shifty transformation of a deal into an intimacy and a genre of communication felt to be central to Russianness" (p. 171). In this way, the threat of an overly calculated relationship was transformed successfully into something of far more diffuse and potentially lasting value. As I read Bourdieu's work, however, he would have agreed entirely that such fundamentally "interested" behavior is, indeed, lived as *real* emotional experience and forges relationships that are *at once* strategic and sincere—this is exactly the nature of misrecognition's "social alchemy"—though he does tend to treat economic capital as the most underlying and basic inspiration for action.

Without prioritizing either economic strategy or "real camaraderie" as the more fundamental truth of the exchanges I observed and discussed with people in Saint Petersburg, I want to shift the focus slightly to consider the role these exchanges played in the larger processes of sense making I have been examining in this book: processes through which people in fact "recognized" and symbolically situated those they supposed to be either utterly distinct from themselves (most notably, New Russians) or in certain significant ways *like* them. I have illustrated at some length how teachers joked about and denigrated the putative moral impoverishment of the wealthy nouveaux riches; what were the parallel realms of practice through which people imagined the members of their society whom they may not have known extremely personally or well, yet with whom they assumed some shared basis of experience and values? Though the discourses of *kul'turnost'* described in chapters 2 and 3 provide one answer, here I argue further that such recognition of a sociomoral community wider than one's own actual friends but narrower than "Russia" or "Saint Petersburg" took place through particular kinds of exchange of gifts and services. Rather than dwelling as have many past analyses of Russian exchange rituals on the formation and maintenance of social networks and their significance for families' survival strategies, I prefer to attend closely to the *items themselves* that were exchanged and to ask why those particular goods should have been chosen. As we shall see, the particular material forms typically taken by gifts helped construct perceived grounds of social commonality and moral legitimacy.

Favors of Access, Shifting Access

Scholars who have sought to understand how the centralized economies of the Soviet Union and Eastern Europe operated in practice have stressed the role of "informal" or "second" economies in helping to fulfill consumer needs and desires (Grossman 1977; Ledeneva 1998; Millar 1981; Sampson 1985–86; Verdery 1991, 1996). Unplanned or "private" economic initiatives provided enhanced access to scarce goods and services, and were manifested in both legal and illegal transactions often normalized or even normative, having taken root during the Stalin era under conditions of dire shortage (Fitzpatrick 1999; Hessler 1996; Osokina 1998). In popular parlance, such techniques were described as operating *po znakomstvu* ("through a contact"), *na levo* (literally, "on the left," or "under the counter"), *na chernom rynke* ("on the black market"), and *po blatu* ("through pull") (Millar 1981, 96; Sampson 1985–86). These activities were conducted through various channels, often utilizing and, indeed, helping to construct friendship and kin relations in everyday life. Thus whereas it is an anthropological truism that acts of consumption and exchange mark and sustain social relationships and distinctions (Appadurai 1981; Bourdieu 1984, 1996; Douglas 1984; Douglas and Isherwood 1996; Mauss 1967), this principle held a special importance in the Soviet Union, where from the Stalin era forward people at all levels of society were likely to be involved in one or another kind of "informal," network-based economic exchange.[2]

At the same time, a crucial stimulus and organizing factor of these activities was the system of state distribution of privileges. Rights to purchase special sets of foodstuffs otherwise in short supply or to shop at elite, well-stocked stores were often allotted through workplaces; alternatively, people could establish social connections with other well-placed individuals. For example, salespeople were known to put aside, as a matter of course, the best inventory for purchase and enjoyment by their own family and friends. Such practices were already commonplace in Stalin's time, as evidenced in a satirical cartoon of the early 1930s in which a store employee confusedly examines a new consignment of shirts: "What should I do? How to distribute them? I received twelve shirts, but there are only eight people in my family."[3] More significant, durable acquisitions such as televisions, washing machines, and cars were also accessible through such channels. The sociologist Alena Ledeneva (1998, 29) observes that, "through official channels, these brand-name products could be bought only with specific allocation slips, which were given to every organisation or enterprise, and then distributed by every work unit to selected employees each year. If one had [pull, connections] in the organisation, one could get to the top of a long waiting-list at one's work unit."

2. E.g., Yang (1994) and Yan (1996) describe a similar phenomenon in China that is known as *guanxixue,* or, roughly, "the art of social relations."

3. *Krokodil* 1932, no. 13, cited in Fitzpatrick 1999, 61.

By taking proper advantage of one's own opportunities of access, then, or by establishing connections with others in privileged positions, Soviet citizens searched out items that would enrich their own consumption and prestige as well as enabling proper hospitality. This exchange of "favors of access" (Ledeneva 1998), whereby people maximized their own consumption and rechanneled state-distributed goods and services, was a lasting feature of everyday life in the Soviet Union, sometimes referred to in Russian as *"blat."* Though the term could refer to a variety of practices, it most typically suggested the practice of obtaining deficit commodities through social channels (ibid.).

English teacher Ivan described a few of the connections from which he had benefited in Soviet days, when "all good things"—including good sausages, smoked fish, caviar, well-made furniture, stylish clothing, and especially shoes—were "deficit" (chronically or episodically in short supply). In Moscow, Ivan remembered, there had been special departments at stores for top members of the Communist Party only. A special department of GUM, the biggest and best-known Moscow department store, served party secretaries. Ivan's uncle, a political slogan writer, was allowed to shop there from time to time, and he gave shirts purchased there to Ivan as presents. Another relative, Ivan's brother-in-law, had been a fisherman and in this capacity had traveled every year to Newfoundland. One year, he brought back a pair of shoes for Ivan's wife; she sold them to someone and got herself another pair more to her liking. Indeed, a common way of obtaining special things was to buy them from friends and at work. For example, Ivan recounted, "You have bought a ring you don't like: you sell it to your colleague who wants a gift for his wife. Of course, it would not necessarily be a ring; it could be shoes, coats, dresses, shirts, blouses—whatever you wanted." Well-placed party officials had the best access to scarce goods and privileges (see Zemtsov 1985; Voslensky 1984), but others might be able to buy or divert items for their own purposes thanks to occupational conveniences (e.g., sailors and others who traveled abroad and brought things home for gifts or sale, and salespeople who put aside special things for "their own people"). Of course, one's consumer possibilities went beyond one's own professional positioning, depending on how much energy one devoted to social networking, how skilled one was at mobilizing and maintaining such connections, and which commodities, services, or public resources ones' acquaintances could offer (e.g., Ledeneva 1998, 114–19).

As Ledeneva (1998, 37) emphasizes, the use of social connections in such transactions was often framed and discussed according to "the rhetoric of friendship or acquaintance: 'sharing,' 'helping out,' friendly support,' mutual care,' etc." Thus while people recognized that transactions *po blatu* (through "pull" or connections) were pervasive in their society, Ledeneva's -informants (Russians of widely varying social backgrounds and geographical origins) were much more hesitant to admit practicing it themselves. "We" engaged in exchanges to "help our friends," while others acted in self-interest through pull (p. 6). In other words, what could appear as self-serving and even corrupt in outsiders' behavior was explained as part of the natural desire to look out for one another in examples that fell closer to home.

The teachers among whom I worked often indicated that they were not really the kind of people who had ever used *blat*. It is true that the teaching profession was not among the most prestigious or lucrative in the Soviet Union; and in the newly market-dominated Russia, some teachers were painfully aware that their importance to society as educators was neither respected nor remunerated sufficiently. However, because teachers exercised some control over students' training and grades, they could be seen as desirable social contacts by parents who wished to secure their children's academic success. Although the exchange strategies commonly used in the USSR to diminish the effects of commodity shortages could not resolve people's current financial difficulties,[4] personalized relationships with service providers were still drawn upon to ensure quality of service or produce satisfactory results at key moments. In fact, the realms of education and health care were often cited as those where having an "acquaintance" and following up with thank-you presents was most crucial; for *blat* practices have long been based upon people's variable access to public resources, which teachers, like doctors, possess along with their specialized professional skills (see Salmi 2000, 2003). In the remainder of this chapter, I examine the range of these exchanges as they were evidenced in teachers' practice and discourse: as part of an ongoing deliberation about the significance of material interests and of affective ties in Russian market society,

---

4. Ledeneva (1998, 176) reports that the most frequent explanation people gave in interviews for the diminishment of *blat* by the mid-1990s was the fact that there was no longer a shortage of personal commodities. Other major factors include the increasing privatization of property, which has changed attitudes toward "favors of access," and the fact that "the system of socialist guarantees ceased to operate—the process of privatisation in combination with severe economic tendencies of the 1990s, such as the decline of industrial production, the investment crisis and the rise of mutual non-payment, etc., ruled out previously dominant forms of solidarity and mutual help between industrial enterprises, a social security system and care about collectives in organisations, and launched a large-scale re-stratification of population" (p. 178).

and about how these defined the membership of postcommunist sociomoral communities.

Intimacy and Reciprocity

When people visit others' homes for the purposes of socializing or celebrating special occasions, their activity is referred to as *"idti v gosti,"* which can be roughly translated as "to go visiting." When a person has spent this kind of time at another's home, she is said to have been *"v gostiakh,"* or "at [someone else's home] as a guest." In its most general usage, being *v gostiakh* can refer, simply, to visiting another's home; but the phrase carries particular understandings of what the social experience of visiting ideally entails. Being properly *v gostiakh* involves sitting around a table (archetypically, heavily laden with many dishes) enjoying a number of salads and other appetizers (*zakuski*), a hot course (usually some kind of meat), and finally, coffee or tea accompanied by some kind of sweet dessert—usually more than one: perhaps some kind of home-baked pie or cake as well as a store-bought tort or box of chocolates and, possibly, a bottle of wine or vodka, or both.

In the late 1990s, such standards were most likely to be met when there was a special occasion to be marked: when friends had not seen each other in a long time or when a holiday was being celebrated, the most festive and carefully prepared of these being New Year's and birthdays. Indeed, this *zastol'e*—the potentially lengthy process of eating, drinking, conversing, and toasting while everyone sits around the table—was acknowledged uniformly as the element most central to the creation of a holiday. For example, one teacher, a single mother in her early forties, explained that she had too little money that year (1998–99) for New Year's presents; but her family would have a decent, if modest, holiday "table," with the traditional dishes that marked such occasions. For example, a salad called "Olivier," composed of diced potatoes, bits of diced ham or other meat, peas, and pickles and held together with mayonnaise, appeared on almost everyone's list of obligatory holiday fare. New Year's would not have been New Year's, teachers said, without some amount of table-centered consumption and interaction with one's loved ones. Holidays considered to be less important and festive might be marked by similar meals but be organized in a more impromptu manner and entail a smaller variety (and volume) of tasty dishes. Still, the special meal might comprise the extent of the "holiday." One woman, Anna, said of her family's celebration of Old New Year's that she had just "baked another pie [*pirog*]," and that this holiday was really "an excuse [means, *povod*] to eat tasty things."[5] In short, enjoying "tasty things" was key to the creation of a convivial atmosphere, and as Anna recognized, a great part of the pleasure of such holidays was the opportunity for such consumption.

Other activities might complement the "table" over the course of an afternoon or evening with guests. The television or stereo might be turned on, or a film on video might be watched. If one was hosting particular friends for the first time, or for the first time in a long while, family photo albums were likely to come out for display and discussion. There might be singing, guitar playing, or dancing by those so inclined. Still, the table figured as the center of activity, structuring a celebration with an ongoing stream of snacking and of toasts, with vodka, liqueur, or wine drunk mainly in small stemmed glasses. The more festive the occasion, the more likely it was that alcohol would be imbibed. Ideally, all these elements helped create a pleasant and celebratory atmosphere in which the stresses of daily life had been forgotten in favor of relaxation, good eating, and enjoyment of one another's company (figures 6.1 and 6.2).

Even brief visits, whether at home or at school, usually entailed drinking a cup of coffee or tea. As one woman put it, "To drink a cup—it's standard; . . . very seldom does it happen otherwise" (*popit' chaiku—eto takaia standartnaia; . . . ochen' redko byvaet po-drugomu*). And for most people, coffee or tea suggested something to nibble on along with it: at least store-bought cookies or crackers, if nothing more elaborate. Considerate guests often brought along some contribution to the table ("something for tea never hurts"). This could be a box of candy or bar of chocolate, a prettily frosted and sugary tort, ice cream, or fruit. Generally it was something sweet (especially if the hosts had children, who would particularly look forward to such treats), but it might also be a piece of cheese or kielbasa easily eaten plain or else put on sliced bread to make open-faced *buterbrody*.

Bringing something to eat along was not always advisable, however. An advice columnist explained her view on the matter:[6]

In Russia, where people, especially the urban intelligentsia, lived meagerly for decades and had to "obtain" foodstuffs, a treat brought along

5. "Old New Year's" is New Year's according to the old Orthodox Church calendar, now celebrated in mid-January.
6. Viktoriia Vol'pina, "Khoroshie manery," *Domashnii Ochag,* June 1998, 25.

Figure 6.1. A meeting room in a public school is set up for tea drinking and refreshments in honor of International Women's Day, March 8, 1999. Photograph by the author.

Figure 6.2. Caviar, cold meats, and pastries are among the treats prepared for an end-of-year party for teachers, 1999. Photograph by the author.

was certainly not superfluous. But now, when there is a choice of goods in stores, the custom of bringing along edible things must be approached with caution. Of course, if you are planning to visit relatives or people relatively close to you, you can bring something tasty "without cere- mony." But in the case of an unplanned or business [*delovoi*] visit sweets or wine brought compel hosts to set the table and go to trouble with ad- ditional provisions [or treats, *ugoshchenie*], and this might not be part of their plans. If you really want to show attention, better to limit it to fruit— it does not require complicated serving and can be put on the table with- out anything additional. If there is a child in the house, it is appropriate to bring chocolate, but do not give it to the little one, but to his mother. And of course, flowers are suitable in any case.

Although Soviet citizens may have been less equivocal about receiving tasty, difficult-to-find treats and in turn sharing whatever it was that they had, Vol'pina suggested, the situation in the late 1990s—simpler at first glance—was in fact more fraught. In the Soviet past, shortages made ob- taining special things for guests and holidays a challenge; one would need to locate them through contacts, stand in long lines for deficit items, or buy things in advance to save for the occasion when they would be needed. Good meat, sausage, fish, and wine had to be sought out, perhaps at one of the fancier stores in downtown Saint Petersburg such as Eliseevskii, where there were always lines for the products that were unavailable elsewhere. In foreigners' accounts of life in Soviet Russia, outsiders were typically confused and surprised by the contrast between the state of local shops' shelves (empty) and of the festive tables set for receiving guests (full of all kinds of treats). The strategies involved were time consuming and required social resources but were not necessarily expensive.

In the early to middle 1990s, money became the primary constraint, and this was particularly true for those, including teachers, who remained on state payrolls. Teachers like Larisa rued the fact that hosting guests had in fact become somewhat of a problem for them, especially after the 1998 cri- sis. Before, even unexpected guests had not affected the family's budget; Larisa could always prepare something, it had always been possible to set something aside and they were always happy about guests. Now the fam- ily had less time to make things from scratch as well as reduced buying power. Sitting next to her, Larisa's husband explained that, for example, "a bottle of wine—okay, I'm not talking about the very worst, but a decent one—costs 60 rubles on average. And if my [monthly] salary is 600, that is too much. Maybe once [in a month], and even this is unlikely." He noted that in communist times, a bottle of wine cost 1 ruble 50 kopecks, while the basic salary had been 150 rubles. The couple set about figuring out what the inflation in the wine to salary ratio had been: It had risen by ten times. Thus while actually *obtaining* something nice to bring one's host was no longer a problem—one could easily stop by a store and find a suitable cake or some pastries—one needed also to be aware that such a gift required the recipient to offer in turn tea or coffee at the very least. Insofar as these circumstances constrained possibilities for socializing *v gostiakh,* unsettling economic developments were interlinked even with relatively close social relationships, affecting how they were conducted and objectified through purchases of food and other gifts.

Celebration of family birthdays and major holidays (especially New Year's Eve) constituted the bare minimum of visiting obligations, and some teachers told of little else in the way of visiting. One woman contrasted this situation to the less formal, more convivial visiting that had taken place more often in earlier years: "It used to be you could visit a friend without a phone call. People were freer before." In fact, teachers often named such table socializing as a distinguishing trait of the Russian people: their propensity for sitting at the table for hour upon hour talking about life, their generosity with one another (and with foreign visitors). Now, despite the much-touted benefits of democracy and capitalism, many felt less free in that they were more occupied with the mundanities of daily work and earning money for their families. Short on time (due to long work hours) and short in cash (due to low salaries), the obligation to host someone with beverages, snacks, and conversation at the table often could not be fulfilled without significant inconvenience or else embarrassment. It was preferable, *Domashnii Ochag* suggested, that one accurately assessed the expectations of her host in advance, or at least plan her choice such that her host would not lose "face" (Goffman 1955) in the process.

Such concerns had come to the fore recently, as the financial crisis of 1998 had made it even more crucial to show consideration of one's host by bringing along something for the table, that is, something edible and appropriate for tea, reducing the burden on the hostess to provide for her guest. Anya was particularly adamant as she explained the propriety and importance of such behavior for guests. "It isn't done to come empty-handed," she said, "not that the rule is written anywhere, but everyone knows. If you don't bring anything, you must apologize [*izvinit'sia*] and explain that it was because you had no money. That is what well-bred [*vospitannye*] people do—for some people, it doesn't come into their heads." As recently as perhaps a few years ago, she continued, though people often did bring things *v gosti,* she would not have thought anything of it if someone did not. Now, to come without anything was dishonorable and not to be done (*"ne chestno—tak nel'zia"*). Anya knew one girl for whom everything was a freeload (*na khaliavu*), always at someone else's expense (*na schet kogo-to*).[7] But in general, she concluded, everyone understood what was expected. What one brought (or did not bring) *v gosti* could be used to draw lines between those whose behavior reflected good intentions and breeding and others who, by contrast, created inconvenience, social discomfort, and even offense for others.

The demands of convention were often portrayed as fuzzier and more situational, however. Liza concurred that, yes, she tried always to bring something when she went visiting, less as an obligation than "as a sign of attention" (*znak vnimaniia*) or consideration—"I don't like to feel that I owe something." Yet at certain moments, she drew attention to the insensitivity of others and the obligatory, morally charged component of being a good guest. As I shared tea with Liza and her friends at school one day, another teacher stopped in on some matter of business. Someone invited her to sit down with us for tea, but she declined. Liza and the others explained afterward what had happened: that woman often had tea with them at school, but she never brought anything. People would bring things in turns, Liza explained. For example, Liza would know that they had run out of tea, and she would buy some, and someone else would bring something else. A cup of coffee does not seem like a big deal, Liza explained, but over the course of the year it adds up. Recently one of them had received a bonus and announced to the group that she was going to buy a cake for their tea with her money. Another teacher, Dima, had then turned to the offending teacher and asked, "And what did you bring?" Dima said he had not intended the comment maliciously, but the woman clearly had been hurt. Though Dima was remorseful, Liza felt his joke had been appropriate: "It was just what was needed," she said: a "point" (*tochka*), a small, prickly reminder of the woman's neglected obligation.

Consideration could also keep her from bringing something, as Liza explained of the case of her old schoolmate, a man with whom she was still

---

7. On *khaliava,* see Borenstein 1999. Dale Pesman points to a possible origin of the term: the Hebrew *khalav,* which referred to distribution of free milk in Odessa (Pesman 2000, 246).

friends and whom she and her husband visited from time to time. Because they had been visiting each other since they were kids and kids do not bring things to each others' homes, they had continued this tradition. This was also related to the fact that he and his wife were in more dire financial straits than Liza's family. When they come to visit Liza, they do not bring anything, and so she also does not, so that he will not feel obligated to bring something the next time he comes to visit her.

The question of whether and what to bring along *v gosti* was not always such a markedly tense one. Participants like Liza could construe such contributions as "signs of attention," indications of sincere consideration and the desire to provide a treat or surprise for someone, especially for the friends and family about whom one cared most—not as something "required" or calculated. Though such offerings are neither strictly disinterested nor altogether optional, they nonetheless are seen as part of the sustenance of friendly relationships built on caring and empathy rather than calculated self-interest. This aspect of the gift explains, for example, why Liza "does not like to feel obligated" yet also understands that her own gifts will obligate her friends to return the consideration. Such actions are supposed to be spontaneous and voluntaristic inclinations rather than being worked out explicitly. Anya's unequivocal insistence on the importance of abiding by generalized norms notwithstanding, Liza's case illustrated how guests' choices were in fact context-specific, sensitive to the state of particular relationships, responsive to the broader economic context, acutely aware of how participating individuals were situated vis-à-vis economic shifts—and required to remain implicit.

This Bourdieuian insight was brought home to me in an uncomfortable conversation with one of my closest teacher friends, Olga. I frequently drank short cups of coffee in her classroom or at her home, sometimes with small pastries, or *pirozhki,* one of us had purchased from the cafeteria, more often with a few bites of a leftover chocolate bar or nothing at all. This seemed to be fine with her. "I can host with a cup of coffee," she once told me, saying that she was not one of those people who felt the table must be spread with food in order to socialize. Our visits were often relatively brief and casual, and because she lived just a few steps away from the school, I would sometimes stop in to chat for half an hour or to use the phone when mine was out of service. I did not always bring things with me for tea; when I did, I sometimes wondered whether I had chosen the right thing or whether she might feel self-conscious about accepting gifts from me, because it seemed that she often politely declined to partake herself of the pastries or other goodies I would bring (true, she also spoke of being careful to maintain her shapely figure).

At one point in the spring, realizing that I was helping to drink quickly through her coffee supply, I brought a can of coffee with me once, and then again a few weeks later. Though she accepted the contribution calmly the first time, she seemed taken aback at the second can, saying that she still had some coffee left in the can I had brought her before. She suggested that perhaps I preferred the coffee I had brought myself to the kind she had been keeping at school. I tried to explain my intentions to her, saying that she had hosted me so often recently, that I had drunk much of her coffee, and that I did not want to "freeload." As became clear, however, what I had meant as a sincere admission of concern about inconveniencing my friend, which reflected my building awareness of some of the "rules" of Russian hospitality, struck her as inappropriate and possibly even offensive: for the fact that I had been (ac)counting suddenly was exposed uncomfortably. She gently instructed me that "here in Russia we don't keep count that way." Indeed, generosity and "willingness to help" were among those traits people in Saint Petersburg mentioned to me as more characteristic of Russians than of people of other nationalities. (It is no coincidence that a popular television commercial running in 1998–99 for a company called "Russia" advertised its boxed collections of chocolate candies on television using the slogan, "Generous Soul," *shchedraia dusha.*) My friend warmly assured me that she liked that I came to visit her often: "It's like a small holiday for me."

In connection with the past decade's increased financial and time constraints, however, such holidays seemed to come less and less often in the lives of most teachers.

Everyday Exchange in a Changing Economy

In contrast to reports from the Soviet period suggesting that workplaces were then important nodes of informal economic activity, not much buying or selling of goods went on among teachers at work in 1998–99. This is not surprising in light of the explosion of goods available on the open consumer market in Saint Petersburg by the start of my field research in 1998. This is also not to say that there was nothing to buy at school; from time to time, merchants set up shop for a few hours in the teachers' room, hawking anything from classroom maps to clothing and perfume to theater tickets. Certain forms of exchange among teachers did take place, though often they were perceived by participants as insignificant compared with the kinds of transactions that had been common a few years earlier. Colleagues and friends borrowed money from one another, and though no one seemed to find it worthy of mention in our discussions of mutual help, items such as films on videotape and women's magazines were circulated at work, to be eventually returned to their owners. In the Soviet Union, people passed around hand-typed underground (*samizdat*) copies of novels excluded from state publication; by contrast, some of the women teachers with whom I worked exchanged glossy fashion and advice magazines such as the Russian version of *Cosmopolitan* published in Moscow (and whose price doubled over the course of the several months following the August 1998 depreciation of the ruble). Also, whether within or outside work-based networks, occasional purchases still could be made through contacts. Olga purchased a kilogram of chocolate from the son of a friend who was in the business. She also gave me a pair of official Baltika beer mugs, obtained through an acquaintance who worked at the Baltika factory; for Women's Day, she presented me with a bouquet of cuttings prepared by a friend who worked at the local botanical gardens. Among teachers and between teachers and pupils at school, gifts were presented for particular favors considered to be relatively small but deserving of some extra sign of gratitude. Thus Olga gave bars of chocolate to a boy in her class who responsibly brought photocopies for class, which his mother had copied for free. I occasionally received boxes of candy or chocolate as thanks for helping with English classes and for my assistance in correcting advanced students' essays.

Contrasting the Soviet past to the current moment, an English teacher in her forties suggested how shifts in households' material needs and resource bases had affected relationships with a range of friends and acquaintances. Lidia said that it was probably in the pre-perestroika era, especially under Brezhnev, that day-to-day conversation had been most focused on the goods people had seen on sale. At that time, one would say to others, "Oh! I saw shoes there" or "Oh!—good detergent." Back then, people would buy things for each other. For example, if you saw a good book on sale, you might buy one copy for yourself and another for a friend. Or, perhaps, detergent; if you saw some good detergent and knew your neighbor used it, why not buy it? Now there was no point, because everything was available and even if you saw something on sale inexpensively, your friend could see the same thing somewhere else, perhaps yet cheaper. Now, as always, help from friends was necessary; they were there to support you if you were having a difficult time. Yet more depended these days on how much one could earn, Lidia said, citing onerous increases in the costs of transportation and rent. Thus, whereas necessities had been much cheaper relative to salaries before, "now we depend more on money than our friends. Can friends pay your rent?"

If connections to friends were less necessary and less useful for obtaining food products and other commodities, they remained almost as important as before in the realm of services, where service providers, whether doctors or hairdressers, were understood to exercise judgment as to which clients were deserving of more time and attentive care.[8] Lidia went on: "If you have a good hairdresser, she will do better for you by *blat*—not just like that [*ne prosto tak*]." Indeed, many did seek to establish friendly relations, sometimes involving reciprocal exchange, with service providers and, less usually, merchants or salespeople.

Teacher Liza and her husband bargained and even became friendly with merchants at their local open-air market (*rynok*), getting better deals and enjoying themselves along the way. Obtaining reliably good quality cuts of meat at a decent price is a general problem in the city, but Liza and her husband managed to make a connection with a butcher at the market. They had gone to this butcher repeatedly and begun exchanging pleasantries, and eventually the butcher had given her the address of another store where he worked so that they could visit him there as well as at the *rynok*. The result of the relationship was that Liza and her husband were able to purchase the particularly good cuts put aside for the butcher's "own people." Not everyone found it so comfortable to interact with merchants at the *rynok*, however; others preferred making the transactions as quickly as possible, and some admitted wanting to avoid the merchants there of "southern" or Central Asian descent, who were reputed to deceive buyers and to be pushy— telling you why not buy two kilos and not just one, not taking no for answer, or even flirting in an unwelcome manner.

Merchants and service professionals certainly would provide goods and services for cash without any personal relationship, but it was assumed that

---

8. In her study of relations between patients and doctors in a Saint Petersburg gynecological clinic in the mid-1990s, Rivkin-Fish (1997, 2005) found, along the same lines, that patients expected that doctors would provide "better care" to patients who visit them by acquaintance. "Better" care was understood to refer not to a more qualified physician but to one who was motivated to offer personal attention and a caring attitude not afforded to most of the clinic's patients: "Physicians found through acquaintance were perceived as 'trustworthy' not because their medical skills are reputed to be better, but because they were expected to care for a patient-acquaintance out of *personal* concern, *rather than* bureaucratic obligation" (Rivkin-Fish 1997, 320).

an acquaintance or friend of a friend would do a better job. Of course, these relationships did carry obligations, and for this reason they were not always sought out nor accepted when proposed; also, the specific expectations involved could remain somewhat vague and implicit, making some teachers nervous about how the relationship might develop. At schools, pupils' parents who worked in service professions sometimes offered their talents and resources to teachers. A doctor, dentist, or cosmetologist might propose that a teacher pay him or her a visit. Maria noted that parents were particularly likely to do this when they were not financially capable of contributing extra money to the school, a practice common among some affluent families. From a teacher's perspective, parents appeared to believe that it was desirable to have something extra to offer directly to the teacher, intended for his or her *personal* convenience and perhaps with the goal of currying favor or lenience toward one's child. Maria herself had become the patient of a heart specialist whose child attended her school. She was grateful for the good care she had received as a result, for which she subsequently had shown her appreciation with a gift of flowers and a box of candy. By contrast, Nastia, an English teacher whose family was more comfortable financially than many, preferred to avoid such relations, especially with the parents of her pupils at school. Some parents offered their services to Nastia, but she explained that she did not like to feel that she was dependent on or indebted to anyone. Furthermore, "it could be connected with [trying to influence decisions about students'] grades—I don't like it." Thus, though the implicit and often vague nature of obligations incurred by participants in accepting gifts or services was part of their affective power, as Bourdieu (1996) would highlight, those in less practical need of such collaborations sometimes preferred to avoid such uncertainty and the possibility of being asked favors they would rather not perform.

Even Nastia, however, could not avoid certain types of exchanges through contacts, as when she told me one day that she would not be able to make a meeting we had scheduled because the head of the English Department had asked her to tutor a particular student: the child of the head of the History Department at the State University. Even though Nastia was overloaded with pupils, she simply could not refuse this new one, because soon her own daughter would be trying to get into a (different, but competitive) department of a local university—and Nastia would probably need the help of these influential individuals to achieve the desired result. In other words, though different teachers might engage in such relationships more or less frequently and willingly, it was generally acknowledged that they were important and useful for achieving things that could otherwise be quite difficult or pricey.

In fact, connections could be essential for deciding questions of education, particularly when it came to getting children into well-reputed schools or prestigious university departments. Liza told me about helping the child of an acquaintance get into her school. The process had involved speaking with various players: the school's director, the school psychologist, and the directors of the upper and lower schools. These people had received gifts, which were chosen to correspond to the degree to which each person had had to go out of her way to help the pupil in question. For example, Liza had found out from the school psychologist what would be asked in the psychological evaluation and had prepared the child accordingly. (It had not been a question of the school's accepting a weak student, Liza said; just of preparing her to make sure things would go well.) As thanks for her contribution, the psychologist had been given a large box of candy. This relatively modest gift was appropriate, Liza explained, because she had not had to do anything that particularly crossed usual boundaries of conduct; she had more or less simply been doing her job. One of the other school administrators, however, had agreed to go a bit against what she normally was supposed to do, and so she had been given the more substantial gift of a gold bracelet. A third woman, a relatively influential administrator (*zavuch*) whose disposition toward the case probably could have determined its outcome, had been given the particular (and expensive) perfume that, when asked what she would prefer, she had requested without hesitation. When the family asked Liza what she would like, she named a book on English teaching methodology that she had had her eye on, and they gave it to her along with a bottle of wine or liqueur. In conclusion, Liza said that the family could have gotten their daughter into the school without her help, but it would have entailed becoming a school "sponsor" and paying $2,000. "So you understand the difference," said Liza: $2,000 versus some perfume and candy.

In telling this story, which to an American reader might sound rife with "corruption," Liza singled out for critique the administrator who had asked for the expensive perfume. Liza said that she herself would willingly do such favors without any presents; but in Liza's view that woman had *counted* on receiving a gift. "She is a very mercantile person," Liza explained with some distaste, illustrating how an appearance of overt calculation and self-interest struck people as unpleasant, even in such situations of carefully orchestrated exchange, because it violated the morality of friendly, disinterested gestures of spontaneous generosity. How else, I asked Liza, could this woman's "mercantilism" be observed? "She really loves presents—expensive ones." She received presents for many holidays throughout the year, more than any other teachers, and according to Liza had made it quite clear ("in open text," that is, in so many words) to the parents of her class that she wanted to receive expensive window bars for her home as a gift. For Liza, such "mercantilism" provided one more reason to dislike her professional superior, a woman whom she considered to be generally unpleasant and with whom she and her close colleagues shared little sympathy or society. Liza's story shows how judgments about the ways people engaged in such exchanges could be used to demarcate sociomoral categories, separating those who would gladly accept presents but did not "expect" them from those who appeared to value the things received over the help enacted and persons engaged.

Teachers received presents from pupils and their parents throughout the year, primarily for national holidays (including New Year's and International Women's Day) school holidays (Teacher's Day and the beginning and end of the school year), and sometimes for their own birthdays. Some were given by individual children and their parents, whereas others were presented by groups of parents in a class who pooled their contributions. Flowers, coffee, and boxes of candy were common gifts to teachers, along with some cosmetics and toiletries such as bath gels and shampoos. More expensive and distinctive gifts were sometimes given, but were rarer. I came in one day in March to see Olga wearing a new silk scarf that closely matched the suit she had on, and she told me she had received the scarf for International Women's Day (March 8) from the wealthy parent of a child she was tutoring. She had also been pleasantly surprised to receive a very expensive imported eyeliner from another parent.

These gifts could have mixed and shifting meanings for teachers. On the whole, those among whom I worked seemed to enjoy receiving the presents; while recognizing such holiday presents to be conventional gestures (not so unlike, though more frequent than, the holiday presents American children give their teachers), they also accepted the sweets and trinkets as measures of the good feeling of a child or class toward them. At the same time, however, such gifts were open to interpretation by teachers as indicators of the need felt by parents to please them, in the sense that it was assumed that *displeasing* them could result in unpleasant repercussions for one's child.

It will not be surprising to scholars of Russia, nor to those familiar with gift economies elsewhere, that Saint Petersburg teachers' descriptions of their own gift practice mixed frequent insistence on the disinterested and affective content of such exchange with a carefully managed awareness that these relationships did, indeed, have strategic aspects, enabling people to access services and resources they would otherwise be hard pressed to gain. Below, I continue to examine just how teachers negotiated these concerns. More important, a closer examination of how they managed to make concrete decisions concerning the material *items* to be given in gratitude for favors received provides further insights into the role of gifts in reproducing particular social cosmologies in the post-Soviet context.

Serviceable Gifts

My initial questions to teachers about what kinds of "connections" (*sviazi*) they used and how dependent they were on *blat,* today and in the past, did not usually yield very forthcoming answers. This was part of the general aversion to seeing one's own favors for and dependence on friends in the slightly negative light of *sviazi* and *blat;* it was likely also a reflection of the fact that the practices in which they engaged most often (giving thoughtful presents to doctors or receiving them from students; arranging to visit a new doctor or cosmetologist through a mutual acquaintance; nurturing friendly relations with school parents) did not seem significant or strategic enough to garner immediate mention as such.

In interviews, I began framing the issue specifically around the *gifts* involved themselves, placing those presented for services and favors against the backdrop of a wider range of gift practices and of questions of taste and style. (Who knows your taste well enough to choose a good present for you? How do you choose a present for someone whom you do not know well? What situations necessitate giving such gifts?) This strategy opened the possibility of thinking about this form of gift exchange not only as a practical, goal-oriented effort at maintaining strategic relationships but also in the context of broader repertoires of material culture, raising the question of why particular kinds of commodities tended to serve as gifts in different settings and how those commodities were being used to objectify a particular kind of community. This especially became relevant as it became clearer to me that while gifts were always intended as signs of personal "attention," they were often chosen based on relatively little personal knowledge of the individual recipient.

It is significant that informants themselves were careful in their comments to define what these presents were and what they were not. A gift to a doctor who had been particularly helpful, for example, might be referred to "not as a payment" but rather as simply a "sign of attention." This particular phrase came up again and again, not just about these gifts but also about presents for loved ones. It was said that one wanted to thank a person who had done you a good turn. One interviewee, the husband of a music teacher, took care to highlight for me that such presents were intended

> to thank, not in the sense of a payment of some kind or something like that, but simply as if, well I liked a person, yes, and I want to thank him, only in this sense. That is, well, some kind of present.

Though some highlighted the normative aspect of such decisions, noting that this was something that was "done" or accepted (*priniato*)—an unquestioned standard—to others it was more important that this was, as one person put it, an action "not required, but possible" (see Ledeneva 1998, 154; cf. Yang 1994, 51–58). In other words, the box of chocolate was a spontaneous expression of gratitude, a recognition of, or "sign of attention" to, an individual's good work or consideration.

A conversation with three longtime friends and former colleagues illustrates the mixture of elements understood to be involved in these exchanges, both practical (oriented toward maintenance of a relationship that might be useful again in the future) and supposedly disinterested, "symbolic" ones. Let me reiterate that in contrasting the practical ends served by these exchanges with their "disinterested" aspects, I do not intend to give the impression that their "symbolic" content is merely a cover for other intents. It is important, rather, to consider how the significance attached to disinterestedness reflects upon the social relationships and distinctions that are produced thereby. In this particular example, it is worthy of note that all three of the women had grown up and spent most of their adult lives in the same provincial town a few hours from Saint Petersburg. Though they, like other informants, talked about the affective content of such gifts and the importance of expressing sincere gratitude, they also had observed that such gift giving was accepted practice specifically here in the big city. In their smaller town, such exchanges were unnecessary. Relationships were more familiar and "pure" there, from their perspectives.

One of the interlocutors, Elena, defined three different types of day-to-day gift exchange (i.e., excluding holiday and birthday gifts): (1) a gift presented to another person for no particular reason, which is a sincere and unexpected expression of concern or affection (she highlighted this as obviously the most pleasant kind of gift for the recipient); (2) a gift presented to someone from whom one needs a particular favor (this one felt more like a bribe, she said, and therefore made people feel uncomfortable; despite feelings of displeasure, they may feel obligated to comply); and (3) the gifts, such as those to doctors and teachers, which are given because it is considered to be proper, *priniato.* Elena noted that in this last type of case, the words spoken along with the presentation of the gift could help set the proper tone. With a box of candy, one could say, "So you'll sit for a while and have candy with your tea" or "This is so that your evening will be a little bit sweet [*Pust' u vas nemnozhko vecher budet sladkii*]." This presentation normally took place after a service had been performed, which further helped distinguish it from a "bribe" intended to influence a future outcome.[9]

In the same conversation, another woman, Natasha, recounted how some of her students at the institute where she taught gave her such presents—not that she would do anything differently because of it, but they seemed to consider it to be the right thing to do. "I do the same thing when I go to the doctor," she noted, and told of a particular case in which she had not behaved so appropriately. Her son had undergone surgery, but she had not given a present to anyone at the hospital. It had been unclear to her whom she should thank, because a team of five surgeons had been involved. Friends she told about the situation later had admonished her: "What were you thinking? You should have gone to the surgeon with a bottle of cognac!" The confusion caused by multiple doctors did not excuse her, they said; she should have pursued the question and ascertained which surgeon had actually performed the operation. Natasha now agreed with some chagrin that, indeed, this was what she should have done:

Natasha: Even though I might go to the surgeon with my bottle of vodka and maybe he wouldn't drink cognac, or maybe he would turn out to be a woman. . . .[10]

Elena: But that's what is necessary.

Natasha: So that they remember you.

---

9. Rivkin-Fish's (1997, 2005) ethnography of relations between doctors and patients in a Saint Petersburg gynecological clinic provides a more detailed and nuanced account of the factors that determine how doctors perceive the gifts offered by their clients, including the question of whether or not a person has come to see a doctor "through an acquaintance."

10. Hard alcohol generally is considered to be a good gift for a man, but less appropriate for a woman.

Elena: Yes, so that you have shown your gratitude [*otblagodaril*] to them—this is a sign. A sign that, there [*Znak, chto vot*].

In this last passage, Elena does not even complete the thought of what exactly the gift symbolizes (the Russian *vot*, much like the French *voilà*, serving to draw attention to the presence of something or the completion of an action or thought—that thing or idea here being rather underdefined). An abstract "symbolic" function is contrasted to any practical, goal-oriented interests that might motivate such a gift, though it also is juxtaposed rather seamlessly with Natasha's reminder that gifts helped people "remember you."[11]

These definitions seem to provide prime examples of the principle of misrecognition; for while the women insisted that such practices were "optional" and spontaneous expressions of emotion, their comments bespoke, too, a deep sense of obligation and the notion that these exchanges must be carried out in the proper way. They did at times mention that they gave these gifts to "keep up relations" with recipients, though they generally did not suggest that such a gift was related to the fact that they would need this person's help again. Instead, speakers were rather explicit about what such gifts were *not:* not payments, not bribes, but "attentiveness." Stated otherwise, the gift was to convey a personal message of gratitude; it was important that it not be read as an overt effort to manipulate the recipient into future service. Nor should it allow interpretation as an abstracted, impersonal provision of payment for services already received. Rather, it was to be a spontaneous, voluntary, and moral response to another's actions. Indeed, as an expression of instinctive propriety and sensitivity to others, attentiveness reflected as much on the giver as on the recipient. Even as the giver of a present, one was at pains to avoid appearing so "mercantile" and calculating as Liza's greedy school administrator.

It was in part through the items chosen themselves that individuals could manage these impressions. Most important, money generally was not to be given, for it was felt to signal bribery; "it would deprive the relationship of a personal basis, and insult the recipient" (Ledeneva 1998, 165; see also Yang 1994, 128–29).[12] Nadezhda explained that she had given a present of a box of chocolate to someone at the hospital after her mother had been treated there:

---

11. An article in a women's magazine articulates a similar principle; see "Meloch', a priiatno," *Domashnii Ochag,* December 1997, 21.

12. More recently, money seems to be becoming more acceptable as a personal gift in Saint Petersburg (Elena Zdravomyslova, personal communication, 2003).

Which is to say, not just candy, but precisely an impressive [*shikarnaia*] box, so that it would be pretty, and, again, something that a person would never buy for oneself—we simply regret [*pozhaleem*] spending the money on ourselves. . . . Candies and flowers are nice for a person, and I feel good handing a person such a present. It doesn't look like a bribe, let's put it that way.

Along similar lines, teacher Liliia and her husband addressed the issue of why chocolates were more appropriate than money for such gifts. Liliia explained that in the Soviet past, people had really paid each other with goods, because in the age of deficits one had to do this to accomplish anything. Now, she explained, money was the only deficit, so it was preferable to earn money for one's work. "But you won't show a sign of attention with money, so . . ." (*No znak vnimaniia dengami ne okazhesh', poetomu vot kakim . . .*). Her husband chimed in that money would give the interaction a bad tone, and Liliia finished that, "that's why there are these *dezhurnye* flowers and chocolate" (*po-etomu tut vot est' takie dezhurnye tsvety, shokoladki*).

The adjective *dezhurnyi,* deriving from the French *du jour,* can refer to something that is either commonplace or available at the moment,[13] as in *dezhurnoe bliudo* (*plat du jour*), and this is probably the sense in which Liliia intended it. Interestingly, though, in another frequent usage *dezhurnyi* refers to one who is "on duty," as in, for example, a military officer or hotel attendant serving her shift (in fact, a woman who sits in the hallway to dispense room keys in a hotel is called a "*dezhurnaia*"). We might pause to consider what kind of "duty" or service flowers and chocolates are called upon to perform.

Individuals were, as we have seen, careful to distinguish their gift giving from the kind of exchange that is conducted among independent market transactors.[14] They did not conceive of their gifts as payments or com-

13. I thank Serguei Oushakine for bringing this usage to my attention.
14. In *Gifts and Commodities,* C. A. Gregory (1982, 12) articulates Marx's theory of the commodity in this way: "That commodity exchange is an exchange of alienable things between transactors who are in a state of reciprocal independence." Here participants are seen as free agents, and their exchange establishes not an ongoing relationship between persons but rather one of equivalence or commensurability between different objects (ibid.; Humphrey and Hugh-Jones 1992, 7). Implicit in Marx's formulation, Gregory argues, is a corollary subsequently demonstrated by Mauss and others: that noncommodity (gift) exchange is the exchange of *inalienable* things between transactors in a state of reciprocal *dependence,* i.e., already bound by social ties and obligations. In Mauss's terms, objects circulated in a gift economy bear enduring, compelling connections to the

pensation for services performed; the objects and services exchanged were not understood to be commensurable and, it was said, should not be calculated for equivalence (at least not explicitly). Money could not be used to strike the affective tone so crucial to a successful gift encounter. But other objects such as chocolate and bottles of liquor, despite the fact that they were purchased and sold on the open market and were in this sense "alienable" commodities, *could* be pressed into such service. That is, chocolates and cognac were mobilized in certain kinds of social contexts to establish or confirm particular kinds of social relationship, in which the specific contributions of each participant and the unique nature of their social link were quite important. Yet, as we shall see, the gifts in question need not be chosen according to any specific connection they bear to participating actors; that is, they were not intended to reflect individualized tastes or other aspects of the giver's identity, nor were they oriented toward special needs or personality traits attributed to the recipient. How, then, did chocolates and cognac carry out the work of social recognition at stake in these exchanges?

Choosing Gifts

Gifts given in gratitude for a favor or service might be very carefully chosen, but there were conventional categories from which one usually chose. A school psychologist, Anna, told of a case when she had needed to buy a present for a doctor who had treated her son—a typical case for teachers in

---

people who exchange them; by virtue of this inextricability, gifts establish ongoing relationships and obligate recipients to engage in reciprocal gift giving (Mauss 1967, 31). (But see Sahlins 1976 for a critique of Mauss's interpretation of the connection between the *hau* of objects as gifts and of people.) Annette Weiner refined the notion of the inalienable object and its significance to exchange and social reproduction by highlighting those items that people strive to *keep out* of circulation: unique possessions (modern examples include land, inherited titles, and precious works of art) that are transferable to one's own descendants and that confer *difference* among competing social parties as well as sustaining a "vision of permanence" and social identity through time (Weiner 1992, 8, 10). Most important, the categories of "gift" and "commodity" themselves have been critiqued usefully by anthropologists of value; see Appadurai 1986 and Miller 2001. In this case, though acquired as mundane commodities, items such as chocolates and cognac serve as gifts that establish *qualitative* relationships between *dependent* transactors (as opposed to the *quantitative* relationship between *objects* usually assumed to be the result of commodity exchange) (Gregory 1982, 71, 100–1; cf. Miller 1998). At the same time, they clearly are not "inalienable" possessions in the sense intended by Mauss (1967) nor that of Weiner (1992).

which they needed to choose and present gifts to individuals outside their most immediate circle of friends and family. Anna felt they had been lucky to have ended up at that hospital and met that doctor. She knew that for a man, a standard present was a bottle of something alcoholic. She began discussing the question with colleagues, talking about what brands would be suitable to give. "And it was Martini, Campari," Anna said. These were quite expensive, and in the end, Anna decided to buy a small bottle of French cognac that was somewhat more affordable. It was not usual (*priniato*) in these situations, she explained, to give "things" (*veshchi*, i.e., products that are not perishable items), such as gloves or pens (which would make fine gifts for friends or relatives). Another teacher, Nadezhda, noted that in choosing such bottled gifts for men, one could consider that not everyone likes whiskey but that gin and tonics are "universal," such that even a person who does not drink himself can serve it to others whom he might host with confidence (boldly, *smelo*) and "with a clean conscience." Thus it makes a good present.

In such situations, then, the most appropriate gifts were those described as "neutral" and "universal" as well as "traditional." This category generally included boxes of chocolate, flowers, bottle of alcoholic beverages (especially cognac for men, and champagne or perhaps wine for women), and possibly cosmetics for women. They stood in contrast to the more open field of items one might consider for a closer friend or family member. In the latter case, one would know what a person needed: precisely what cosmetics she used, what color of clothing predominated in her wardrobe (for the purpose of matching new clothes or jewelry), what kinds of books he or she favored, what his general interests were, and so on. In fact, chocolate and alcohol would not be particularly desirable gifts for family members, due to their "neutrality." As Anna explained, "If I know a person well, then maybe I will want to set him apart [*vydelit'*] somehow, to find something specifically for him."

By contrast, when thanking someone for a service, or if for some reason one needed to get a present for a person less well known—perhaps a colleague or friend of a friend—she had the option of choosing a less distinctive, more "traditional" gift. As teacher Lena put it:

> Then I will just traditionally give candy, say, champagne and flowers, if it is a woman. Because to buy cosmetics, let's say, for a woman I don't know well is. . . . She might not like it and she might need something else. So a traditional present. Then no questions come up, because I am

not going and picking it, thinking what can I give. I make use of what is accustomed and reliable.

Referring specifically to gifts for doctors, Anna contrasted these presents to more personalized ones, emphasizing that "this isn't a birthday present, this is more just some signs of attention than . . . that is, it isn't some 'thing' [*veshch'*]."

Such gifts, then, like the relationships they objectified, struck a balance between *personalization* and *anonymity;* or to put it differently, they fell somewhere between close kin (or kinlike) relations and depersonalized, ephemeral market transactions. From one perspective, the decision to give a gift may represent an effort to personalize (in the sense of making more personal, affective) an interaction that might otherwise be more formal, impersonal, and generally unsatisfactory; it has been said that *blat* exchanges and relations of mutual help serve to define and set apart "one's own people" (*svoi*) from everyone else, "constructing and reaffirming a kind of intimacy or closeness" (Rivkin-Fish 1997, 294; see also Ledeneva 1998 and Rivkin-Fish 2005). I found, however, that these gift themselves were not very personalized. That is, they were not necessarily customized to satisfy a particular individual and her tastes, nor necessarily to reflect something unique about the giver (aside from conveying her stance of gratitude toward the recipient). Instead, these gifts were discussed as things that everyone "needed" (and sometimes, alternatively, that no one needed—*chachki*), that would not prove conspicuously superfluous or inappropriately chosen. Some noted, too, that these items, due to their relative frivolity, were things that one normally would not buy for oneself: prettily packaged boxes of chocolate candy filled with liqueur (more expensive than a simpler chocolate bar or candy sold by the kilogram), flower bouquets (which were expensive and would soon wilt), or pretty soaps and imported bath supplies. At the same time, these things were "needed" in the sense of being consumable or usable by the recipient. For example, one could give a woman shampoo labeled "for all types of hair" or facial cream appropriate "for all types of skin." Presumably (the logic goes) all women would welcome certain toiletries of this nature, and the "universality" of certain products made them safe choices.

Teacher Lidia provided another example of the "universal" desirability and appropriateness of certain items over others as gifts. Commenting on a women's magazine that she was leafing through while we discussed the topic of gift options, Lidia noted that she had seen somewhere within the magazine an advertisement for mascara: "—Yes exactly good mascara, which will always be a good gift, because you won't buy such an expensive one for yourself." She excluded, however, those that came in a variety of bright, unconventional shades. "How is it possible to give these, for example, as gifts? This is a dangerous gift." In general, presents of cosmetics were more likely to be chosen for personal friends than for doctors, though teachers occasionally received them from students' parents; and with a very close friend, one might discuss exactly what she needed or even observe when visiting her home what products were standing on her shelves. Otherwise, candy and flowers were standbys.

Some teachers complained of the impact of the country's financial situation on their family lives, and how there recently had been a regrettable, if sensible and unavoidable, turn toward not only selecting more modest gifts but also shifting the focus to gift items that were relatively "necessary" ones. Teacher Elizaveta spoke of the last several years as "nasty times" (*protivnye vremena*), noting ruefully that whereas in the past she had gone out with her daughters before holidays to search for things that would make everyone happy (or glad, *poradovat'*), absolutely necessary things that used to be purchased "just because" (*prosto tak*), such as winter outerwear or shoes, had now become family presents. Such purchases had to be made in any case, and this was a way to get them while saving money by not buying other (relatively unnecessary, if pleasant) things.

In the midst of financial crisis, economic factors also influenced extrafamilial exchange. Teachers' students were not giving so many flowers anymore this year, Liza told me, because they were expensive, and pleasant, but quickly gone. On March 8 of the year before, she had received "two tubs" of them, she said, but this year only four bouquets, along with various boxes of candy, cosmetics, and deodorant; for people were trying to give "things" such as toiletries and cosmetics more often. Parents gave her "not lipstick, of course" (which one would want to choose for oneself) but toiletries such as expensive soap, bath gel, and shampoo.

One teacher noted that it was interesting to see which things were considered appropriate gifts as the years went on. There had been a period in the Soviet era, she said, when soap was difficult to find, and thus a piece of soap had been considered a good present. Others observed that books had once been reliable presents, for there had been a certain group of books that were considered desirable but difficult to find. Thus if one found a good book, it made an appropriate, rather neutral gift for a friend or acquaintance whose more specific desires were not known. More recently, though, these had become more problematic gifts because the variety of books available meant that it was difficult to guess what someone might prefer or might already own. Books, like cosmetics today, were perhaps more favored as gifts for personal acquaintances as opposed to, for example, doctors, even if the latter were often found thanks to acquaintances who paved the way for a good visit. Nonetheless, these reflections on how shifting market conditions have shaped gift preferences bring into sharper relief how it is, more generally, that certain products are constructed as not only "traditional" or conventional gifts but also "needed," "universal," and "neutral."

For however matter-of-factly such assessments may be presented by informants, the "neutral" "necessity" of these products is not inherent in them (Baudrillard 1988). There is some evidence, as seen here, that in the USSR's prolonged periods of consumer shortage, those products that were "deficit" —available from time to time but difficult to find, and often requiring significant investment of time and social resources to locate and to purchase— more or less automatically fell into the category of goods that were self-evidently "needed" by all. In other words, the shortage economy and centralized distribution system helped individuals and, by power of convention, the larger social body, to narrow the field of possibilities in gift giving. In this situation, a good's relative scarcity (or real exchange value, not necessarily reflected by its market price) could help determine its perceived "usefulness" (or use value) as well as its symbolic power, in that an item that was hard to get spoke well of the social position of and/or the care taken by the giver. That is, the considerable obstacles one met in obtaining these goods helped to produce their general desirability, quite aside from the tastes of any particular individual. The personal effort involved in obtaining such a product made it that much more suited to a show of disinterested appreciation and goodwill.[15]

As Lidia reminded me in speaking of the past of several years previous, even if one simply went into a store back then to choose a gift for someone, there was not much variety available, while everything was accessible in terms of price. There might be, she went on, three choices of a particular type of good from which to make a selection; you chose one and left. Now, when there were thirty variants from which to choose, it is overwhelming and you might stand there for two or three hours trying to make a decision.

---

15. Indeed, Ledeneva (1998, 154) claims that acceptable *blat* gifts such as French perfume and cognac served as effective symbols because they "were cheap but difficult to obtain. The cost of a present was not important; what counted was that it could not be bought."

This raises the important question of what new standards, categories, and limitations facilitated the process of gift giving by the late 1990s—a question that became particularly important in cases where givers wanted to convey a certain kind of concern and attention but did not know the would-be recipients very intimately. Meanwhile, cost rather than access was now the primary obstacle people faced in acquiring desirable goods, though entrance to some institutions (e.g., schools) and good treatment within them remained manipulable through social connections and exchange; hence the continued need for appropriate gifts. But how were they now to be chosen— simply by properly gauging the cash amount that must be spent? Many items from the "traditional" gift repertoire did, in fact, seem to be long-standing favorites; but it is crucial to investigate why these "traditional" items seemed appropriate to people in the late 1990s, how their "neutrality" was constructed, and what significance these objects and their qualities had in teachers' imaginations of Russian society and its members.

Price must certainly play a role in these decisions, given the financial constraints many Russians now experienced. However, overly explicit, quantitative calculation of gift choices was likely to conflict with the "sincere," affective content givers wish to convey, as demonstrated above. Furthermore, though price limited the *range* of possibilities, it could *determine* which of those possibilities was chosen only to a certain extent. The problem remained to choose things that were undoubtedly appropriate, desirable, and "needed," despite the fact that one might not know much about the personal hobbies and preferences of the person in question. Flowers were acceptable and neutral (if only for women) perhaps because, like *chachki,* they had no presumed use value at all; they were just "pretty" and pleasurable, and so were suited to use as a *"znak"* (sign) of positive, warm relations (though they may be seen as especially frivolous and superfluous when everyone has fewer resources). But what of the chocolates and cognac?

Arguably, chocolates and cognac were products that many people, quite simply, enjoyed consuming. But more important for this discussion, I think, is the fact that these goods were recognized to be appropriate socializing consumables. That is, as earlier sections of this chapter illustrated, these items were commonly brought out for visiting guests; indeed, social interaction *v gostiakh* (and even in workplaces) almost invariably centered on the table. Their material qualities, too, helped make them thoughtful gifts and effective vehicles for exchange (Weiner 1992; see also Myers 2001b), because chocolate, cognac, coffee, and the like did not go bad quickly and could be saved for the right moment. Unlike other products, such as *kolbasa* or smoked fish, chocolate and coffee could always be part of having "tea," the most common kind of table socializing. In the absence of shortage as a structuring force in suggesting to a gift giver what "everyone wanted," it was important that standardized gift choices were related to basic aspects of sociability. These were understood to be more or less shared, predictable, and regular; thus one did not expect that anyone would let a box of candy sit to rot or would not bring out the extra bottle of cognac on a special occasion with friends. In short, such gifts were unlikely to be judged superfluous or to be met with displeasure. Some informants noted that doctors seemed to be of the same socioeconomic stratum (layer, *sloi*) as teachers, surviving with about the same financial means, inhabiting similar social milieus; this offered teachers extra assurance that norms of sociability would be shared among them. By the same token, the fact that such exchanges were so common among teachers and doctors undoubtedly contributed to the participants' sense of their being part of the same social milieu or "layer," that is, as sharing certain problems and sensibilities.

Some of the specific items most commonly mentioned as favored gifts can be contrasted to more mundane analogues that served similar purposes in daily life but were less festive or special. Coffee was a habit for many, but tea is the archetypical Russian day-to-day beverage; though nicely packaged teas were sometimes given as gifts, for example by pupils to teachers, coffee was much more frequently mentioned as a gift item. One teacher told me that his family rarely bought coffee, because his sister, a doctor and frequent coffee drinker, received so much from her patients (though it was unclear to what extent they knew of her consumption habits). Though fruit teas and black Lipton tea in sachets were now available in Russia and preferred by some, no one seemed to complain about the basic, loose black tea leaves that could be purchased in inexpensive paper boxes. By contrast, a jar of "good" instant coffee such as Nescafé or Tchibo was rather expensive. Vodka was a staple of family celebrations but was not so appropriate as a gift to a doctor as, for example, a bottle of French cognac, which was more expensive and presumably outside the ordinary products one might buy for one's own family. And though cookies or individual pastries were fully appropriate as offerings to one's host and her "table," thank-you gifts required the more festive appearance—as well as easy transportability and storability—of nicely wrapped chocolate bars or boxes of chocolate candy. The latter, though not necessarily much more expensive than a cake or other treat one might bring *v gosti,* were ideally suited to presentation as gifts. Packagings carried images of local and national culture (Pushkin, the

Saint Petersburg–based national naval fleet) or suggested refined settings for sociability and consumption (such as a photo of a fancy table setting for tea service). Some referenced the very situation of holiday gift giving and offers of good wishes and congratulations, representing, for example, a floral bouquet accompanied by the inscription *"Pozdravliaiu!"* (Congratulations!)—a greeting that can pertain to any holiday, as in "I congratulate you on your birthday." In short, the symbolic value of chocolates, cognac, and similar gifts was not arbitrary but indexical, referring to familiar contexts of sociability and helping to produce the gift encounter as akin to these (figures 6.3 and 6.4).

These observations can enrich an anthropological understanding of gifts' potential significance in the social imagination. Without a doubt, gifts have been part of people's strategies for getting things that they need and want, and which they might not get otherwise. In late-1990s Saint Petersburg, attentive health care and favorable treatment from a child's schoolteacher often could not be purchased outright; rather, they might depend on the shared understanding that a relationship existed between doctor and patient, or teacher and parent. "Signs of attention" can be analyzed in terms of the misrecognition through which participants in these exchanges described their

Figure 6.3. At home, the table is set for a small birthday celebration. Photograph by the author.

Figure 6.4. The celebration concludes with tea, cakes, and assorted chocolates. Photograph by the author.

"disinterested" behavior. Yet there was also a particular form of *recognition* instantiated and performed in these transactions: not only a recognition of "good work" but also a recognition of the good terms on which the relationship had been conducted thus far; and finally, a recognition of social commonality, which was expressed in the gift choices themselves. This recognizable commonality had to do with the relatively private worlds in which people consumed chocolate and cognac with friends and family, realms one did not necessarily witness if the recipient was not a close acquaintance but rather were assumed to exist. The social body recognized (and constructed) through such exchanges was something less abstract than "the general public" or "Russians"; yet it frequently went beyond one's intimate circle of friends, and it necessarily extended beyond one's own professional group.

If gifts serve as "signs of attention," we can think about this as "attention" to and recognition of a person: not as a fully individuated person with idiosyncratic likes and dislikes—the kind of person for whom one would desire and have the appropriate knowledge to choose a highly individualized gift—but at least as more human (or perhaps, more fully *social*) than the indifferent bureaucrat or service provider who bears only a public face.[16] The recipient, in other words, is "recognized" as a meaningfully social person who has dealt with one personally and well, whom one may never get to know much better but who has made herself known as a valuable social actor. Gifts of chocolate and cognac draw extra attention, sometimes implicitly, to the recipient as a social being who as well as providing skilled and amiable service drinks tea with family and friends. With the gift, the giver also expresses her *own* social value through her appropriate "attentiveness" to the social relations in which they have engaged.

In so doing, it can be said that she also encounters—or constructs—a particular dimension of her social world, made up of potentially likeminded and like-moraled individuals connected to one another through webs of mutual help and respect. The "neutrality" of the goods chosen as gifts suggests that, despite an explicit intention to signal personal attention and good feeling, this kind of networking helps to create for participants the sense of something like an urban public in a slightly more generic and abstractable sense: a realm, ideally, governed by the morality of sincere interpersonal relations and mindful of how people are situated in contexts of sociability. Rooted in the Soviet experience of confrontations with and manipulations of bureaucratic structures and systems of distribution, this social stance has remained morally persuasive as well as practically expedient in some arenas. It will remain to be seen, as years pass, how this public, as imagined from the perspective of teachers and others of their social milieu, may accommodate itself to the market relations emerging since the 1990s.

"Neutral" Gifts and the Worlds They Create

If we can assume, for the moment, that socioeconomic differentiation and inequality will continue to increase in urban Russia and that new commodity markets will continue to expand, what role will the exchange relations described in this chapter play? Will items such as boxes of chocolate, cans of coffee, and flowers persist as anchors of a shared social ground and perceived consumer commonality, at least among some sectors of society? Might it become increasingly difficult for the relevant actors to discern what is "needed" by the recipient? Now that cash has become a scarcer and more important resource than it was in the past, to what extent is the need for such

16. For a related analysis of the social significance of exchange relationships in the realm of medical treatment, see Rivkin-Fish 1997, 2005.

gifts itself at issue? It has already been suggested that in certain spheres of Russian life today (most notably, business), prices are named and cash payments are beginning to be offered where, just a few years ago, gift exchanges and/or favors of access would have been expected (Ledeneva 1998; Rivkin-Fish 2000).

Some Saint Petersburg teachers expressed dissatisfaction about wealthy parents who presumed that because they had become contributing "sponsors" of a school, they were at liberty to criticize and control teachers' work. According to a similar logic, teachers (among others) tended to speak negatively of the city's new private schools where, it was believed, wealthy parents paid so that their children would receive high grades, while no one particularly attended to standards of children's education. As state-employed, qualified professionals who felt that they still deserved a measure of respect and authority in society, teachers resented—even as they recognized the practical need for—parents' cash interventions in the school system. Conversely, I heard no particular objection to the idea of selling one's services to other individuals at an hourly rate; many teachers gave private lessons, and though they complained of overwork, they appreciated the extra income tutoring brought. But pupils' parents, including and perhaps especially those whose children took private lessons, gave their teachers gifts for holidays throughout the year.

In short, gifts and the relationships they established were still understood in the late 1990s to be desirable and necessary, even in situations where people were able, willing, and in fact did pay in cash for privileged access and certain services rendered. At the same time, interactions between privately wealthy individuals and representatives of state institutions gave rise to disquieting uncertainties, for teachers at least, as to how (and by whom) terms of exchange would be set. How will their greater "gifts"—the bases of social value (education, culturedness) upon which they judge their own personhood—be appreciated (or depreciated) as time goes by? That is, according to what logic(s) will the value of individuals and their relationships be appraised?

Russian gift practices will continue to offer critical insights into people's positionings vis-à-vis shifting structures of access to wealth, commodities, and authority, because these gifts are prime examples of how material things can hold meaning for and draw connections between a variety of practices and knowledges (economy, friendship, ritual) that all too often are perceived as discrete and easily separable realms. As Mauss insisted in his classic essay:

> It is only by considering [gift systems] as wholes that we have been able to see their essence, their operation and their living aspect, and to catch the fleeting moment when the society and its members take emotional stock of themselves and their situation as regards others. (Mauss 1967, 77–78)

In other words, the care with which things are exchanged is part of the same process through which social actors assess selves and self-worth—their own and others'—over time. In a situation of rapid economic and social change, such "fleeting moments" are particularly examined and are particularly revealing of an emergent social world.

Saint Petersburg teachers, like most everyone else in postsocialist Russia, must address everyday needs, solve logistical problems, and allot scarce resources, and they seek the information that will enable them to act in ways that feel both profitable and honorable. The categories and judgments according to which individuals, families, and networks of friends and acquaintances fulfill these material and emotional interests will reflect and, in turn, generate the shifting moral foundations of Russia's socioeconomy. As Russia continues into the twenty-first century, what principles will be articulated to justify market and exchange relations—not just as means to fulfill tangible, concrete ends but also as ways of recognizing selves and others as the constituents of something like a new society, connected by rewoven webs of obligation and power?

Chapter 7

A More "Normal" Future?

The individuals whose stories have been told here hold little in the way of economic resources or political influence. In that sense, it can be said that the past few decades' rapid transformations of state and market have been imposed upon them, giving them little choice but to adapt in response. At a closer look, however, they have been engaged in a process far more active than simple adaptation. We have seen how, in self-conscious and outspoken as well as implicit and tentative ways, the teachers were interrogating relationships among consumers and reframing the questions one needed to ask about goods, persons, and populations to compare and value them properly. For a recouping intelligentsia, the work of consumption also has been the work of researching value itself, so that they may stake educated claims in the nation's future. Judgments about value and social difference are acts of investment: not mere commentary from the sidelines, but small parts of a collective process through which social relations at large are being restructured and reimagined in post-Soviet Russia. Indeed, as I have said, these engagements are not just "personal"; their collective ramifications are far-reaching, because people's ways of either legitimating or challenging inequality help, in turn, either to cement or to undermine those structures in the long run.

To tell the story of postsocialist upheaval from the perspective of teachers—this group with such a tenuous hold on middle-classness—is also to clarify how the everyday expectations and moralities of Soviet life have overlapped with and informed contemporary experiences of privatized commerce and ideals of global consumer citizenship. This study of a post-Soviet, state-employed professional class has yielded a more ambiguous picture of reactions to marketization than those offered by previous ethno-

207

graphic accounts. Ries's 2002 study of urban entrepreneurs, for example, highlighted moral discourses dominated by stark and fatalistic cynicism, whereas Caldwell's (2004, 204) account of the elderly poor in a Moscow soup kitchen focused upon their continuing mobilization of familiar "ideals about social networks, collective responsibility, and cooperative action" they viewed as "authentically Russian." The Russian teachers portrayed in this book were neither given over to a seemingly amoral cynicism nor staunch defenders of a classically Russian collectivism. Rather, while they continued to be influenced by the expectations of social justice and rational redistribution raised by Soviet modernity (Kotkin 1995), these orientations came along with long-standing desires to participate as consumers equally entitled to the perks of "civilization" as their neighbors to the west—an attitude *also* linked to the goals and assumptions of the Soviet project. Indeed, these impulses toward both social justice and consumerist plenty are not entirely contradictory to one another (Patico 2005). Both have been shaped by Soviet social and discursive formations, and both necessarily have taken on new significance in the 1990s and 2000s.

At the end of the twentieth century, the logic that framed the Saint Petersburg teachers' evaluations of the fruits of marketization—from imported food products to New Russian "sit-at-home" wives, and, most poignantly, their own personal and professional prospects—could be stated this way: that worthy, cultured subjects deserved, and ideally were recognizable by, their similarly civilized consumption. In the late 1990s, this logic, in many ways resonant with the experiences and prevailing rhetorics of Soviet life, did not always represent a true set of expectations so much as a set of ideals—and a critical stance toward the contemporary socioeconomy that violated it. Those violations had inspired angry resentment and the sense that things had gone very wrong in a systemic way. At the same time, insofar as one's personal civilization was supposed to be visible through one's appropriately civilized consumption, it seemed impossible for teachers not to feel personally implicated in their own relative poverty. A lack of consumer access reflected negatively upon their capacities to contribute meaningfully to society and to have those contributions recognized by others (or even themselves).

In fact, in the midst of the 1998–99 crisis, it was clear that by comparison with the outraged litanies more widespread in the late 1980s and early 1990s (Ries 1997), the questions teachers were raising from day to day were relatively open-ended. They left room for systemic critiques of Russia's contemporary socioeconomy but also for occasional *self*-indictments to explain nagging problems and inequalities. As representatives of a highly educated, poorly paid contingent of culture workers, teachers spoke assuredly about the sins and inadequacies of New Russians and their wives. But now and again, they showed that it was also conceivable that one's inability to live comfortably in the New Russia could be due in part to one's *own* shortcomings and failures. For where moral legitimacy and material respectability were assumed (or at least hoped) to be organically linked, people could account variously for disjunctures in the proper way of things. Was it because society was failing us, devaluing that which should be valued? Or were we less worthy than we had thought ourselves to be? Though it is the former attitude—litanies more consonant with notions of the Russian *narod*'s endless suffering—that has been most recorded in the ethnographic literature, the stories recounted in this book show how *both* interpretive moves were being made. Indeed, such self-interrogation is part of what has made post-Soviet transformation so personally unsettling, in such emotionally charged and embodied ways.

In 1994, Ries observed a "growing sense of isolation in . . . private struggles" among her acquaintances in Moscow, as compared with the shared experience and populist solidarity more prominent in the conversations of the late 1980s and early 1990s (Ries 1997, 162). I saw a similar and intensified sort of isolation, introspection, and mulling over of individual problems and solutions during the financial crisis of 1998–99—for example, in Lidia's rhetorical question about how effectively friends could really help one another now, given that the neighbors could hardly pay one's rent; in Larisa's conflicted consideration of a new job scheme and its moral delicacy; and in Olga's melancholy and her strained hope that she was "still a woman in her soul" despite lacking the money to buy stylish clothes and good cosmetics. Such moments of self-doubt and small efforts to rethink daily strategies suggested that the teachers were, at least at some moments, open to the idea that individuals were personally responsible for their own financial success and, correspondingly, their capacity to consume respectably; and that their own internal culturedness and personal integrity, and the respect of their peers, could not be counted upon to count toward material respectability in the new Russia. Something more or other than what they perceived as meaningful contributions to society seemed to be necessary. Still, this was not usually seen as a "normal" or acceptable state of things.

Consumption, Inequality, and Value in 2003

When I returned to Saint Petersburg in 2003, I was struck immediately by certain visible and perhaps, in themselves, superficial changes in city life. Over the course of three and a half years, scores of cafes had sprouted all over the city, even in the less touristy areas. They represented a breed of establishment that had scarcely existed before, a Starbucks-type fast-food-meets-European-cafe (figure 7.1). Well frequented by all kinds of people, especially college students, they provided one of the most tangible signs of economic recovery. And though a few years before only the New Russians had distinguished themselves by having loud public conversations on cellphones, the ringing of "mobiles" (*mobil'nye*), or "horns" (*trubki*) as they have been dubbed affectionately, now punctuated the rituals of urban existence from cafe to classroom.

When I explained to teachers and other friends and acquaintances that I had returned to see how the general situation had changed during my absence, there was a standard and usually immediate answer: "Nothing has changed, everything is the same." This was sometimes followed by a comment along the lines of "Things were difficult [or expensive] then, and they're difficult [or expensive] now." When I reminded them that the year I had lived and worked in Saint Petersburg had been the one immediately following the financial crisis of 1998–99, some acknowledged that the economy seemed to be more stable now and that, in this regard at least, things might be a little better. But though salaries in rubles were at least twice what they had been in 1998–99, prices had continued to rise, leading one woman to assure me that "we lived better before the crisis than now." When they talked about low salaries and high taxes, about the new law that required annual car insurance almost as costly as some people's cars, or about the lack of public toilets at Saint Petersburg's massive 300th birthday celebration downtown, people still decried the dysfunction of Russia, using epithets such as *dur dom* (roughly, "looney bin"). "Russia was never up to standard [*standartnaia strana*]," a visiting Muscovite told me as he complained that, like Saint Petersburg, even Moscow still had no good Chinese restaurants.

Yet with the crisis behind them, the bitter jokes about living in Africa and half-ironic references to Russia's utter lack of civilization had quieted. And as I walked up and down the aisles with Larisa at Lenta, one of Saint Petersburg's new "hypermarkets," I could not resist the impression that something, somehow really had gotten easier or at least more comfortable for my

Figure 7.1. A new coffee franchise in downtown Saint Petersburg, 2003. Photograph by the author.

friends (despite my own pang of nostalgia for the cramped spaces and contrary cashiers of Soviet-style shops). Lenta and other new stores like it approximated America's suburban supermarkets and warehouse discount clubs—a far cry from the smaller twenty-four-hour shops that called themselves *supermarkety* in the late 1990s. As Larisa pushed her shopping cart in front of her and thoughtfully examined the goods stocked there, I was reminded of Olga's conviction in 1999 that certainly, given the choice, she would have preferred to shop at an indoor supermarket where she could put what she wanted in her basket "culturedly" and be on her way, rather than wading through crowds and dusty stalls and dealing with putatively wily merchants at the outdoor *rynok*. Though her family was still struggling financially, with Ivan working multiple jobs to make ends meet, Larisa seemed to be living out such a long-desired improvement.

If there is, indeed, some sense of dignity to be found through shopping at Lenta and other new stores like it, it seems to derive from the fact that these outlets are fairly "democratic"—that is, broadly accessible, appropriate, or versatile, as I heard Russian friends appropriate the political term—in clear contrast to the few large, expensive, and sparsely populated Scandinavian supermarkets that had been on the local scene since the mid-1990s.

"Everyone has [his or her] favorite one now," Larisa's daughter explained. From an increased range of options in price and style, one could identify a more or less desirable and attainable niche. Families must have cars to take full advantage of Lenta's abundance, but prices there are comparatively low and its foods and housewares themselves include much that is standard, domestically produced fare—not delicacies for elites—all in a convenient and more "Western" setting. Significantly, credit plans have become available once again for big-ticket items like home appliances. In short, though salaries still as meager as $100 a month provided teachers with little cause to proclaim tangible improvement or comfort in 2003, a modicum of stability did, at least for the moment, seem to be allowing for an atmosphere of relative predictability, normalcy, and consumer participation.

This might also help explain why, despite people's continuing sense of inequity and injustice in distributions of wealth, the image of the "New Russian" was already less salient. No one told those jokes anymore, teachers and others told me in 2003. (In fact, teacher Dima claimed that no new jokes had replaced them; for a time, he said, there had been a lot of jokes about the "GAI"—Russia's notoriously corrupt traffic police—but now no one seemed to be telling any jokes in particular.) Those with whom I spoke that summer were unanimous in saying that the very notion of the "New Russian" as a social type had become a thing of the past. The men who had been completely ignorant but had earned a lot of money all the same (through less than honorable means) were no longer visible to them on the social landscape. "The raspberry-colored jackets are gone," Kseniia admitted. As Liliia explained it, those people had either adjusted to life here—she emphasized that some of them had come to Saint Petersburg from provincial towns and southern republics to make their fortunes—or had ultimately failed and departed.

Even those teachers I had known in 1998–99 to be most skeptical about the morality of commerce now indicated that it had become more possible to *earn* money through one's own active and respectable work. Local industry had picked up; formerly shut-down factories had reopened, and a look in any grocery store showed that a far greater proportion of the foods for sale were now domestically and locally produced. This, too, helped explain the disappearance of "New Russians," according to Liza; there were fewer people just buying and selling (you cannot make money that way forever without producing anything, Liza reasoned), so more of them were earning money in honest ways (*chestno*). It was no longer fashionable to be a *bandit.* "Now there's an idea of the *kommersant* [businessman], a *delevoi chelovek* [businesslike person]—a positive view," Liliia affirmed. And, Liza added, people had simply gotten better used to the polarization of wealth that had been so painful and difficult to accept initially.

What was more, the teachers agreed that others around them were now properly recognizing the importance of education as a key foundation for a good career. Even wealthy parents understood this and did everything they could to provide their children with a good education, yet in the teachers' estimation they were still so busy working that they had too little time to spend actually raising (*vospitat'*) their children. Babysitters and nannies had become more popular, though they were not necessarily qualified for the work but rather were "*sluchainye liudi*" (random people). Children were coming to the first grade "wild," without proper manners or any idea of how to behave in school, I was told. The eyes of the energetic, poised, and typically positive teacher and administrator Svetlana welled up with tears as she admitted that "working as a teacher now is very difficult, . . . very difficult." The low pay they received made it understandable, though discouraging, that fewer and fewer of the teachers who worked under her supervision appeared to her truly committed to their work, she said, and that none of her graduating students were planning to become teachers. None of them were headed even for the philological department at the prestigious State University in Saint Petersburg, once a logical choice for top students at this English specialization school. "Those aren't money professions," Svetlana quoted one talented young man who had briefly considered such a path before opting instead for a law degree. She felt that "to be able to raise a worthy Russian citizen, a teacher should be lifted up," but clearly she believed that this was far from the case.

Thus the financial strains and social cleavages I had observed in 1998–99 persisted. And yet, if in 1998–99 there had been a sharp sense among teachers that the most undeserving Russians were reaping material rewards unjustly and not giving cultural authorities like them their due share of respect, in 2003 the same teachers now seemed to be finding somewhat less cause for suspicion and offense in the behavior of others and were more willing to grant that many of their compatriots were earning, as opposed to stealing, good money. Though opportunities for economic mobility unquestionably had expanded after the 1998 crisis, and teachers were in ideal positions to observe some of these processes through their interaction with so many families in the schools, their shifting commentaries about Russian society also need to be acknowledged as a key social practice in itself. For these were not simple observations of new realities but new styles of perceiving and conceptualizing the possibilities and pitfalls of the marketplace.

That is, whereas by 2003 teachers said they had observed more people "working hard" and fewer "stealing" (or, as Larisa had put it in 1999, transgressing "spiritual rules"), these observations have as much to do with interpretation as with changes in activities; in other words, the speakers had become a bit more willing to see "work" in the commercial transactions and businesses where they might once have seen primarily "theft" and deception. If in 1998–99, Larisa, Ivan, and their children had debated whether a member of their own extended family was a New Russian and decided that she was not—in part because her success was based upon what they knew to be her true effort and expertise (chapter 2)—by 2003, discussions with the N. family and their colleagues about how things had changed suggested that such benefit of the doubt was being extended more widely these days. The teachers seemed to meet the idea that transcendent values such as culturedness and education did not translate directly into material security more and more with market-wise resignation rather than with the righteous resentment and ironic humor of the 1990s. Liza's description of how the *kommersant* had replaced the bandit hinted that commercial success was increasingly open to interpretation as, in itself, a legitimate reflection of one's personal merit and meaningful labor. What are the implications of such a shift?

As even the fallen intelligentsia has gained some faith that the Russian market is not entirely at odds with useful work and other measures of value and humanity, they also might find "culturedness" in the familiar sense to be a less and less persuasive proof of their own entitlement to material security. In this shifting logic of value, the assumption that social worth and personal integrity take material form in respectable consumerism appears to have weakened; at the same time, it has become more possible to interpret private enterprise as a locus of such social value—bringing the logic slightly closer to something like a Protestant Ethic. To raise another comparison: If culturedness is losing its capacity to convince teachers of their own deservingness, such professionals may be less and less likely to attribute ongoing and emergent hardships to structural factors larger than themselves, and more likely—like the laid-off American engineers interviewed by Newman (1988)—to place the blame upon the deficiencies of their own characters or actions. Could this be why Dima had observed that the joke-as-social-critique seemed to be in decline as a genre?

In short, by 2003, with the latest economic crisis past, the teachers' most indignant discourses about post-Soviet society's violation of a fundamental logic of value had dissipated, pointing to their heightened sense of predictability and normalcy. Yet this apparent easing of tensions can be understood, too, as a diminishment of the rhetorical resources whereby teachers had managed, just a few years earlier, to produce such biting critiques of economic inequality.

With these observations, I do not suggest that Russia is moving headlong, in a linear and entirely predictable fashion, toward Western-style, capitalist-driven individualism in its archetypal and idealized sense, nor that the teachers suddenly have been duped into accepting full blame for the difficulties they have faced in the wake of the Soviet Union's collapse. For one thing, as a Saint Petersburg friend of mine was fond of saying, one never knew when the next *kriziz* was coming, and it could be right around the corner—bringing with it, no doubt, new occasions for complaint and styles of interpretation. More to the point, as Adrie Kusserow (2004) observes in an ethnography of education and child rearing in the United States, "American individualism" is a mythologized master term that masks more than it reveals about what is in fact a range of assumptions, ideologies, and styles of interaction that vary greatly according to class position and locality—even within the presumed global hub of market-led individualism, the United States (see also Carrier 1995, 1997). Extending this observation to the case at hand, to conclude that Russia in 2003 was a bit more individualistic or culturally capitalistic than it had been a few years before is valid to the extent that we can hold these terms a bit at arm's length, continuing to define and locate the sentiments they are meant to describe within the specificity of twentieth-century and twenty-first-century Russian histories and class positionings. Today's deliberations about how individuals are (and should be) valued in the capitalist marketplace continue to be contextualized and, to some degree, challenged by comparisons with the remembered experiences of socialism and in light of ongoing social conflicts, such as those that play out between teachers and wealthy parents at school.

By the same token, the teachers' stories have illustrated how misleading it would be to say that Russian consumers have approached post-Soviet transformation from timelessly Russian or even Soviet, collectivist, anti-market moral perspectives. Rather, historically fleeting interpretive formations such as New Russian stereotypes and Africa jokes reveal how value logics—ideas about how social contributions and moral legitimacy are causally and organically related to the possession of material things—are themselves not only shifting with time but also ambivalent and flexible, usually cutting at least two ways. (Did ownership of a Mercedes make someone worthy of vilification, in the teachers' eyes? Or were the teachers also questioning their *own* value to a society that had not seen fit to bestow a Mercedes upon *them?* Yes, and yes.) The culture of capitalism emerging in today's Russia should not be seen as a battle won for the capitalist West, nor lost in terms of more local visions of social justice, but rather viewed as a site of ongoing struggle to define meanings, garner resources, and achieve self-respect.

What is clear is that ideas about what is possible and pragmatic in one's own life, and about what is morally legitimate or suspect, have transformed noticeably as moods have shifted away from ironic critique and toward unsurprised acceptance of the security lost and shame endured in the wake of the Soviet system's collapse. The advent of more affordable Western-style supermarkets might be a welcome development for Saint Petersburg schoolteachers and others who, like them, are tenuously "middle class"; but if life looks a bit more normal for them today, this is connected not only with consumer improvements but also with a process of *normalization* that has dulled their earlier lines of social critique and made them less convincing. Through this gradual shift in sensibilities, widened socioeconomic inequalities are seen more and more as inevitable, expected, and logical—and perhaps, with time, even as natural and legitimate.

Working Onward

When I called Olga to wish her a happy New Year's Day in 2001, she informed me that she had started a new job, "the kind I've been dreaming about." Through an acquaintance, she had found a position as a service operator for a cellphone company. She worked long hours and the work was not stimulating, but her salary had increased enough that she was finally able to buy her own room, at least, in a communal apartment. Two years later, she was becoming tired of the routine and assured me that she had little time or energy these days for any kind of "refined life" (*svetskaia zhizn'*); she got home late in the evenings and did not feel like going to the theater or anywhere else, even on her days off. Yet in the meantime she had remarried and had managed, with her husband, to buy an entire new apartment as well as a dacha in the suburbs of Saint Petersburg. Her now eighteen-year-old daughter was pursuing higher education in tourism management. Optimistic and forward looking as always, at forty Olga was planning to study for a master's degree in economics.

She was not alone in moving on from teaching. A few of the teachers in the two collectives had left for private schools in pursuit of higher salaries. Two young women had gotten married and had babies, and stayed home for some time with their children. One teacher had moved on to an administrative position in a nearby scientific institute, though for similarly low pay. Larisa continued on much as before, having seriously considered the idea of starting a day care center with a colleague. After carefully planning budgets and calculating what they would have to pay in taxes and salaries, they had realized that the enterprise simply would never be profitable and had given up the dream. Meanwhile, now-retired teacher Veronika had become a nanny for the children of several wealthy families, and longtime retiree Tatiana had begun selling Tupperware—a hobby that did not seem to be making her much extra money but was a source of pleasure and occasional free Tupperware gifts. Liliia, Liza, and many others continued to live with the satisfactions and disappointments of post-Soviet education. Some, especially the older, career teachers, felt they had no place else to turn; and some would not really have wanted to work anywhere else, despite everything.

References

Abu-Lughod, Lila. 1990. The Romance of Resistance: Tracing Transformations of Power through Bedouin Women. *American Ethnologist* 17, no. 1: 41–55.

———. 1993a. Editorial Comment: On Screening Politics in a World of Nations. *Public Culture* 5: 465–67.

———. 1993b. Finding a Place for Islam: Egyptian Television Serials and the National Interest. *Public Culture* 5: 493–513.

———. 1995. The Objects of Soap Opera: Egyptian Television and the Cultural Politics of Modernity. In *Worlds Apart: Modernity through the Prism of the Local,* ed. Daniel Miller. New York: Routledge.

Alapuro, Risto. 1998. Reflections on Social Networks and Collective Action in Russia. Paper prepared for the conference "Education and Civic Culture in Post-Communist Societies," London, November 13–15.

Anderson, Benedict. 1991. *Imagined Communities.* New York: Verso.

Andrusz, G. D. 1980. Housing Ideals, Structural Constraints and the Emancipation of Women. In *Home, School and Leisure in the Soviet Union,* ed. Jenny Brine, Maureen Perrie, and Andrew Sutton. Boston: George Allen and Unwin.

Appadurai, Arjun. 1981. Gastro-Politics in Hindu South Asia. *American Ethnologist* 8, no. 3: 494–511.

———. 1986. Introduction: Commodities and the Politics of Value. In *The Social Life of Things: Commodities in Cultural Perspective,* ed. Arjun Appadurai. New York: Cambridge University Press.

———. 1988. How to Make a National Cuisine: Cookbooks in Contemporary India. *Comparative Studies in Society and History* 30, no. 1: 3–24.

———. 1990. Disjuncture and Difference in the Global Cultural Economy. *Public Culture* 2, no. 2: 1–24.

Appadurai, Arjun, and Carol Breckenridge. 1988. Why Public Culture? *Public Culture* 1, no. 1: 5–9.

Ashwin, Sarah. 2000. Introduction: Gender, State, and Society in Soviet and Post-Soviet Russia. In *Gender, State, and Society in Soviet and Post-Soviet Russia,* ed. Sarah Ashwin. New York: Routledge.

Ashwin, Sarah, and Elaine Bowers. 1997. Do Russian Women Want to Work? In *Post-*

Soviet Women: From the Baltic to Central Asia, ed. Mary Buckley. New York: Cambridge University Press.

Attwood, Lynne. 1990. *The New Soviet Man and Woman: Sex Role Socialization in the USSR.* Bloomington: Indiana University Press.

———. 1999. *Creating the New Soviet Woman: Women's Magazines as Engineers of Female Identity, 1922–1953.* New York: St. Martin's Press.

Azhgikhina, Nadezhda, and Helena Goscilo. 1996. Getting under Their Skin: The Beauty Salon in Russian Women's Lives. In *Russia-Women-Culture,* ed. Helena Goscilo and Beth Holmgren. Bloomington: Indiana University Press.

Balzer, Harley. 1998. Russia's Middle Classes. *Post-Soviet Affairs* 14, no. 2: 165–86.

Baranskaya, Natalya. 1989. Just Another Week (*Nedelya kak Nedelya*), ed. Lora Paperno, Natalie Roklina and Richard Leed. Columbus, Ohio: Slavica Publishers. Orig. pub. 1969.

Barth, Fredrik. 1998. *Ethnic Groups and Boundaries: The Social Organization of Culture Difference.* Prospect Heights, Ill.: Waveland Press.

Barthes, Roland. 1997. Toward a Psychosociology of Contemporary Food Consumption. In *Food and Culture: A Reader,* ed. Carole Counihan and Penny van Esterick. New York: Routledge.

Bassin, Mark. 1999. Asia. In *The Cambridge Companion to Modern Russian Culture,* ed. Nicholas Rzhevsky. New York: Cambridge University Press.

Baudrillard, Jean. 1988. *Selected Writings,* ed. Mark Poster. Stanford, Calif.: Stanford University Press.

Berdahl, Daphne. 1999. *Where the World Ended: Re-unification and Identity in the German Borderland.* Berkeley: University of California Press.

Berman, Marshall. 1982. *All That Is Solid Melts into Air: The Experience of Modernity.* New York: Simon & Schuster.

Bezgodov, A., and N. Sokolov. 1999. *Biznes v Zerkale Svobodnykh Vyskazyvanii Peterburzhtsev. "Teleskop": Nabliudeniia za Povsednevnoi Zhizniu Peterburzhtev.* No. 1: 19–25.

Blakely, Allison. 1986. *Russia and the Negro: Blacks in Russian History and Thought.* Washington, D.C.: Howard University Press.

Borenstein, Eliot. 1999 Public Offerings: MMM and the Marketing of Melodrama. In *Consuming Russia: Popular Culture, Sex, and Society since Gorbachev.* Durham, N.C.: Duke University Press.

Bourdieu, Pierre. 1977. *Outline of a Theory of Practice,* trans. Richard Nice. New York: Cambridge University Press.

———. 1984. *Distinction: A Social Critique of the Judgment of Taste,* trans. Richard Nice. Cambridge, Mass.: Harvard University Press.

———. 1990. *The Logic of Practice,* trans. Richard Nice. Stanford, Calif.: Stanford University Press.

———. 1996. The Work of Time. In *The Gift: An Interdisciplinary Perspective,* ed. Aafke E. Komter. Amsterdam: Amsterdam University Press.

Bourdieu, Pierre, and Loic J. D. Wacquant. 1992. *An Invitation to Reflexive Sociology.* Chicago: University of Chicago Press.

Boym, Svetlana. 1994. *Common Places: Mythologies of Everyday Life in Russia.* Cambridge, Mass.: Harvard University Press.

Bridger, Sue, Rebecca Kay, and Kathryn Pinnick. 1996. *No More Heroines? Russia, Women and the Market.* New York: Routledge.

Bruno, Marta. 1997. Women and the Culture of Entrepreneurship. In *Post-Soviet Women: From the Baltic to Central Asia,* ed. Mary Buckley. New York: Cambridge University Press.

Buchli, Victor. 1999. *An Archaeology of Socialism.* New York: Berg.

Burawoy, Michael, and Katherine Verdery. 1999. Introduction. In *Uncertain Transition: Ethnographies of Change in the Postsocialist World,* ed. M. Burawoy and K. Verdery. Lanham, Md.: Rowman & Littlefield.

Burda Woman. 1999. Solnechnyi azart v kazhdoi kaple. May, 24–25.

Burke, Timothy. 1996. *Lifebuoy Men, Lux Women: Commodification, Consumption, and Cleanliness in Modern Zimbabwe.* Durham, N.C.: Duke University Press.

Caldwell, Melissa. 2002. The Taste of Nationalism: Food Politics in Postsocialist Moscow. *Ethnos* 67, no. 3: 295–319.

———. 2004. *Not by Bread Alone: Social Support in the New Russia.* Berkeley: University of California Press.

Campbell, Colin. 1995. The Sociology of Consumption. In *Acknowledging Consumption: A Review of New Studies,* ed. Daniel Miller. New York: Routledge.

Carrier, James. 1997. Introduction. In *Meanings of the Market: The Free Market in Western Culture,* ed. J. Carrier. New York: Berg.

———, ed. 1995. *Occidentalism: Images of the West.* New York: Oxford University Press.

Chakrabarty, Dipesh. 1997. The Difference-Deferral of a Colonial Modernity. In *Tensions of Empire: Colonial Cultures in a Bourgeois World,* ed. Frederick Cooper and Ann Laura Stoler. Berkeley: University of California Press.

Chatterjee, Partha. 1989. Colonialism, Nationalism, and Colonized Women: The Contest in India. *American Ethnologist* 16, no. 4: 622–33.

Clark, Katerina. 1993. Not for Sale: The Russian/Soviet Intelligentsia, Prostitution, and the Paradox of Internal Colonization. In *Russian Culture in Transition: Selected Papers of the Working Group for the Study of Contemporary Culture, 1990–1991.* Stanford, Calif.: Stanford University Press.

———. 1995. *Petersburg: Crucible of Cultural Revolution.* Cambridge, Mass.: Harvard University Press.

Clements, Barbara Evans. 1991. Later Developments: Trends in Soviet Women's History, 1930 to the Present. In *Russia's Women: Accommodation, Resistance, Transformation,* ed. Barbara Evans Clements, Barbara Alpern Engel, and Christine D. Worobec. Berkeley: University of California Press.

Clements, Barbara Evans, Barbara Alpern Engel, and Christine D. Worobec, eds. 1991. *Russia's Women: Accommodation, Resistance, Transformation.* Berkeley: University of California Press.

Clifford, James. 1986. Introduction: Partial Truths. In *Writing Culture: The Poetics and Politics of Ethnography,* ed. James Clifford and George Marcus. Berkeley: University of California Press.

Collier, Jane, Michelle Rosaldo, and Sylvia Yanagisako. 1997. Is There a Family? New Anthropological Views. In *The Gender/Sexuality Reader: Culture, History, Political Economy,* ed. Roger N. Lancaster and Micaela di Leonardo. New York: Routledge.

Comaroff, Jean, and John Comaroff. 1990. Goodly Beasts, Beastly Goods: Cattle and Commodities in a South African Context. *American Ethnologist* 17, no. 2: 195–216.

———. 2001. Millennial Capitalism: First Thoughts on a Second Coming. In *Millen-*

nial Capitalism and the Culture of Neoliberalism, ed. J. Comaroff and J. Comaroff. Durham, N.C.: Duke University Press.

Condee, Nancy, and Vladimir Padunov. 1993. Makulakul'tura: Reprocessing Culture. In *Russian Culture in Transition: Selected Papers of the Working Group for the Study of Contemporary Russian Culture, 1990–1,* ed. Gregory Freidin. Stanford Slavic Studies 5. Stanford, Calif.: Stanford University Press.

———. 1995. The ABC of Russian Consumer Culture: Readings, Ratings, and Real Estate. In *Soviet Hieroglyphics,* ed. Nancy Condee. Bloomington: Indiana University Press.

Cook, Ian, and Philip Crang. 1996. The World on a Plate: Culinary Culture, Displacement and Geographical Knowledges. *Journal of Material Culture* 1, no. 2: 131–53.

Creed, Gerald. 1998. *Domesticating Revolution: From Socialist Reform to Ambivalent Transition in a Bulgarian Village.* University Park: Pennsylvania State University Press.

———. 1999. Deconstructing Socialism in Bulgaria. In *Uncertain Transition: Ethnographies of Change in the Postsocialist World,* ed. M. Burawoy and K. Verdery. Lanham, Md.: Rowman & Littlefield.

de Certeau, Michel. 1984. *The Practice of Everyday Life.* Berkeley: University of California Press.

Douglas, Mary. 1984. Standard Social Uses of Food: Introduction. In *Food in the Social Order: Studies of Food and Festivities in Three American Communities,* ed. Mary Douglas. New York: Russell Sage Foundation.

———. 1992a. *Purity and Danger: An Analysis of the Concepts of Pollution and Taboo.* New York: Routledge.

———. 1992b. Why Do People Want Goods? In *Understanding the Enterprise Culture: Themes in the Work of Mary Douglas,* ed. Shaun Hargreaves Heap and Angus Ross. Edinburgh: Edinburgh University Press.

———. 1997. Deciphering a Meal. In *Food and Culture: A Reader,* ed. Carole Counihan and Penny van Esterick. New York: Routledge.

Douglas, Mary, and Baron Isherwood. 1996. *The World of Goods: Towards an Anthropology of Consumption.* New York: Routledge. Orig. pub. 1979.

Draitser, Emil. 1998. *Taking Penguins to the Movies: Ethnic Humor in Russia.* Detroit: Wayne State University Press.

Dubrovina, I. V. 1989. *My zhivem sredi liudei: Kodeks povedeniia* (We live among people: A codex of behavior). Moscow: Politizdat.

Dunham, Vera. 1976. *In Stalin's Time: Middle-Class Values in Soviet Literature.* New York: Cambridge University Press.

Dunn, Elizabeth. 1999. Slick Salesmen and Simple People: Negotiated Capitalism in a Privatized Polisg Firm. In *Uncertain Transition: Ethnographies of Change in the Postsocialist World,* ed. M. Burawoy and K. Verdery. Lanham, Md.: Rowman & Littlefield.

———. 2004. *Privatizing Poland: Baby Food, Big Business, and the Remaking of Labor.* Ithaca, N.Y.: Cornell University Press.

Einhorn, Barbara. 1993. *Cinderella Goes to Market: Citizenship, Gender and Women's Movements in East Central Europe.* New York: Verso.

———. 1995. Ironies of History: Citizenship Issues in the New Market Economies of East Central Europe. In *Women and Market Societies: Crisis and Opportunity,* ed. Barbara Einhorn and Eileen Janes Yeo. Brookfield, Vt.: Edward Elgar.

Eiss, Paul K., and David Pedersen, eds. 2002a. *Cultural Anthropology* 17, no. 3. Special Issue on the Anthropology of Value.

———. 2002b. Introduction: Values of Value. *Cultural Anthropology* 17, no. 3: 283–90.

Elias, Norbert. 1978. *The Civilizing Process,* trans. Edmund Jephcott. New York: Urizen Books.

Engels, Friedrich. 1942. *The Origins of the Family, Private Property, and the State.* New York: International Publishers.

Epstein, Mikhail. 1995. *Na Granitsakh Kul'tur: Rossiiskoe- Amerikanskoe-Sovetskoe* (On the Boards [*sic*] of Cultures: Russian-American-Soviet). New York: Slovo Publishers.

Eremicheva, Galina. 1996. Articulating a Catastrophic Sense of Life. In *Women's Voices in Russia Today,* ed. Anna Rotkirch and Elina Haavio-Mannila. Brookfield, Vt.: Dartmouth Publishing Company.

Etienne, Mona, and Eleanor Leacock, eds. 1980. *Women and Colonization: Anthropological Perspectives.* New York: Praeger.

Farquhar, Judith. 1999. Technologies of Everyday Life: The Economy of Impotence in Reform. *Cultural Anthropology* 14, no. 2: 155–79.

Fedorov, Sergei. 1999. Moi khoroshii, moi liubimyi margarin. *Reklama-SHANS,* May 3, 41.

Fehervary, Krisztina. 2002. "American Kitchens," Luxury Bathrooms and the Search for a Normal Life in Post-Socialist Hungary. *Ethnos* 67 (forthcoming).

Fikes, Kesha, and Alaina Lemon. 2002. African Presence in Former Soviet Spaces. *Annual Review of Anthropology* 31: 497–524.

Fitzpatrick, Sheila. 1992. *The Cultural Front: Power and Culture in Revolutionary Russia.* Ithaca, N.Y.: Cornell University Press.

———. 1999. *Everyday Stalinism: Ordinary Life in Extraordinary Times—Soviet Russia in the 1930s.* New York: Oxford University Press.

Fitzpatrick, Sheila, Alexander Rabinowitch, and Richard Stites, eds. 1991. *Russia in the Era of NEP: Explorations in Soviet Society and Culture.* Bloomington: Indiana University Press.

Foster, Robert. 2002. *Materializing the Nation: Commodities, Consumption, and Media in Papua New Guinea.* Bloomington: Indiana University Press.

Friedl, Ernestine. 1967. The Position of Women: Appearance and Reality. *Anthropological Quarterly* 4, no. 3: 97–108.

———. 1986. The Position of Women: Appearance and Reality. In *Gender and Power in Rural Greece,* ed. Jill Dubisch. Princeton, N.J.: Princeton University Press.

Frykman, Jonas, and Orvar Lofgren. 1987. *Culture Builders: A Historical Anthropology of Middle-Class Life.* New Brunswick, N.J.: Rutgers University Press.

Funk, Nanette. 1993. Introduction: Women and Post-Communism. In *Gender Politics and Post-Communism: Reflections from Eastern Europe and the Former Soviet Union,* ed. Nanette Funk and Magda Mueller. New York: Routledge.

Funk, Nanette, and Magda Mueller, eds. 1993. *Gender Politics and Post-Communism: Reflections from Eastern Europe and the Former Soviet Union.* New York: Routledge.

Gal, Susan. 1994. Gender in the Post-Socialist Transition: The Abortion Debate in Hungary. *East European Politics and Societies* 8, no. 2: 256–86.

———. 2002. A Semiotics of the Public/Private Distinction. *Differences* 13, no. 1: 77–95.

Gal, Susan, and Gail Kligman. 2000. *The Politics of Gender after Socialism: A Comparative-Historical Essay.* Princeton, N.J.: Princeton University Press.

Gewertz, Deborah, and Frederick Errington. 1991. *Twisted Histories, Altered Contexts: Representing the Chambri in a World System.* New York: Cambridge University Press.

———. 1996. On PepsiCo and Piety in a Papua New Guinea "Modernity." *American Ethnologist* 23, no. 3: 476–93.

———. 1999. *Emerging Class in Papua New Guinea: The Telling of Difference.* New York: Cambridge University Press.

Gillette, Maris. 2000. *Between Mecca and Beijing: Modernization and Consumption among Urban Chinese Muslims.* Stanford, Calif.: Stanford University Press.

Gleason, Abbott. 1999. Ideological Structures. In *The Cambridge Companion to Modern Russian Culture,* ed. Nicholas Rzhevsky. New York: Cambridge University Press.

Goffman, Erving. 1955. On Face-Work: An Analysis of Ritual Elements in Social Interaction. *Psychiatry: Journal for the Study of Interpersonal Processes* 18: 213–31.

Golenkova, Z. T. 1998. Dinamika Sotsiostrukturnoi Transformatsii v Rossii. Sotsiologicheskoe *Issledovanie* 10: 77–84.

Goody, Jack. 1982. *Cooking, Cuisine, and Class: A Study in Comparative Sociology.* New York: Cambridge University Press.

Gorham, Michael. 2000. *Natsiia ili Snikerizatsiia?* Identity and Perversion in the Language Debates of Late and Post-Soviet Russia. *Russian Review* 59: 614–29.

Gosden, Chris, and Chantal Knowles. 2001. *Collecting Colonialism: Material Culture and Colonial Change.* New York: Berg.

Graeber, David. 2001. *Toward an Anthropology of Value: The False Coin of Our Own Dreams.* New York: Palgrave.

Grant, Bruce. 1995. *In the Soviet House of Culture: A Century of Perestroikas.* Princeton, N.J.: Princeton University Press.

Gray, Francine du Plessix. 1989. *Soviet Women: Walking the Tightrope.* New York: Doubleday.

Gregory, C. A. 1982. *Gifts and Commodities.* London: Academic Press.

Grossman, Gregory. 1977. The "Second Economy" of the USSR. *Problems of Communism* 26, no. 5: 25–40.

Gullestad, Marianne. 1984. *Kitchen-Table Society.* Oslo: Universitetsforlaget.

———. 1993. Home Decoration as Popular Culture. Constructing Homes, Genders, and Classes in Norway. In *Gendered Anthropology,* ed. Teresa del Valle. New York: Routledge.

Gupta, Akhil, and James Ferguson. 1990. Beyond "Culture": Space, Identity, and the Politics of Difference. *Cultural Anthropology* 7, no. 1: 6–23.

Hann, Chris. 1996. Introduction: Political Society and Civil Anthropology. In *Civil Society: Challenging Western Models,* ed. Chris Hann and Elizabeth Dunn. New York: Routledge.

Hannerz, Ulf. 1996. *Transnational Connections: Culture, People, Places.* New York: Routledge.

Herzfeld, Michael. 1996. *Cultural Intimacy: Social Poetics in the Nation-State.* New York: Routledge.

Hessler, Julie Marie. 1996. Culture of Shortages: A Social History of Soviet Trade, 1917–1953. PhD dissertation, Department of History, University of Chicago.

Holt, Alix. 1980. Domestic Labor and Soviet Society. In *Home, School and Leisure in the Soviet Union,* ed. Jenny Brine, Maureen Perrie, and Andrew Sutton. Boston: George Allen and Unwin.

Howes, David. 1996. Introduction: Commodities and Cultural Borders. In *Cross-Cultural Consumption: Global Markets, Local Realities,* ed. David Howes. New York: Routledge.

Humphrey, Caroline. 1995. Creating a Culture of Disillusionment: Consumption in Moscow, a Chronicle of Changing Times. In *Worlds Apart: Modernity through the Prism of the Local,* ed. Daniel Miller. New York: Routledge.

———. 1999. Traders, "Disorder," and Citizenship Regimes in Provincial Russia. In *Uncertain Transition: Ethnographies of Change in the Postsocialist World,* ed. M. Burawoy and K. Verdery. Lanham, Md.: Rowman & Littlefield.

———. 2002. *The Unmaking of Soviet Life: Everyday Economies after Socialism.* Ithaca, N.Y.: Cornell University Press.

Humphrey, Caroline, and Stephen Hugh-Jones. 1992. Introduction: Barter, Exchange and Value. In *Barter, Exchange and Value: An Anthropological Approach,* ed. Caroline Humphrey and Stephen Hugh-Jones. New York: Cambridge University Press.

Humphrey, Caroline, and Ruth Mandel. 2002. The Market in Everyday Life: Ethnographies of Postsocialism. In *Markets and Moralities: Ethnographies of Postsocialism,* ed. R. Mandl and C. Humphrey. New York: Berg.

Ignatjev, Yuri. 1996. Consumers Union Promotes Safe Food in St. Petersburg. *Central European Health and Environment Monitor* 4, no. 2: 4–5.

Inda, Jonathan Xavier, and Renato Rosaldo, eds. 2002. *The Anthropology of Globalization: A Reader.* Malden, Mass.: Blackwell.

Jaschok, Maria. 1995. On the Construction of Desire and Anxiety: Contestations over Female Nature and Identity in China's Modern Market Society. In *Women and Market Societies: Crisis and Opportunity,* ed. Barbara Einhorn and Eileen Janes Yeo. Brookfield, Vt.: Edward Elgar.

Jones, Anthony. 1991. Teachers in the Soviet Union. In *Professions and the State: Expertise and Autonomy in the Soviet Union and Eastern Europe,* ed. Anthony Jones. Philadelphia: Temple University Press.

Kay, Rebecca. 1997. Images of an Ideal Woman: Perceptions of Russian Womanhood through the Media, Education and Women's Own Eyes. In *Post-Soviet Women: From the Baltic to Central Asia,* ed. Mary Buckley. New York: Cambridge University Press.

Keane, Webb. 1998. *Signs of Recognition: Powers and Hazards of Representation in an Indonesian Society.* Berkeley: University of California Press.

———. 2001. Money Is No Object: Materiality, Desire, and Modernity in an Indonesian Society. In *The Empire of Things: Regimes of Value and Material Culture,* ed. Fred R. Myers. Santa Fe: School of American Research Press.

Kelly, Catriona. 1998a. Creating a Consumer: Advertising and Commercialization. In *Russian Cultural Studies: An Introduction,* ed. Catriona Kelly and David Shepherd. New York: Oxford University Press.

———. 1998b. Introduction: Iconoclasm and Commemorating the Past. In *Constructing Russian Culture in the Age of Revolution: 1881–1940,* ed. Catriona Kelly and David Shepherd. New York: Oxford University Press.

———. 1998c. The Retreat from Dogmatism: Populism under Khrushchev and Brezhnev. In *Russian Cultural Studies: An Introduction,* ed. Catriona Kelly and David Shepherd. New York: Oxford University Press.

————. 1999a. *Kul'turnost'* in the Soviet Union: Ideal and Reality. In *Reinterpreting Russia,* ed. Geoffrey Hosking and Robert Service. New York: Oxford University Press.

————. 1999b. Popular Culture. In *The Cambridge Companion to Modern Russian Culture,* ed. Nicholas Rzhevsky. New York: Cambridge University Press.

————. 2001. *Refining Russia: Advice Literature, Polite Culture, and Gender from Catherine to Yeltsin.* New York: Oxford University Press.

Kelly, Catriona, and Vadim Volkov. 1998. Directed Desires: *Kul'turnost'* and Consumption. *In Constructing Russian Culture in the Age of Revolution: 1881–1940,* ed. Catriona Kelly and David Shepherd. New York: Oxford University Press.

Khotkina, Zoya. 1994. Women in the Labour Market: Yesterday, Today and Tomorrow. In *Women in Russia: A New Era in Russian Feminism,* ed. Anastasia Posadskaya and others at the Moscow Gender Centre; trans. Kate Clark. New York: Verso.

Kiblitskaya, Marina. 2000a. "Once We Were Kings": Male Experiences of Loss of Status at Work in Post-Communist Russia. In *Gender, State and Society in Soviet and Post-Soviet Russia,* ed. Sarah Ashwin. New York: Routledge.

————. 2000b. Russia's Female Breadwinners: The Changing Subjective Experience. In *Gender, State and Society in Soviet and Post-Soviet Russia,* ed. Sarah Ashwin. New York: Routledge.

Kideckel, David. 1976. The Social Organization of Production on a Romanian Cooperative Farm. *Dialectical Anthropology* 1, no. 2: 267–76.

————. 1993. *The Solitude of Collectivism: Romanian Villagers to the Revolution and Beyond.* Ithaca, N.Y.: Cornell University Press.

Kligman, Gail. 1988. *The Wedding of the Dead: Ritual, Poetics, and Popular Culture in Transylvania.* Berkeley: University of California Press.

————. 1994. The Social Legacy of Communism: Women, Children, and the Feminization of Poverty. In *The Social Legacy of Communism,* ed. James R. Millar and Sharon L. Wolchik. New York: Cambridge University Press.

Konrad, George. 1984. *Antipolitics,* trans. Richard E. Allen. San Diego: Harcourt Brace Jovanovich.

Kopytoff, Igor. 1986. The Cultural Biography of Things. In *The Social Life of Things: Commodities in Cultural Perspective,* ed. Arjun Appadurai. New York: Cambridge University Press.

Kotkin, Steven. 1995. *Magnetic Mountain: Stalinism as a Civilization.* Berkeley: University of California Press.

Krestianka. 1999. Maslo maslianoe? No. 5, 15.

Krishtanovskaia, Olga, and Stephen White. 1999. From *Nomenklatura* to New Elite. In *The New Elite in Post-Communist Eastern Europe,* ed. Vladimir Shlapentokh, Christopher Vanderpool, and Boris Doktorov. College Station: Texas A&M University Press.

Krylova, Anna. 1999. Saying "Lenin" and Meaning "Party": Subversion and Laughter in Soviet and Post-Soviet Society. In *Consuming Russia: Popular Culture, Sex, and Society since Gorbachev,* ed. Adele Marie Barker. Durham, N.C.: Duke University Press.

Kukhterin, Sergei. 2000. Fathers and Patriarchs in Communist and Post-Communist Russia. In *Gender, State and Society in Soviet and Post-Soviet Russia,* ed. Sarah Ashwin. New York: Routledge.

Kusserow, Adrie. 2004. *American Individualisms: Child Rearing and Social Class in Three Neighborhoods.* New York: Palgrave McMillan.

Lamont, Michele. *Money, Morals and Manners: The Culture of the French and American Middle Class.* Chicago: University of Chicago Press.

Lampland, Martha. 1995. *The Object of Labor: Commodification in Socialist Hungary.* Chicago: University of Chicago Press.

Lane, David. 1985. *Soviet Economy and Society.* New York: New York University Press.

———. 1990. *Soviet Society under Perestroika.* Boston: Unwin Hyman.

Lankauskas, Gediminas. 2001. On "Modern" Christians, Consumption, and the Value of National Identity in Post-Soviet Lithuania. *Ethnos* 67, no. 3: 320–44.

Lapidus, Gail. 1983. Social Trends. In *After Brezhnev: Sources of Soviet Conduct in the 1980s,* ed. Robert F. Byrnes. Bloomington: Indiana University Press.

Leacock, E. 1981. *Myths of Male Dominance: Collected Articles on Women Cross-Culturally.* New York: Monthly Review Press.

Ledeneva, Alena V. 1998. *Russia's Economy of Favours: Blat, Networking and Informal Exchange.* Cambridge: Cambridge University Press.

Leitch, Alison. 2000. The Social Life of *Lardo:* Slow Food in Fast Times. *Asia Pacific Journal of Anthropology* 1, no. 1: 103–18.

Lemon, Alaina. 2000. *Between Two Fires: Gypsy Performance and Romani Memory from Pushkin to Postsocialism.* Durham, N.C.: Duke University Press.

———. 2002. Without a "Concept"? Race as Discursive Practice. *Slavic Review* 61, no. 1: 54–61.

Leont'eva, Elizaveta. 1999. Smotri v oba, ili Kak ne otravit'sia khlebom (Look at both, or How to not be poisoned by bread). *Sankt-Peterburgskie Vedemosti,* October 5.

Levi-Strauss, Claude. 1997. The Culinary Triangle. In *Food and Culture: A Reader,* ed. Carole Counihan and Penny van Esterick. New York: Routledge.

Liechty, Mark. 1995. Media, Markets and Modernization: Youth Identities and the Experience of Modernity in Kathmandu, Nepal. In *Youth Culture: A Cross-Cultural Perspective,* ed. Vered Amit-Talai and Helena Wulff. New York: Routledge.

———. 2003. *Suitably Modern: Making Middle-Class Culture in a New Consumer Society.* Princeton, N.J.: Princeton University Press.

Lipovskaya, Olga. 1994. The Mythology of Womanhood in Contemporary "Soviet" Culture. In *Women in Russia: A New Era in Russian Feminism,* ed. Anastasia Posadskaya and others at the Moscow Gender Centre; trans. Kate Clark. New York: Verso.

Lonkila, Markku. 1997. Informal Exchange Relations in Post-Soviet Russia. A Comparative Perspective. *Sociological Research Online* 2, no. 2. http://www.socres online.org.uk/socresonline/2/2/9.html.

Malinowski, Bronislaw. 1984. *Argonauts of the Western Pacific.* Prospect Heights, Ill.: Waveland Press.

Mankekar, Purnima. 1993. National Texts and Gendered Lives: An Ethnography of Television Viewers in a North Indian City. *American Ethnologist* 20, no. 3: 543–63.

Marx, Karl. 1990. *Capital: A Critique of Political Economy, Volume 1,* trans. Ben Fowkes. New York: Penguin Books. Orig. pub. 1887.

Mauss, Marcel. 1967. *The Gift,* trans. Ian Cunnison. New York: W. W. Norton. Orig. pub. 1925.

Medvedev, Roy. 1997. Novyi Klass Rossiiskogo Obshchestva. *Svobodnaia Mysl'* 8: 58–71.

McCauley, Martin. 1997. *Who's Who in Russia since 1900.* New York: Routledge.

McCracken, Grant. 1988. *Culture and Consumption: New Approaches to the Symbolic Character of Consumer Goods and Activities.* Bloomington: Indiana University Press.

Mehnert, Klaus. 1962. *Soviet Man and His World,* trans. Maurice Rosenbaum. New York: Frederick A. Praeger. Orig. pub. 1958.

Millar, James. 1981. *The ABCs of Soviet Socialism.* Urbana: University of Illinois Press.

———. 1990. *The Soviet Economic Experiment,* ed. Susan J. Linz. Urbana: University of Illinois Press.

Miller, Daniel. 1987. *Material Culture and Mass Consumption.* New York: Basil Blackwell.

———. 1992. The Young and the Restless in Trinidad: A Case of the Local and the Global in Mass Consumption. In *Consuming Technologies: Media and Information in Domestic Spaces,* ed. Eric Hirsch and Roger Silverstone. New York: Routledge.

———. 1994. *Modernity: An Ethnographic Approach—Dualism and Mass Consumption in Trinidad.* Oxford: Berg.

———. 1995a. Consumption and Commodities. *Annual Review of Anthropology* 24: 141–61.

———. 1995b. Consumption Studies as the Transformation of Anthropology. In *Acknowledging Consumption: A Review of New Studies,* ed. Daniel Miller. New York: Routledge.

———. 1995c. Consumption as the Vanguard of History: A Polemic by Way of an Introduction. In *Acknowledging Consumption: A Review of New Studies,* ed. Daniel Miller. New York: Routledge.

———. 1995d. Introduction: Anthropology, Modernity, and Consumption. In *Worlds Apart: Modernity through the Prism of the Local,* ed. Daniel Miller. New York: Routledge.

———. 1997. *Capitalism: An Ethnographic Approach.* Oxford: Berg.

———. 1998. *A Theory of Shopping.* Ithaca, N.Y.: Cornell University Press.

———. 2001. Alienable Gifts and Inalienable Commodities. In *The Empire of Things: Regimes of Value and Material Culture,* ed. Fred R. Myers. Santa Fe: School of American Research Press.

———. N.d. Alienable Gifts and Inalienable Commodities. Unpublished ms.

Mintz, Sidney. 1985. *Sweetness and Power.* New York: Viking Press.

Molyneux, Maxine. 1981. Women in Socialist Societies: Problems of Theory and Practice. In *Of Marriage and the Market: Women's Subordination in International Perspective,* ed. Kate Young, Carol Wolkowitz, and Roslyn McCullagh. London: CSE Books.

Moore, Henrietta. 1988. *Feminism and Anthropology.* Minneapolis: University of Minnesota Press.

Mukhopadhyay, Carol C., and Patricia Higgins. 1988. Anthropological Studies of Women's Status Revisited: 1977–1987. *Annual Review of Anthropology* 17: 461–95.

Munn, Nancy D. 1986. *The Fame of Gawa: A Symbolic Study of Value Transformation in a Massim (Papua New Guinea) Society.* Durham, N.C.: Duke University Press.

Myers, Fred R., ed. 2001a. The Empire of Things: Regimes of Value and Material Culture. Santa Fe: School of American Research Press.

———. 2001b. Introduction: The Empire of Things. In *The Empire of Things: Regimes of Value and Material Culture,* ed. Fred R. Myers. Santa Fe: School of American Research Press.

Newman, Katherine. 1988. *Falling from Grace: The Experience of Downward Mobility in the American Middle Class.* New York: Free Press.

Ninetto, Amy. 2001. "Civilization" and Its Insecurities: Traveling Scientists, Global Science, and National Progress in the Novosibirsk *Akademgorodok. Kroeber Anthropological Society Papers* 86: 181–202.

——. 2005. "An Island of Socialism in a Capitalist Country": Postsocialist Russian Science and the Culture of the State." *Ethnos* 70, no. 4: 443–64.

Nove, Alex. 1992. *An Economic History of the USSR: 1917–1991.* New York: Penguin Books.

O'Dougherty, Maureen. 2002. *Consumption Intensified: The Politics of Middle-Class Daily Life in Brazil.* Durham, N.C.: Duke University Press.

Ohnuki-Tierney. 1993. *Rice as Self: Japanese Identities through Time.* Princeton, N.J.: Princeton University Press.

Ong, Aihwa. 1987. *Spirits of Resistance and Capitalist Discipline: Factory Women in Malaysia.* Albany: State University of New York Press.

——. 1990. State versus Islam: Malay Families, Women's Bodies, and the Body Politic in Malaysia. *American Ethnologist* 17, no. 2: 258–76.

Orlinkova, Marina. 1998. Zamuzh za bogatogo. *Cosmopolitan* (Russian edition), October, 88–92.

Ortner, Sherry. 1974. Is Female to Male as Nature Is to Culture? In *Woman, Culture and Society,* ed. Michelle Rosaldo and Louise Lamphere. Stanford, Calif.: Stanford University Press.

Osokina, Elena. 1998. *Za Fasadom "Stalinskogo Izobiliia": Raspredelenie i Rynok v Snabzhenii Naseleniia v Gody Industrializatsii, 1927–1941.* Moscow: Rossiiskaia Politicheskaia Entsiklopediia.

Oushakine, Serguei. 1999. The Quantity of Style: Imaginary Consumption in the New Russia. Paper presented at the conference "1989–1999 Transformations: Triumph or Tragedy?" Annual Graduate Student Conference, Harriman Institute and East European Center, Columbia University, New York, February 26–27.

——. 2001. The Fatal Splitting: Symbolizing Anxiety in Post-Soviet Russia. *Ethnos* 66, no. 3: 291–319.

Patico, Jennifer. 2000. "'New Russian' Sightings and the Question of Social Difference in St. Petersburg." *Anthropology of East Europe Review* 18, no. 2: 73–77.

——. 2001a. Consumption and Logics of Social Difference in Post-Soviet Russia. PhD dissertation, Department of Anthropology, New York University.

——. 2001b. Globalization in the Postsocialist Marketplace: Consumer Readings of Difference and Development in Urban Russia. *Kroeber Anthropological Society Papers* 91.

——. 2002. Chocolate and Cognac: Gift Exchange and the Recognition of Social Worlds in Post-Soviet Russia. *Ethnos* 67, no. 3: 345–68.

——. 2003. Consuming the West but Becoming Third World: Food Imports and the Experience of Russianness. *Anthropology of East Europe Review* 21, no. 1: 31–36.

——. 2005. To Be Happy in a Mercedes: Culture, Civilization and Transformations of Value in a Postsocialist City. *American Ethnologist* 32, no. 3: 479–96.

Patico, Jennifer, and Melissa L. Caldwell. 2002. Consumers Exiting Socialism: Ethnographic Perspectives on Daily Life in Post-Communist Europe. *Ethnos* 67, no. 3: 285–94.

Pesman, Dale. 2000. *Russia and Soul: An Exploration.* Ithaca, N.Y.: Cornell University Press.

Petryna, Adriana. 2000. *Life Exposed: Biological Citizens after Chernobyl.* Princeton, N.J.: Princeton University Press.

Piirainen, Timo. 1997. *Towards a New Social Order in Russia: Transforming Structures in Everyday Life.* Brookfield, Vt.: Dartmouth Publishing Company.

Pilkington, Hilary. 1992. Whose Space Is It Anyway? Youth, Gender and Civil Society in the Soviet Union. In *Women in the Face of Change: The Soviet Union, Eastern Europe, and China,* ed. Shirin Rai, Hilary Pilkington, and Annie Phizacklea. New York: Routledge.

———. 1996a. Farewell to the Tusovka: Masculinities and Femininities on the Moscow Youth Scene. In *Gender, Generation and Identity in Contemporary Russia,* ed. Hilary Pilkington. New York: Routledge.

———. 1996b. Introduction. In *Gender, Generation and Identity in Contemporary Russia,* ed. Hilary Pilkington. New York: Routledge.

———. 1996c. Youth Culture in Contemporary Russia: Gender, Consumption and Identity. In *Gender, Generation and Identity in Contemporary Russia,* ed. Hilary Pilkington. New York: Routledge.

Pilkington, Hilary, Elena Omel'chenko, Moya Flynn, Ul'iana Bliudina, and Elena Srakova. 2002. *Looking West? Cultural Globalization and Russian Youth Cultures.* University Park: Pennsylvania State University Press.

Rausing, Sigrid. 2000. Re-constructing the "Normal": Identity and the Consumption of Western Goods in Estonia. In *Markets and Moralities: Ethnographies of Postsocialism,* ed. R. Mandl and C. Humphrey. New York: Berg.

Reiter, Rayna. 1975. Men and Women in the South of France. In *Toward an Anthropology of Women,* ed. R. Reiter. New York: Monthly Review Press.

Ries, Nancy. 1997. *Russian Talk: Culture and Conversation during Perestroika.* Ithaca, N.Y.: Cornell University Press.

———. 2002. "Honest" Bandits and "Warped People": Russian Narratives about Money, Corruption, and Moral Decay. In *Ethnography in Unstable Places,* ed. C. Greenhouse, K. Warren, and E. Mertz. Durham, N.C.: Duke University Press.

Rivkin-Fish, Michele. 1997. Reproducing Russia: Women's Health and Moral Education in the Construction of a Post-Soviet Society. PhD dissertation, Department of Anthropology, Princeton University.

———. 2000. Gifts, Bribes, and Unofficial Payments: The Moral Economy of Healing in Post-Soviet Russia. Paper presented to the Soyuz Conference on Post-Communist Cultural Studies, Columbia University, New York, February 11–12.

———. 2005. *Women's Health in Post-Soviet Russia: The Politics of Intervention.* Bloomington: Indiana University Press.

Rogers, Douglas. 2005. Moonshine, Money, and the Politics of Liquidity Rural Russia. *American Ethnologist* 32, no. 1: 63–81.

Rogers, Susan Carol. 1975. Female Forms of Power and the Myth of Male Dominance: A Model of Male/Female Interaction in Peasant Society. *American Ethnologist* 2: 727–56.

———. 1978. Woman's Place: A Critical Review of Anthropological Theory. *Comparative Studies in Society and History* 20, no. 1: 123–62.

———. 1985. Gender in Southwestern France: The Myth of Male Dominance Revisited. *Anthropology* 9: 65–85.

Rosaldo, Michelle Z. 1974. Women, Culture, and Society: A Theoretical Overview. In *Woman, Culture and Society,* ed. Michelle Rosaldo and Louise Lamphere. Stanford, Calif.: Stanford University Press.

————. 1980. The Use and Abuse of Anthropology: Reflections on Feminism and Cross Cultural Understanding. *Signs* 5, no. 3: 389–417.

Rouse, Roger. 2000. Mexican Migration and the Social Space of Postmodernism. In *The Anthropology of Globalization: A Reader,* ed. Jonathan Xavier Inda and Renato Rosaldo. Malden, Mass.: Blackwell.

Rozin, Paul. 1998. Food Is Fundamental, Fun, Frightening and Far-Reaching. *Social Research* 66, no. 1: 9–30.

Rutman, Emma. 1997. Novye russkie papy. *Domashnii Ochag,* December, 148–49.

Sacks, Karen. 1975. Engels Revisited: Women, the Organization of Production, and Private Property. In *Toward an Anthropology of Women,* ed. Rayna Reiter. New York: Monthly Review Press.

Sagatovskii, V. N. 1982. *Vesy feminida i sud sovesti: Populiarnye ocherki ob etike i etikete.* Moscow: Molodaia Gvardiia.

Sahlins, Marshall. 1976. *Culture and Practical Reason.* Chicago: University of Chicago Press.

————. 1996. On the Sociology of Primitive Exchange. In *The Gift: An Interdisciplinary Perspective,* ed. Aafke E. Komter. Amsterdam: Amsterdam University Press.

Salmi, Anna-Maria. 2000. Bonds, Bottles, Blat and Banquets. Birthdays and Networks in Russia. *Ethnologia Europaea* 30: 31–44.

————. 2003. Health in Exchange: Teachers, Doctors and the Strength of Informal Practices in Russia. *Culture, Medicine and Psychiatry* 27: 109–30.

Sampson, Steven. 1976. Feldioara: The City Comes to the Peasant. *Dialectical Anthropology* 1, no. 3: 321–48.

————. 1985–86. The Informal Sector in Eastern Europe. *Telos* 66: 44–66.

Sampson, Steven, and David Kideckel. 1988. Anthropologists Going into the Cold: Research in the Age of Mutually Assured Destruction. In *The Anthropology of War and Peace: Perspectives on the Nuclear Age,* ed. Paul R. Turner and David Pitt. Granby, Mass.: Bergin and Garvey.

Sankt-Peterburgskie Vedemosti. 1999. Maionez maionezu rozn'. February 17.

Schein, Louisa. 1997. The Consumption of Color and the Politics of White Skin in Post-Mao China. In *The Gender/Sexuality Reader: Culture, History, Political Economy,* ed. Roger N. Lancaster and Micaela di Leonardo. New York: Routledge.

————. 1999. Of Cargo and Satellites: Imagined Cosmopolitanism. *Postcolonial Studies* 2, no. 3: 345–75.

————. 2002. *Minority Rules: The Miao and the Feminine in China's Cultural Politics.* Durham, N.C.: Duke University Press.

Sharov, A., ed. 1965. *Moral'nyi kodeks stroitelia kommunizma* (Moral codex of the builder of communism). Moscow: Politizdat.

Shcherbakova, Anna. 1999. Price Controls Decreed for Essentials. *Saint Petersburg Times,* September 18.

Shevchenko, Olga. 2002a. Between the Holes: Emerging Identities and Hybrid Patterns of Consumption in Post-Socialist Russia. *Europe-Asia Studies* 54, no. 6: 841–66.

————. 2002b. "In Case of Fire Emergency": Consumption, Security and the Meaning of Durables in a Transforming Society. *Journal of Consumer Culture* 2, no. 2: 147–70.

Shlapentokh, Vladimir. 1999. Social Inequality in Post-Communist Russia: The Attitudes of the Political Elite and the Masses (1991–1998). *Europe-Asia Studies* 51, no. 7: 1167–81.

Silverblatt, Irene. 1988. Women in States. *Annual Review of Anthropology* 17: 427–60.

Silverman, Bertram, and Murray Yanowitch. 2000. *New Rich, New Poor, New Russia: Winners and Losers on the Russian Road to Capitalism.* Armonk, N.Y.: M. E. Sharpe.

Simpura, Jussi, Galina Eremitcheva, Elena Evdokimova, Simo Mannila, Tatjana Nosova, Teela Pakkasvirta, and Evguenia Poretzkina. 1999. No Limits to Patience? Experiences of the Russian Economic Crisis of 1998 in the Everyday Lives of Ten Middle-Class Families in St. Petersburg. *Finnish Review of East European Studies* (Idantutkimus) 2: 49–68.

Slezkine, Yuri. 1994a. Arctic Mirrors: Russia and the Small Peoples of the North. Ithaca, N.Y.: Cornell University Press.

———. 1994b. The USSR as a Communal Apartment, or How a Socialist State Promoted Ethnic Particularism. *Slavic Review* 53, no. 2: 414–52.

Smith, Raymond. 1984. Anthropology and the Concept of Social Class. *Annual Review of Anthropology* 13: 467–94.

Stacey, Judith. 1983. *Patriarchy and Socialist Revolution in China.* Berkeley: University of California Press.

Startsev, Boris. 1998. Iskomaia Seredina. *Itogi,* April 15.

Stryker, Rachael, and Jennifer Patico. 2004. The Paradoxes of Progress: Globalization and Postsocialist Cultures. *Kroeber Anthropological Society Papers* 86: 1–8.

Taussig, Michael. 1980. *The Devil and Commodity Fetishism in South America.* Chapel Hill: University of North Carolina Press.

Temkina, Anna. 1996. Entering Politics: Women's Ways, Gender Ideas and Contradictions of Reality. In *Women's Voices in Russia Today,* ed. Anna Rotkirch and Elina Haavio-Mannila. Brookfield, Vt.: Dartmouth Publishing Company.

Temkina, Anna, and Anna Rotkirch. 1997. Soviet Gender Contracts and Their Shifts in Contemporary Russia. In *Russia in Transition: The Case of New Collective Actors and New Collective Actions,* ed. Anna Temkina. Helsinki: Kikimora Publishers.

Thomas, Nicholas. 1991. *Entangled Objects: Exchange, Material Culture, and Colonialism in the Pacific.* Cambridge, Mass.: Harvard University Press.

Timofeev, Lev. 1985. *Soviet Peasants, or, The Peasants' Art of Starving.* New York: Telos Press.

Turner, Terence. 1980. The Social Skin. In *Not Work Alone,* ed. J. Carfos and R. Lewin. Beverly Hills: Sage Publications.

Ule, Mirjana, and Tanja Rener. 1996. Nationalism and Gender in Postsocialist Societies: Is Nationalism Female? In *Ana's Land: Sisterhood in Eastern Europe,* ed. Tanya Renne. Boulder, Colo.: Westview Press.

Vann, Elizabeth. 2003. Production Matters: Consumerism and Global Capitalism in Vietnam. *Anthropological Perspectives on Economic Development and Integration Research in Economic Anthropology* 22: 225–57.

———. 2005. Domesticating Consumer Goods in the Global Economy: Examples from Vietnam and Russia. *Ethnos* 71, no. 4: 465–88.

Varoli, John. 1998. Panic Spurs Run on Food Staples, New Ladas. *Saint Petersburg Times,* September 1.

Veblen, Thorstein. 1994. *The Theory of the Leisure Class.* New York: Dover Thrift Editions. Orig. pub. 1899.

S.-P. Vedemosti. 1999. "Kurinyi skandal'" vyshel na obshcheevropeiskii uroven (The "chicken scandal" is now affecting all of Europe). June 3.

Verdery, Katherine. 1983. *Transylvanian Villagers: Three Centuries of Political, Economic, and Ethnic Change.* Berkeley: University of California Press.

———. 1991. Theorizing Socialism. *American Ethnologist* 18, no. 3: 419–39.

———. 1994. From Parent-State to Family Patriarchs: Gender and Nation in Contemporary Eastern Europe. *East European Politics and Society* 8, no. 2: 225–55.

———. 1996. *What Was Socialism, and What Comes Next?* Princeton, N.J.: Princeton University Press.

———. 1999. Fuzzy Property: Rights, Power, and Identity in Transylvania's Decollectivization. In *Uncertain Transition: Ethnographies of Change in the Postsocialist World,* ed. M. Burawoy and K. Verdery. Lanham, Md.: Rowman & Littlefield.

———. 2003. *The Vanishing Hectare: Property and Value in Postsocialist Transylvania.* Ithaca, N.Y.: Cornell University Press.

Vinokur, Aaron, and Gur Ofer. 1987. Inequality of Earnings, Household Income, and Wealth in the Soviet Union in the 1970s. In *Politics, Work, and Daily Life in the USSR: A Survey of Former Soviet Citizens,* ed. James R. Millar. New York: Cambridge University Press.

Virkunen, Tamara. 1998. Radioaktivnaia kliukva: Est' ili ne est'? (Radioactive cranberries: To eat or not to eat?). *Argumenty i Fakty,* no. 40, October, 11.

Virkunen, Tamara, and Natal'ia Mironenko. 1999. Khleb-ubiitsa (Killer bread). *Argumenty i Fakty,* no. 39: 9.

Visson, Lynn. 1998. *Wedded Strangers: The Challenges of Russian-American Marriages.* New York: Hippocrene Books.

Volkov, Vadim. 1999. Violent Entrepreneurship in Post-Communist Russia. *Europe-Asia Studies* 51, no. 5: 741–54.

———. 2001. *Violent Entrepreneurs: The Use of Force in the Making of Russian Capitalism.* Ithaca, N.Y.: Cornell University Press.

Von Bruck, Gabriele. 1997. Elusive Bodies: The Politics of Aesthetics among Yemeni Elite Women. *Signs* 23, no. 1: 175–214.

Voronina, Olga. 1994. Virgin Mary or Mary Magdalene? The Construction and Reconstruction of Sex During the Perestroika Period. In *Women in Russia: A New Era in Russian Feminism,* ed. Anastasia Posadskaya and others at the Moscow Gender Centre; trans. Kate Clark. New York: Verso.

Voslensky, Michael. 1984. *Nomenklatura: The Soviet Ruling Class,* trans. Eric Mosbacher. Garden City, N.Y.: Doubleday.

Wanner, Catherine. 1998. *Burden of Dreams: History and Identity in Post-Soviet Ukraine.* University Park: Pennsylvania State University Press.

———. 2005. Money, Morality and New Forms of Exchange in Postsocialist Ukraine. *Ethnos* 70, no. 4: 515–37.

Waters, Elizabeth. 1993. Finding a Voice: The Emergence of a Women's Movement. In *Gender Politics and Post-Communism: Reflections from Eastern Europe and the Former Soviet Union,* ed. Nanette Funk and Magda Mueller. New York: Routledge.

Watson, James L., ed. 1997. *Golden Arches East: McDonald's in East Asia.* Stanford, Calif.: Stanford University Press.

Weber, Max. 1946. *From Max Weber: Essays in Sociology,* ed. H. H. Gerth and C. Wright Mills. New York: Oxford University Press.

———. 1992. *The Protestant Ethic and the Spirit of Capitalism.* New York: HarperCollins. Orig. pub. 1904–5.

Wedel, Janine. 1998. *Collision and Collusion: The Strange Case of Western Aid to Eastern Europe 1989–1998.* New York: Palgrave Macmillan.

Weiner, Annette. 1992. *Inalienable Possessions: The Paradox of Keeping-While-Giving.* Berkeley: University of California Press.

Weiss, Brad. 1996. *The Making and Unmaking of the Haya Lived World.* Durham, N.C.: Duke University Press.

Westbrook, Marie, Lev Lurie, and Mikhail Ivanov. 1994. The Independent Schools of St. Petersburg: Diversification of Schooling in Postcommunist Russia. In *Education and Society in the New Russia,* ed. Anthony Jones. Armonk, N.Y: M. E. Sharpe.

Wolf, Margery. 1985. *Revolution Postponed: Women in Contemporary China.* Durham, N.C.: Duke University Press.

Yan, Yunxiang. 1996. *The Flow of Gifts: Reciprocity and Social Networks in a Chinese Village.* Stanford, Calif.: Stanford University Press.

Yanagisako, Sylvia. 1987. Mixed Metaphors: Native and Anthropological Models of Gender and Kinship Domains. In *Gender and Kinship: Essays toward a Unified Analysis.* Stanford, Calif.: Stanford University Press.

Yang, Mayfair Mei-Hui. 1994. *Gifts, Favors, and Banquets: The Art of Social Relationships in China.* Ithaca, N.Y.: Cornell University Press.

Zavisca, Jane. 2003. Contesting Capitalism at the Post-Soviet Dacha: The Meaning of Food Cultivation for Urban Russians. *Slavic Review* 62, no. 4: 786–810.

Zdravomyslova, Elena. 1996. Problems of Becoming a Housewife. In *Women's Voices in Russia Today,* ed. Anna Rotkirch and Elina Haavio-Mannila. Brookfield, Vt.: Dartmouth Publishing Company.

Zemstov, Ilya. 1985. *The Private Life of the Soviet Elite.* New York: Crane, Russak, and Company.

Index

gimnaziia (public schools), 28, 28*n*12
glasnost, 50
global community of consumers, 14, 104, 137, 139, 207
Good Housekeeping (magazine), 2, 123, 163. *See also Domashnii Ochag* and *Home Hearth*
Gorbachev, Mikhail, 37, 50, 65
Goscilo, Helena, 140
Gosden, Chris, 137
Graeber, David, 8
gratitude, expressions of, 191, 193, 195
Gregory, C.A., 194*n*14

hierarchies of access, 40–44
holiday celebrations: birthdays, 132, 181, *202, 203;* discussed in teacher interviews, 28; importance of, 177–78; as school events, 29, *179;* shortages affecting, 180; symbolic value of, 202; teachers receiving gifts for, 189, 205
Home Hearth (magazine), 168. See also *Domashnii Ochag*
homemaking: gender roles of, 148, 149–57; lack of good homemakers, 150–57, 168; and new Russian women, 158, 166; in Soviet era, 45, 143–50; teachers' views of, 141
home visiting, 29, 68, 177, 181–83, 200
hospitality, 28, 154, 175, 184
Humphrey, Caroline, 18, 88, 108, 110, 114, 136, 160
hygiene, 44, 45, 144

iarmarki (indoor bazaars), 3, 113
Ignatjev, Yuri, 121*n*11
image. *See* personal appearance and grooming
imported goods: availability of, 1, 2, 17, 51, 102–03, 117; desirability of, 116, 117, 160; domestic goods vs., 110, 125; fear of, 118–22, 123, 128, 135; preferences for, 111, 119; quality of, 61; in Soviet era, 115. *See also individual countries (e.g., China and Chinese goods)*

income disparities. *See* income gaps
income gaps, 43, 52, 63*n*18
Indian goods, 110, 112–13
individualism, 17, 70, 215
indoor bazaars. *See iarmarki*
industry and industrialization: privatization of, 17, 50; revitalization of, 212; Russia as center of, 12, 23, 37; as focus of anthropological research, 9–10; in Soviet economy, 41, 42
inequality. *See* social inequality
inflation: and affordability of consumer goods, 164, 181; in 1990s, 51, 52, 55, 58, 153; rate of, 21
intelligentsia: and *kul'turnost'*, 48; and measures of value, 214; new Russians as, 65; parents of schoolchildren as, 82; respect for, 69–71, 79; teachers as, 62–64, 69–71, 93. *See also* mass intelligentsia
International Women's Day, 169, *179,* 185, 189
intimacy and reciprocity, 177–84
Italy and Italian goods, 110, 113, 114, 115, 139, 165
Itogi (magazine), 66, 66*n*19

job loss. *See* unemployment
job security, 64, 153
Jones, Anthony, 14*n*4, 63

Kay, Rebecca, 164
Kelly, Catriona, 111
Khakamada, Irina, 163
khoziaiki. See homemaking
Khrushchev, Nikita, 42
Kligman, Gail, 142
Knowles, Chantal, 137
Korea, 3, 109–10, 112, 113, 114
Krest'ianka (Peasant Woman magazine), 2, 48, 163, 164
kriziz. See crisis of 1998-99
Krylova, Anna, 99
kul'turnost': and gender relations, 144; idealization of, 11; and leisure time, 161; and material security, 100, 214;

zastoi (economic stagnation), 37, 42
Zhurnal Mod (magazine), 163
znak vnimaniia (sign of attention):
  contrasted with bribes, 193; doctors
  receiving, 191; and home visiting,
182, 183; and misrecognition of
gifts, 202; and money, 194; and
personal knowledge of recipient,
190; as personal recognition,
203